Make Money to Write About Your Kids

Get Published in Regional, National & Online Parenting & Family Magazines (285 markets)

BY KERRIE MCLOUGHLIN

ISBN: 1508603464
ISBN-13: 978-1508603467

DEDICATION

To my ever-supportive husband and best friend, Aron, and our amazing kids, Joel, Michael, Callie, Eva and Samuel.

To my parents, who have always been on my side.

To all those writers out there who want to share their words and experiences … and get paid to do so.

CONTENTS

INTRODUCTION

Welcome, writers! I'm so excited you decided to purchase this book because it shows that you're ready to head into the paid writing world (print and online). Let's jump right in with the answers to some questions you probably have.

A Regional Parenting Magazine (RPM) is a publication that caters to parents and families in a specific geographic area. The articles in RPMs range from newborn sleep issues to teenagers on Facebook to living with an aging parent. RPMs depend on freelancers to fill their pages with articles, essays, fillers, how-tos, etc. They make most of their money from advertisers and give out their magazine for free, with the exception of some paid subscriptions people pay for so they can have the magazine mailed to their home. This means pay to writers is usually low ($15-150 per article in general).

While writing for RPMs is a great stepping stone on your way to writing for national markets, there's no reason you can't keep writing for the RPMs and sell your reprints while you are also writing for other markets nationally, internationally or online. Or you can tailor your $1,000 article that you had published in *Parents Magazine* into 25 more sales to the RPMs. The sky is the limit once you get into the groove of writing for this special market. You own your work and can also upload it to blogs or other revenue-making sites, as long as you are slightly changing the material so as not to anger the almighty Google search engine!

I compiled this book for you because it made my own submission process so much more efficient. Back in 2008 I spent many hours gathering the information I needed to even sit down and *begin* to submit my first piece to a regional parenting magazine. I printed every single entry from the Parenting Publications of America (PPA) website, then started Googling every search term I could think of to come up with more regional parenting magazines. The PPA list was not complete by any means and had a lot of misinformation. It also did not share writer's guidelines or pay information.

I want to share everything I've learned with you and save you the time and effort I've already spent. This book is the fast-track way to get published! I want you to enjoy the success (and paychecks!) I've enjoyed the last few years and continue to enjoy. Imagine writing just one 750-word article that takes minimal research and minimal time because you have personal experience with the subject and plenty of parent friends to offer you quotes, and then selling it 20 times and getting checks in your mailbox on almost a daily basis.

This book works because I'm also submitting my work to the places I'm telling you about. I'm in this business *with* you, and I believe there is enough business to go around. As some writers drop out of the RPMs to write for larger markets, YOU will take their place as the person RPMs go to for reprints and original articles! Then others will take YOUR place as you move on up!

I wish you writing success! Please email me at mommykerrie@yahoo.com if you have any questions at all!

1. STEPS TO TAKE TO GET PUBLISHED

"All the so-called 'secrets of success' will not work unless you do."
– Author Unknown

1. Read up on your craft (see RESOURCES section in Chapter 16).
2. Check out other writers who inspire you. It's easy to find great writers on BlogHer, Mamalode, Huffington Post Parents and so many more places. There are women and men who are inspirational to me and (without even realizing it) have given me the courage to write on.
3. Consider taking an online writing course. Honestly, this is not something I've done, but I have heard good things about them. It may seem like a large outlay of money, but if it helps you hone your craft, give it a shot!
4. Come up with a good idea (see GENERATING IDEAS in Chapter 2).
5. Before you start writing, do an Internet search for your article idea to make sure it hasn't already been overdone and that you have a new or different angle on it. Some writers like to flesh out their piece a little before hunting down others like it. It's up to you.
6. Research your topic, and try to put a different spin on the idea.
7. Collect quotes to support your article. It's always a good idea to get national quotes from both "real" people *and* experts if you can because they add to an article. I've sold plenty of pieces with just quotes from moms in my city (local quotes), but I probably would sell more if I got national quotes (from outside my area).

8. Proofread your work by reading it on paper out loud. Then have someone you trust check for errors as well.

9. Read over the GENERAL SUBMISSION GUIDELINES section of this book in Chapter 3.

10. Read the writer's guidelines included in this book for the publications that provide them. If you're consistently not breaking in to a publication with specific guidelines, focus on them for a while and see what happens. For example, I might send an article to 200 publications in this book every time I write one. After a year I notice there are a few who are never contacting me and so I read their writer's guidelines more closely if they have provided them and try to follow them. Some publications might want you to use a specific font when submitting or may want you to submit your manuscript as an attachment (most don't), so look for their idiosyncracies.

11. Be patient and stay busy. I've found that the more projects I have in the works, the less time I have to worry about why I haven't heard back from a specific editor. I think most RPMs are like fickle teenagers on a Saturday night: they have many invitations (submissions) and are just waiting for the perfect one before they commit to go out (print your piece).

12. Keep good records of your submissions so you can keep track of your publishing credits and any money owed to you. The spreadsheet ideas included with this book in the KEEPING TRACK section in Chapter 12 make it a snap!

13. Start an author website (see YOUR AUTHOR WEBSITE in Chapter 8).

14. Keep those reprints in circulation with your reprint list and by reworking pieces you've already written (see YOUR REPRINT LIST in Chapter 9).

2. GENERATING IDEAS

Half the battle of seeing an article in print is coming up with an idea editors want to publish. Set aside some time to brainstorm article and essay ideas using the list below. Then choose your best ideas and work the steps to getting published from the previous section.

1. Eavesdrop on conversations everywhere you go.
2. Go through your old blog posts, email messages and journal entries to find essay or article material.
3. Read letters to the editor in your local newspaper.
4. Rework something you have now that you've abandoned.
5. Write the birth stories of your kids.
6. Come up with some inspirational stories.
7. Solve a problem you have now or have had in the past.
8. Write about something you wonder about.
9. Write about something you know how to do.
10. Write the opposite of your experience with a subject.
11. Report on a negative or positive trend.
12. Read editorial calendars.
13. Read writer's guidelines.
14. Read magazines you want to write for.
    - Read them for free at the library

- Peruse them at major bookstores
- Check out some RPMs online
- Put the word out to family, friends and neighbors that you'll take all their old magazines

15. Think about what's missing from publications you read. Should there be more articles about single parenting? Attachment parenting? Special needs? Adoption? Large families? Homeschooling? Daycare issues? Pet care? Chores? Meal planning?

16. Watch TV in your downtime if you enjoy it. There are lots of ideas on reality TV shows, the news and talk shows.

17. Do you find yourself leaving a long comment on someone else's online piece? That could be the start of your own essay or article!

3. GENERAL SUBMISSION GUIDELINES

"Opportunities are never lost; someone will take the one you miss." – Author Unknown

In an ideal writing world, you would have time to read back copies of every parenting magazine to get a feel for what kinds of articles they publish. But with so many demands on our time, that's just not possible. So if there are no writer's guidelines available, follow the rules below.

- Make sure you have a copy of the *Associated Press Stylebook* because most RPMs like articles to follow "AP style" (a few prefer the *Chicago Manual of Style*).
- Always include your name, address, phone number, email address and word count with every submission.
- Use one space after periods so your piece is print-ready for most publications. RPMs like to save as much space as they can, and that gives them more room for advertising and sidebars.
- Include a general service sidebar of where readers can go to get more information (websites, books, etc.).
- If you can, include either local quotes in your article or quotes from experts around the country, not just from your hometown.
- Photos may be submitted with the story, but since many editors don't read email with attachments (or it goes to their Spam folder), just offer and describe the photo in your "cover letter." I sometimes put a fitting photo on my author site with the synopsis of the story.

- Unless otherwise stated, the subject line in your email should be "Submission: [Article Name]."
- Submit a "cover letter" in your email.
- Submit seasonal pieces (e.g., Christmas, Mother's Day) three months in advance as a general rule, unless writer's guidelines state otherwise.
- Add a one to two sentence bio at the end of each article. For instance, "Kerrie McLoughlin is the homeschooling mom of five naughty kids and wife of Aron. Catch up with her at www.TheKerrieShow.com."
- Make sure your submission says it's available for "purchase."
- You'll save hours if you make every piece general, but put in your cover email letter that you are happy to include a local sidebar of resources (e.g., local meal prep stores, local food bank donation centers, etc.) depending on the topic of your article.
- Don't submit your article as an attachment unless the editor asks for it that way in written guidelines, or it may end up in the editor's Spam folder. Instead, place the submission in the body of the email.
- Keep your piece under 1,000 words.
- Editors always reserve the right to edit for clarity, length and style.
- Most publications receive many more submissions than they can use.
- Proofread your work by reading it on paper out loud. Then have someone you trust check for errors, as well.
- Many publications like it when you include a "pull quote." A pull quote is a sentence taken from your article which basically summarizes it and makes the reader want to read the entire article.

4. TWENTY-FIVE MISTAKES TO AVOID

"As you grow older, you'll find the only things you regret are the things you didn't do." – Zachary Scott

Hey, we're all only human and are bound to make a few mistakes here and there, right? Lucky for you, I've made many mistakes and will be thrilled if you learn from some of mine … instead of making your own. Below are some don'ts for you to ponder during your writing journey.

1. Don't mix up a query with a submission. A query is a detailed letter outlining what you propose to write for a magazine. A submission is when you send the entire article or essay, sometimes offering to grab local sources and quotes if the editor is interested in publishing your work. RPMs want you to submit the entire article or essay.
2. Don't submit your article as an attachment unless writer's guidelines specifically ask for it that way because otherwise it will likely end up in the editor's Spam folder. If a magazine is interested in your submission, they can always ask you to submit it as an attachment later.
3. Don't forget to do a little research. Set aside a little time to check out some of the RPMs online. Many even have back issues so you can get a feel for what they have already published.
4. Don't make international mistakes. Watch out when submitting to other countries. Check over your article and make sure you aren't mentioning a business they don't have in Canada, for example, or that you don't send a piece on the 4th of July to England.

5. Don't forget to proofread your work by reading it on paper out loud. Then have someone you trust check for errors, as well. Don't freak out if you find an error after you've submitted your article. In researching this book, some of the RPMs with the most anal-retentive writer's guidelines were the ones where I found the most errors!

6. Don't assume your piece isn't wanted if you don't hear back immediately. I've gotten acceptances from editors over two years after submitting.

7. Don't take it personally if an editor asks to see a particular piece in full … and then never writes you again. Your piece probably just didn't fit their editorial needs, which doesn't mean they won't ever publish your work.

8. Don't get upset if you never hear back from an editor. They receive far too many submissions to personally reject or accept every submission.

9. Don't give up! Getting published is a numbers game. Even with a well-written piece, there are a lot of writers out there competing for limited print space. You may not hear back from the majority of magazines you submit to. This doesn't mean they hate you; it means they get a lot of material to wade through. Your piece may not fit in with what they need or they may already have something similar. They may also contact you months later. It's like if you're dating a lot of people: you won't get obsessed over the one who doesn't call. Keep sending out different articles constantly, and you won't have time to worry about rejection!

10. Don't forget to talk money upfront. Make sure you know what you're getting paid for (print, Web rights or both). The rare RPM might want to buy all rights. Watch out for them because you can't sell your piece anywhere ever again. If you are asked how much you want for an article, consider where the RPM is located and how many copies they distribute.

11. Don't promise to write a piece and then change your mind at the last minute. You will be blacklisted by that publication. If something comes up and you are unable to write the piece, let the editor know as soon as possible so she can re-assign the piece.

12. Don't forget to get a concrete deadline from the editor on rewrites or on getting local quotes/sources. In other words, don't bust your butt to get an assignment in if an editor is going to be on vacation for the next two weeks and doesn't even need it yet.

13. Don't be afraid to write for free sometimes in the beginning. Larry Getlen (larrygetlen.com) advises in the 2007 *Writer's Market*, "When you're just starting out, clips and experience are more important than money."

14. Don't be afraid to write for online sites. You can print it as a clip for your portfolio and add the website as a publishing credit on your author site.

15. Don't forget that you can choose to hunt down local quotes or not. It's often time-consuming when you're just starting out, before you have a large networking database. Of course RPMs all love a local angle, but it's not practical to research a local sidebar for over 200 RPMs and email each one separately. Instead, send your general article with an email cover letter stating that you would be happy to come up with a local sidebar if they are interested in your article. Another option is to focus on a few of the larger or better-paying RPMs and localize just for them.

16. Don't expect to see a final draft of your article before it prints. In fact, don't expect to see a tear sheet of your article even *after* it prints. If you get a tear sheet, consider it a bonus. If you get an entire copy of the magazine, jump up and down.

17. Don't slack off once you get a few articles published. Pick a month and submit 30 articles or essays in 30 days. Keep up the hard work, and head to the higher-paying publications!

18. Don't forget to keep records for tax time.

19. Don't waste too much time on networking sites like Twitter, Facebook, Café Mom, Tumblr, StumbleUpon, LinkedIn, Instagram, Pinterest, etc. Get in, do your business, and get out.

20. Don't get in a rut of only writing feature-type articles because many RPMs love personal and humorous essays.

21. Don't forget to send your seasonal pieces out again next year.

22. Don't forget to send out some of your best pieces in their entirety if you see that an RPM has a new editor. Different editors print different things.

23. Don't forget to look for other markets for your already-published piece. Just because you sold all rights to an article doesn't mean you can't rework it with a different angle, and then sell it to a different market.

24. Don't be too shy to ask for assignments. An editor may love your work but assume you are too busy to take on assignments.

25. Don't think an author website (see YOUR AUTHOR WEBSITE in Chapter 8) is too costly for you to set up. You don't need a professional website developer to show your writing credits and synopses of your published pieces.

5. LOCAL SIDEBARS AND QUOTES

LOCAL SIDEBARS

In your general email cover letter, you might want to offer a local sidebar with any article you send out. These are usually easy to come up with, such as tracking down some local volunteer opportunities by zip code to go with an article about volunteering during a specific holiday season. If you need help or ideas, don't be afraid to ask the editor.

LOCAL QUOTES

Getting local quotes can be a pain, so you can decide whether you want to do this or not, and then ask for more money. If so, you have a few options:

1. Go to your network. Email everyone you know in a specific area of the country and put out a request on all of your social media.
2. Try PeterShankman.com. Type in your request and see if he can get you some quotes from the region you need.
3. Grab national quotes from real people and experts instead.
4. Ask the editor of the RPM for some ideas of where to get local quotes. The editor may want a "regular" person and/or an expert quoted in the article. Recently I had a local assignment and knew not one soul in the city I was writing about. The editors put out a call for quotes on their Facebook page, and I got my sources!
5. Track down local mom groups online and let the head of the group know what you're after.
6. Sometimes a magazine will let you put a call for quotes on their Facebook or Twitter page.

6. EXCLUSIVITY, SIMULTANEOUS SUBMISSIONS AND RIGHTS

EXCLUSIVITY

When an RPM says they want "exclusivity," they mean magazines in the same geographic area don't want to run the exact same article during the same month. It's kind of like how you wouldn't want to wear the same outfit to a party as a friend. They also don't want to run a piece that just ran in their competitor's publication.

EXAMPLE: Publication A in southern Florida wants to buy your article and print it in March. You accept. Then Publication B (also in southern Florida) wants the same piece, and they want to print it in May. You email Publication A, who wants exclusivity for 6 months, to ask who their competitors are, and they tell you Publication B is a direct competitor. You would then email Publication A to let them know you already sold the piece to a competitor, but they may use it in their October issue if they are still interested.

SIMULTANEOUS SUBMISSIONS

When an RPM's guidelines say they don't want simultaneous submissions, this means they don't want you sending to them <u>and</u> to other publications at the same time. If they pay well, try offering your piece to them first, wait a few weeks, then offer it to all the other pubs on the list.

RIGHTS

When an editor wants to buy your piece, assume they are offering you First North American serial rights. This means the rights revert back to you once the piece is published, and that it's fine for your piece to be in more than one publication in the same month. If an RPM has different terms, they will let you know, most often in the form of a contract they want you to sign and return. Different terms could include something like they want to use your piece exclusively online forever and they will pay you a decent rate. Ask if you could perhaps change the piece by about 20% and change the title and then shop it around other places. You want to maintain as much freedom with your work as possible so you can resell it other places.

7. COVER AND QUERY LETTERS

Most RPMs want to see your entire submission so they'll know if they want to buy it or not. For most RPMs, I send a cover letter to introduce my piece and my experience. And yes, I do this with every article or essay I send out because I can't expect every editor to remember my name when they receive hundreds of submissions per month.

Some RPMs and most national markets want you to send a query to them before you actually write the piece. This saves you time since this way you don't have to angle a piece to each separate market.

I recommend you buy the ebook called *Cash in on Your Kids: Parenting Queries That Worked* by Kris Bordessa, Teri Cettina and Jeannette Moninger because it contains sample query letters sent to national magazines, as well as the "secret code" of formatting email addresses for the large magazines like *Parenting*, *American Baby*, *BabyTalk* and many more.

SAMPLE E-MAIL COVER LETTER

This is a basic email "cover letter" similar to the one I send out, whether the piece is an original or a reprint. I consider even an original piece to be a reprint if I am sending it to everyone in my Excel database because I assume more than one publication will want to buy it, thus making it a reprint somewhere. Note how I send it to myself and then BCC the editors.

To: mommykerrie@yahoo.com
Bcc: editor@regionalpub.com; editor@otherpub.com
Subject: Submission: Dreaming of a Peaceful Holiday

The problem of where to go on Christmas day and who to spend the holidays with is one that's universal, and it only gets more difficult when you have kids. Many new (and not-so-new) parents find themselves being pulled in too many directions during a time that is already stressful.

My article, titled "Dreaming of a Peaceful Holiday," (below as text) aims to help solve this dilemma. At 861 words, I believe it would be a great fit for your December issue. If you decide to purchase this piece, I would be happy to include a local sidebar of your choice (e.g., local volunteer holiday opportunities).

I have been published in several publications, including *Kids VT*, *Pittsburgh Parent*, *Houston Family*, *Kansas City Parent*, *Memphis Parent*, *Calgary's Child* and *Georgia Family* (links available at KerrieMcLoughlin.blogspot.com) and would be honored to have my article featured in your publication.

I look forward to hearing from you!

SAMPLE QUERY LETTER

Following is an email query letter that I sent to *American Baby*. They loved the idea so much they had already assigned it to another writer a few weeks before they received my query! Ah, timing!

To: tricia.obrien@bonniercorp.com
Subject: Query: Desperately Seeking Sleep

Dear Tricia,

Being pregnant five times has practically made me an expert on sleep disturbances. If I wasn't rubbing out a leg cramp, I was wrestling with four pillows, eating Tums like they were M&Ms or lying awake worrying.

I would like to write a piece for you called, "Desperately Seeking Sleep," which would offer solutions to eight of the most common sleep disruptions experienced during pregnancy. This piece was originally published as "Pregnancy Sleep Solutions" in *Kansas City Baby* [insert a link to your article here, Reader] and several other regional parenting magazines, and I know it would be a great help for your national readership, as well.

To make this article a knockout, I would interview national experts about the latest sleep solutions, research and recommendations (e.g., if Ambien is alright to take during pregnancy, whether or not calcium tablets work for leg cramps, etc.) and would get quotes from moms all over the country about their pregnancy sleep woes and solutions they found helpful. It would also include a sidebar of relaxation exercises to try before bedtime.

I have been published in over two dozen regional parenting magazines, including *Calgary's Child*, *Columbus Parent*, *San Diego Family*, *Family Time* and *Washington Family*. You can find all of my publishing credits, as well as links to published pieces, at KerrieMcLoughlin.blogspot.com.

I would be happy to customize this piece in any way you might need and look forward to hearing from you.

Sincerely,

8. YOUR AUTHOR WEBSITE

"Perseverance is not a long race; it is many short races one after another."
– Walter Elliott

Even though the pay is relatively low, writing for RPMs can earn you valuable publishing credits. You'll need those clips and credits in order to make your move to writing for national publications in the future. Don't think an author website is unnecessary and too costly for you to set up. You don't need a professional website developer to showcase your writing credits and synopses of your published pieces. For now, in fact, my author website is on Blogger, and I hear amazing things about WordPress, whether you host it yourself or let them do it.

Once you get a body of work under your belt, you'll want to periodically send an email to all editors to let them know about your author website, which will list all of your available reprints. (If you don't have time for this right now, just send out YOUR REPRINT LIST). The reason you'll do this is to keep your work fresh in their mind for when they need filler pieces.

Your author website is important and should include the following:

- Something about you as a writer and a person
- A photo of you
- Summaries of articles you have written or have had published
- Links to the places where you have been published (your publishing credits), serving as a type of online resume
- A list of available reprints you have for sale

- Testimonials/references. Don't be afraid to ask for these from editors you have worked with. I have found LinkedIn to be a great resource for asking for recommendations.
- Links to your online writing so editors can see your writing style
- A way to contact you

With a little patience and a lot of hard work, your author website will grow as you write more pieces, are published more places and as you gain testimonials.

9. YOUR REPRINT LIST

Below is a short example of what I send to publications on a regular basis, sometimes monthly and sometimes more like quarterly. It's also nice to have it updated for when I find new publications I might want to work with and they ask me for samples or for my reprint list. I put a link to *Calgary's Child* (I did a search for my name on their site and all of my pieces came up) so any publications can get a feel for my writing style and see many of my pieces in full.

Kerrie McLoughlin Reprint List
updated 6/19/15
mommykerrie@yahoo.com

I would love to work with you! All pieces are available as Web-only posts, and you can find many of my pieces in full here at *Calgary's Child* [add link]. Please contact me first if you would be interested in reviewing one of these pieces for possible purchase so you don't overlap coverage in your area without realizing it. A synopsis of most can be found at http://kerriemcloughlin.blogspot.com, as well as pieces I have in the works!

1. *5 St. Patrick's Day Traditions to Start* (507 words)
2. *8 Birthday Traditions* (679 words)
3. *8 Egg-citing Easter Traditions* (816 words)
4. *8 Holiday Traditions for EVERYONE!* — (802 words)
5. *8 Tips for Saving on Birthday Gifts* (570 words)
6. *10 Fun Halloween Traditions* (625 words)

10. TAKING ON ASSIGNMENTS: JUST DO IT!

After you've sold a few articles to a specific editor, he/she may ask you if you are available to start writing articles assigned by the editor, or even a weekly online blog segment. This is wonderful because you often don't have to come up with the idea, and you get to sell the piece later as a reprint (ask about terms, as many sites will want your piece retooled by 20% and the title change). Often the editor will give you the specific information they want to see in the article, so all you have to do is research and write. Sometimes they'll even give you contact information for local sources to interview.

Never, never, never promise to write a piece and then change your mind at the last minute. If something comes up and you are unable to write the piece, let the editor know as soon as possible so she or he can re-assign the piece.

11. GETTING PAID AND SAMPLE INVOICE

INVOICING

Most of the time when a magazine wants to use your piece they will request an invoice from you. You can find invoice templates online, and maybe you even have a financial program that will invoice for you. I just use a simple Word document and enter my name and mailing address, the article name, month it was used and how much the charge is. I put an invoice number at the top (such as 2015-001) and make sure to put the name of the publication and save each invoice separately in case I need to resend.

HOW MUCH TO CHARGE

If an RPM asks you how much you want for an article, considerations include:

- the size of the RPM (i.e., how many copies they print and how often)
- the word count of the article
- whether or not they would like a local sidebar or local quotes
- whether or not you are promoting something in your bio like an ebook or book, in which case you might consider offering the piece for free
- the chances of selling the piece many more times as a reprint
- the chances of reworking the piece to sell to a national market
- if the piece will be used online indefinitely
- if you have worked with the publication before

You'll find that most RPMs pay anywhere from $15-100, with some in New York paying as much as $120.

*Because I've written for over 140 of the publications in this book, you can be sure the pay information I share is accurate. If pay seems low to you,

you can always negotiate a higher rate (e.g., if a publication says it pays $20, you could try asking for $30).

Karen Hammond, publisher of *Purchase Area Parenting*, shared some helpful advice: "The newest type of magazine submission is community magazine groups. Here content may be used in up to 50 local magazines owned by a regional publisher and printed simultaneously with only limited "local" content in each market. Writers should be aware if they are submitting to this type of magazine so that they are paid per insertion in all the magazines, not paid as if it was going into just one. They may want to negotiate a bulk rate."

MAKING SURE YOU GET PAID

Some magazines "forget" to email you first to talk payment, etc. before running your piece. To catch your writing and to make sure you're getting paid for your work, sign up for Google News Alerts at alerts.google.com. Enter your name as the search term and have Google notify you via email when it pops up on the Internet.

Unfortunately, Google News Alerts can't catch all mentions of your pieces so another great tip I have for you is to check Issuu.com every month and search for your name in quotes.

When I find that an RPM has used an article of mine without running it by me first, I send them an email like the one below. If I don't hear from them within a week, I email again. If another few days go by with no word, I start calling the magazine to speak with the editor and sometimes even have to find contact info for the publisher.

> Hi there! I recently found an article of mine on your website [*include link for them to see and also do a Print Screen to save it for your records as proof*] on [*date*] and was thrilled to see it! Attached is an invoice for my usual $35 reprint fee.
>
> Thanks so much, and I look forward to working with you again!

IF YOUR MONEY DOESN'T ARRIVE

1. Check the original email from the editor to see if they gave a timeline for sending you a check.
2. If there was no mention of when you would be paid, check this book for the RPM's writer's guidelines. Some RPMs pay 30 days after the publication of each issue; some pay on publication.

3. Resend your invoice not as an attachment, but in the body of the email. Mention the date you sent your original invoice.
4. If you still don't hear from anyone at the RPM, head back to this book for the phone number of the RPM. If I leave a message, I wait a week for a reply. If I don't get one, I call daily because I'm persistent like that!

12. KEEPING TRACK

"Some people dream of success … while others wake up and work hard at it."
– Author Unknown

TRACKING SUBMISSIONS

I like to keep track of which articles I've sent each month, which publications I sent them to and the dates I emailed or mailed them. I keep my logs in one Microsoft Excel document with several sheets, but you can decide which program works best for you. I include a column for where I submitted my piece to (the entire list of RPMs or just to *Brain, Child* magazine, for example); the name of my submission; date sent; amount to be paid; publication date; and when I was actually paid and how much I was paid.

TRACKING TIME

Some of you might want to use something like a time log (used in conjunction with your submissions tracking log), which tracks income and time all in one sheet for a picture of how you are using your time and of your most fruitful ventures. This is nice if you are working for clients as well as submitting to RPMs. You can create an easy time log in Excel with columns for the date; projects like Ebooks, Articles, Paid Blogging, Social Media, etc.; how much time you spent on each project; and how much you will be paid or how much you earned per hour.

TRACKING MONEY

You can also easily track your income with a Payments Received Log using Excel. I like to use something like this so I can track payments received for a quick annual financial picture, plus it makes it easier at tax time. I simply transfer amounts to the Time Log so I can get a picture of which of my ventures are most fruitful. I make columns for Publication, Article Name, Amount Owed and Date Received so I can see when I need to send follow-up emails for nonpayment.

OTHER TRACKING

I also suggest you start a spreadsheet for writing expenditures for your writing business write-offs at tax time (postage, mileage, etc.). You may also want to make a sheet to keep track of where your work has been published (your publishing credits) in alphabetical order by publication so you can easily put that information onto your author website later. I also have a spreadsheet for how many times and article has been published and where each article has been published because some publications ask if a competitor has ever published a piece before.

13. START SUBMITTING

"If you aim at nothing, you'll hit it every time."
– Author Unknown

I used to think sending out submissions to a huge list of editors by using the "blind carbon copy" (BCC) option on my email program was tacky. Then I did it myself with an article, saved a couple of hours per article and had a better success rate than when I sent individual emails addressed to each specific editor. Here's what a couple of editors have to say about what I do:

"Personally, I wouldn't rule out a story just because I received it this way. However, it is certainly possible that I give a bit more attention to a story when submitted directly to me. It would also seem that by taking the time to find out the types of articles that a publication uses that a writer's chance of selling the article would be heightened."

"I am also the publisher of 13 other periodicals ... I personally receive over 100 legitimate emails a day. I understand the importance of saving time. For me, I scan the in box and the subject ... I understand and agree with your sentiment. I just don't have time to do things all separately sometimes."

To increase your chance of article acceptance, check out the writer's guidelines in this ebook because some are extremely specific.

After I've written a piece, I always email it to all the RPMs in the included table. Then when I get more time I check out the guidelines (e.g., attachments only, double space after periods, a specific font, etc.) for the RPMs I really want to be published in and follow them for a better success rate. I have found that if your writing is good and fits an RPM's needs, your formatting (e.g., shorter, longer, more local) can be quickly and easily changed, and isn't generally a deal breaker.

SUBMITTING VIA EMAIL

Whether you buy this book in ebook or print format, you'll probably have to take the time to enter every email address and publication name and then assign it to a category. (Unless, of course, you are a brilliant computer person and know how to import the table into your email program.) For instance, I use Yahoo for my emails, and entered email addresses/publication names into categories of "Submissions 1", then "Submissions 2" and so on (remember: only 50 at a time or sometimes your email program might think you are a spammer).

*Even the magazines who only publish pieces by local writers sometimes need fillers and might need your piece someday so keep trying!

14. MOVIN' UP

"Know your limits, but never stop trying to exceed them." – Author Unknown

Once you've been published in a few Regional Parenting Magazines, you might want to take either some reprints or fresh material to a few national, international or online publications.

You'll notice many of the larger magazines make it practically impossible to track down an editor's email address and prefer to receive submissions and queries via snail mail (don't forget the self-addressed stamped envelope!). Once again, I recommend you buy the ebook *Cash in on Your Kids: Parenting Queries That Worked* by Kris Bordessa, Teri Cettina and Jeannette Moninger because it contains the "secret code" of formatting email addresses for the large magazines like *Parenting*, *American Baby*, *BabyTalk* and many more.

15. PAYING PARENTING AND FAMILY MAGAZINES

(201)family NORTH JERSEY
201magazine.com
editor@201magazine.com

A FINE PARENT (online)
afineparent.com
sumitha@afineparent.com
GUIDELINES: Write for us about Our Current Topic, which can be found online. Submit detailed outline by approximately the 4th of each month. I will let you know if your outline is accepted on approximately the 6th. The first draft of the full article is due by approximately the 13th. Payment will be made within 24 hours of receiving the final draft. Payment per accepted article is $100 + links + a shot at the annual bonus. (NOTE: This page is updated on the 1st of each month with a new topic and submission dates. Please sign up for notifications.) *A Fine Parent* is an online community for parents who believe that *Great Parents are Made, Not Born.* We focus on one topic each month that can help us become better people and better parents. Each week on the blog I publish one in-depth article related to the monthly topic. Initially, I wrote all the articles for this blog myself. After sharing a few readers stories and guest posts however, I realized just how much we can all benefit from shared wisdom and diverse voices. Hence this call for you to write for us. If you are constantly working on becoming a better parent, if you have a few hard-earned nuggets of wisdom under your sleeve, if you see another parent and instantly connect, AND if you happen to be a writer as well … *boy, have we been waiting for you!*

What We Look for In the Articles We Publish:

- the article MUST offer practical and actionable advice/tips
- the article MUST contain personal stories and anecdotes that connect with the other parents in our community (blah list posts won't cut it)
- the article MUST be written in web-format (well-organized; skimmable; short paragraphs; lists and bullets when possible; custom illustrations when possible)
- the article MUST include references to books, research or other authoritative references (you can even link to articles on your own blog as long as it is relevant and offers value)
- the article MUST be original and not published anywhere else before
- the article MUST contain the mandatory "2-minute action plan" (contemplation/reflection questions) and the "long-term action plan" (specific action to take over the next week) sections at the bottom of the article (see the bottom of any article for samples)
- Most articles on the blog are in the 1,500-2,500 words range. I prefer to stick to that range, but will make exceptions on a case-by-case basis.

By submitting the article you agree that if your article is published, I will retain the rights to republish or reuse the material in the future, of course with due credit to you. If you're not familiar with the blog, please spend some time there to get a feel for it first. You may even consider joining our community and just watching what gets posted for a bit before you start writing for us.

How to Submit

- Send me an email with the article outline before the deadline. Include as many details as possible to help me make an informed decision (for instance, mention any background stories that you plan to tie in, a list of the practical tips that will be included, references that will be used, any books that will be mentioned etc.)
- If you have published online before, please send me a few links so I can get a sense of your writing style.
- If your outline is accepted, send the completed article as a word document before the deadline.
- Include the keywords "Kick-ass Article for AFP" in ALL your email subject lines. (I get a LOT of mail, so this is *extremely* important to ensure that you receive a prompt response from me).

Frequently Asked Questions (FAQs)

1. I missed the deadline for this month, or this month's topic does not resonate with me. Do you by any chance have a list of the future topics?

Yes, sort of. A Fine Parent has been evolving into a true community blog and the topics we cover now are picked by our readers through a survey. A link to the response from our latest survey is online, and that should give you an idea of what we will cover next.

2. How do you notify me about the outline?
   I do my best to notify everyone of (a) the receipt of the outline and (b) the final decision. It will help immensely if you include the keywords "Kick-ass Article for AFP" in ALL your email subject lines. I receive a lot of mails and those words are part of an email filter that marks your mails as important so I can respond in a timely manner.
3. What kind of articles are more likely to get selected?
   We've been doing this for a few months now, and a pattern is beginning to emerge. The articles that I end up publishing are the ones where I see that *you personally relate* to the topic you've chosen to write about and hence will be able to connect more authentically and genuinely with the reader. For instance, if you are writing about how to teach kids to be compassionate, then either you've had to deal with your child acting unexpectedly mean, or your child has been a victim of bullying. Also, the "lessons learned"/ "what I'm trying to do"/ "what is working for me now" parts of your article tend to be much more real and not a riff off of a few Google search results. Think of it … You are a parent too. Which one of these would you rather read—a preachy list of things of what you must do in any given situation, or a real-life account of what another parent did in a very similar situation, their thought process, the obstacles they came up against and how they triumphed?
4. Can I submit more than one outline?
   No. Please submit only one outline per month. See #3 above. I'd rather that the focus be on quality than on quantity, and you send me that one article about the topic that most resonates with you.

If you have not written for us before or if you've not been a member of our community for long, please use the suggestions below to send your first outline. Also, please be sure to pick something you have personal experience with—anecdotes, unique perspectives and lessons learnt are highly valued in our community (hashed-up lists compiled using Google search generally don't make the cut). If you can bring professional advice from your day job and apply it in a clever and practical way to this month's topic, please do—these are some of the most highly prized articles we seek out!

APPROXIMATE PAY: $100 per article via PayPal with the chance for a $200 bonus at the end of the year if your piece is the most popular.

ABOUT FAMILIES – BERKS COUNTY
ABOUT FAMILIES – LEBANON COUNTY
Lebanon, PA
www.aboutfamiliespa.com
maric@aboutfamiliespa.com
GUIDELINES: Keep pieces under 600 words.
APPROXIMATE PAY: $10-20 per article.

ACTIVE FAMILY
Pleasanton, CA
activefamilymag.com
info@activekidsbayarea.com

ADDITUDE
additudemag.com
submissions@additudemag.com
GUIDELINES: Thank you for your interest in writing for *ADDitude*. We're always looking for great writers and great stories about attention-deficit hyperactivity disorder, learning disabilities, and related conditions. Most of the articles we publish are written by journalists and mental-health professionals. However, we are generally willing to consider first-person articles by parents, employers, teachers, etc. who have personal experience with ADHD or LD and whose insights might be helpful to *ADDitude*'s readers (most of whom are parents of children with ADHD or a learning disability and/or adults with ADHD). Reading back issues of the magazine is a good way to get a sense of the kinds of articles we publish. Please be aware that story concepts you propose may have been suggested previously by others or may already be planned for publication by our editorial staff. If you'd like to propose an article idea or submit a manuscript you've already written, please send a query letter to *ADDitude*. Your query letter should include: A brief description or outline of your idea; Why you think it belongs in our magazine; Why you should be the one to write it; Any recent clips you may have. If we're interested in your idea, we'll get back to you, generally within six weeks, with details about the assignment (deadline, payment, and so on). We prefer to receive submissions via e-mail, as attachments. But we accept submissions via US mail, as well. It generally takes us 6-8 weeks to respond to a submission. We regret that we are unable to return any materials you submit. Articles are usually 2,000 words or less and payment varies according to the article length, the experience and expertise of the author, and other factors. We consider all submissions on a speculative basis. We cannot guarantee that a proposed article, even one that we've expressed interest in, will be published. Payment is made upon publication of an article. If an assigned article is not accepted for

publication, we will pay a "kill" fee.

Blogger Guidelines

Interested in blogging for ADDitudeMag.com? Take a look at our blogs—written by parents of ADHD children, adults living with ADD, and even a CEO with ADHD—and consider how your blog topic is unique from others already covered. We are currently seeking the following types of ADD bloggers:

- Parent bloggers: Daily stories, victories, and rants from the people who love ADHD kids.
- Professional organizer blogger: Help kids and adults with attention deficit keep their lives in order.

ADDitude bloggers must contribute posts once a week. Compensation varies based on experience and level of contribution. To apply to become an *ADDitude* blogger:

- Please send a 300-word sample blog post covering the topic you'd like to blog about (i.e., your work as an ADHD coach, or a review of an ADHD-friendly product). Additionally, you may send us a sample of previously published work that reflects your ability and interest in blogging on an ADHD-related topic.
- Because our writers are expected to contribute on a weekly basis, we also ask that you send 10 additional post topics, complete with a headline and one-paragraph blurb for each.

Please send all blogging applications, as one attached file (as an .rtf or .doc file, or as a PDF) to webmaster@additudemag.com. Please allow six to eight weeks for a reply.

ADOPTIVE FAMILIES

Bimonthly
adoptivefamilies.com
submissions@adoptivefamilies.com

GUIDELINES: *Adoptive Families* is the leading information resource for families before, during, and after adoption. The award-winning national bimonthly magazine provides independent, authoritative adoption information in an accessible and reader-friendly format. Each issue of *Adoptive Families* is built around stories of adoption written by people who read the magazine closely and regularly. We encourage you to share your insights and experiences with other adoptive families.

CORE TOPICS COVERED IN EVERY ISSUE: Preparing for adoption; health issues; school and education; family, friends, and community; birth families; talking about adoption; parenting tips and guidelines

DEPARTMENTS:

***The Waiting Game:** A special section for pre-adopters

***Parenting the Child Who Waited:** Adopting and raising older children
***About Birthparents:** Stories about, and sometimes by, birth families
***Been There:** Adults speak honestly about their experiences of growing up adopted
***Our Story:** Your stories about how you became a family
***Adoption & School:** Advice from teachers, parents, and experts on education-related issues
***In My Opinion:** An editorial on a controversial subject
***At Home:** A personal essay
***Single Parent:** Single parents share their experiences
***And So It Begins:** Stories about the first year of parenthood
***Living with Diversity:** For and by families who've adopted transracially or from other cultures
***Letters:** Responses from readers to past articles and other readers' letters
In the case of reported articles on adoption-related topics, we prefer that you send a query letter (via e-mail or regular mail) before sending in your article. Again, take a look at recent issues of the magazine; we're less likely to publish a piece on a topic we've recently covered.

Query letters should include: a brief description or outline of your idea, why you think it belongs in our magazine, why you should be the one to write it, if possible, a sense of where in the magazine you believe your story might fit, whether as a feature or in a particular department; see list of departments above, any recent clips you may have

We prefer to receive submissions via e-mail, as attachments. You may also wish to send family photographs with your story, particularly in the case of personal essays. We prefer scanned photos e-mailed as attachments. Know the magazine. Look through past issues. Get a sense of our general tone. Familiarize yourself with the topics we generally cover. Consider which of our departments your story might best fit. Have a clear sense of your central theme. (E.g., "How I included extended family in our adoption process," "Traditions and rituals bind families together," "Networking can help to make the waiting period less agonizing.") Think about what makes your story unique—or what useful information families in similar situations might gain from it. Keep it active. Describe not only what happened to you, but how you chose to deal with it. Focus on choices made and strategies used to deal with a particular situation. (E.g., "We realized our parents weren't ready to be supportive, and we didn't have the energy to deal with their criticism on every single point, so we offered them only general information as we progressed through the adoption process;" "When my daughter started being questioned by her classmates about her adoption, I offered her teacher tips on how to inform the class about adoption in general without invading any individual student's privacy.") Keep it active. Describe not only what happened to you, but how you chose to deal with it.

Be specific. The more specific the details you provide, the more useful—and engaging—your story will be for other adoptive families. And bear in mind, even the most "ordinary" of experiences—the ones many people share—can be extraordinarily inspiring to read about. Other readers can learn from your experiences—even from your mistakes. We do receive many, many "How I Adopted" stories. But each of these can offer something unique if it maintains a strong focus on a central theme. Areas we are currently looking to cover: middle-school and teen years, relatives and community, adoptive parent support groups, school, foster adoption, transracial adoption, domestic adoption, adoptive parents of color

APPROXIMATE PAY: It generally takes us 6-8 weeks to respond to a submission. Writers of personal essays we publish will receive a one-year subscription to the magazine. Payment for reported articles varies. We're a small magazine; our pay rates are scaled accordingly. You should submit a brief, two- or three-sentence biographical note at the end of each submission.

ALAMO AREA KIDS AND FAMILY

alamoareakids.com
graphics@hillcountrytravelguide.com

ALASKA PARENT

alaskaparent.com
editor@alaskaparent.com

GUIDELINES: *Alaska Parent* is a free, full-color family and parenting magazine, published 4 times per year. As Alaska's exclusive, all-in-one parenting resource, our readers include parents with children ages newborn through teens, as well as expectant moms. We publish several stories in each issue, from hard-hitting articles on serious topics to pieces designed for fun and entertainment. Our writing tone is easy-to-read and conversational, yet packed with plenty of punch. Through our pages, we want our readers to feel understood, supported and empowered to make healthy parenting and life choices. We suggest writers examine our Editorial Calendar for information concerning the proposed features/focus of each publication. We also accept submissions on topics not included in the Editorial Calendar. Our ongoing editorial needs include topics relating to parenting and families, such as: health & wellness, education, pregnancy & babies, enrichment activities, holidays, sports & fitness, nutrition, technology, special needs, parties & celebrations, green living, family travel and all ages & stages (toddlers, preschoolers, school-age children, tweens & teens). We do not accept fiction, fantasy pieces, dreamy musings or poetry. Typically, we only give out story assignments to writers that have worked with us previously. In other words, please don't email us saying, "I want to write for you, please give me an assignment." Rather, send us a query letter with an idea for a specific article you'd like to write. We welcome story pitches, especially from local freelancers. These queries should be emailed to editor@alaskaparent.com. We do not accept queries through the mail or fax. You may send multiple queries.

Your query should be no more than 4 paragraphs and include:

- What is the focus of the story? A brief summary written in the style of your proposed piece.
- What are some of the key points you will cover and the sources you will interview?
- Answer the "so what?" Why is this story important to our readers? Why should you be the one to tell it?
- What is the anticipated word length? (In general, articles should be between 400 and 1,200 words in length.)
- If you have not written for us before, include 2-3 writing samples along with your query. Links to online stories are preferable, but PDFs are ok too.

Make your pitches detailed and concise. A vague pitch produces a vague article. Pitch early. Be mindful that content for *Alaska Parent* is determined months in advance. Therefore, story ideas should be pitched 2-4 months before the issue it would run. This is particularly important for seasonally anchored stories. *Alaska Parent* welcomes unsolicited articles that meet our story requirements. Send the complete article to editor@alaskaparent.com. If we are interested in your article, we will contact you prior to publication to negotiate an acceptable rate and obtain permission for use. We are interested in fresh material so reprints are less likely to be accepted. However, you may send us a reprint if you feel it fits perfectly with our magazine. Include the date, previous publisher and what rights they may have to the article. We may ask if we can insert local sources/content. We do require market (Alaska) exclusivity. Due to the high volume of queries/submissions and frequencies of our publications, our response time can take several weeks. Often we consider story ideas for several issues and may delay the publication of some stories for seasonal reasons. However, if you do not hear from us after 3 months of your submission, it is safe to assume that we have decided to pass. Please feel free to pitch us a new idea. If your query/submission is accepted, we will email you an acceptance letter that specifies deadline, word count and writer's fee. With the exception of reprints, we purchase all rights to articles, including the option to republish articles in special editions or post them online at www.AlaskaParent.com. (If you do not want your article to appear on our web site, do not submit it to our magazine.)

Here is an Editorial Checklist for *Alaska Parent.* Please do not send in your article until you have verified the following:

- Did I include a proposed headline? (Subheads are good, too.)
- Did I put my name directly below that?
- Did I write in third person, rather than first person? (If your article can only be written in first person, please refer to FIRST-PERSON SUBMISSIONS.)
- Did I interview local sources (experts, parents, kids)?
- Did I write in an easy-to-read, conversational style? Does the article sound informative but not authoritative (and certainly not lecturing!), while leaving the "voice of authority" to the experts?
- Did I write an interesting, compelling lead that grabs the reader?
- Does my story include unpredictable details and fresh insights?
- Did I include a sidebar? (Most articles benefit from one or two sidebars, which might provide helpful tips, "how-to" steps, additional resources, or other information related to the subject.)
- Does each paragraph logically lead to the next paragraph? Are there transitions, subheads, etc., to guide the reader if these are necessary?
- Did I include the name and phone number of all the sources at the end of story (in case Alaska Parent has any follow-up questions)?
- Are all sources, quotes or references accurate and correct and used with permission of the source?

FIRST-PERSON SUBMISSIONS

Alaska Parent is currently accepting the following, told in first-person:

- Personal Essays: These essays share personal experiences that would appeal to our readers. We are looking for inspiring, thought-provoking and humorous essays that honestly portray life. Make us laugh. Make us cry. Show us the good, the bad or the downright ugly. What did you learn? How did you change? Did it turn out in a way that surprised you? What did it all mean to you? The goal is to entertain, inform and to offer the wisdom gleaned from the experience. *NOTE: We receive many essay submissions, but we can only publish the very best, so make sure your submission is COMPELLING and WELL-WRITTEN.*
- Tips. Help make a parent's life easier by sharing creative ideas and solutions to everyday challenges, including (but not limited to): organization, scheduling, parenting, relationships, traveling, birthdays, holidays and more. These should be between 150-600 words.

PHOTOS

Photographs grab readers' attention, so we want to include them whenever possible. If you have photos or leads for photos, please pass that information along as early in the writing process as possible.

EDITORIAL DISCRETION

All submissions are subject to editorial review and approval by Alaska Parent and may be edited for grammar, clarity, brevity and tone. If major revisions are needed, you will be contacted. For reprints, local content/comments may be added. We reserve the right to reject an article at any stage before publication.

2015 EDITORIAL CALENDAR

SUMMER ISSUE (MAY-JULY)

The Summer Camp & Activities Issue: Get ready for a fun & safe summer: Advice/tips, hot products & special summer camps & programs. PLUS these features:

- Mompreneurs: Balancing the roles of mom & entrepreneur
- Unplug & play: The importance of creative play
- Blow 'em away! Birthday party ideas
- Kids & running: How to get started, stay safe and have fun
- Fido & the family: How to transition into dog ownership

FALL ISSUE (AUG.-OCT.)

The Back-to-School Issue: Everything you need to know to gear up for a great year – from healthy starts to success in school. PLUS these features:

- Technology use & Internet safety
- The 'sandwich generation': Raising kids & caring for aging parents
- Flag football: A touchdown for girls' sports?
- Childhood obesity: Strategies for helping kids lose weight
- Hit the road for a great fall family trip

WINTER ISSUE (NOV.-JAN.)

The Ultimate Holiday Issue: Holiday planning, activities and events, cheery crafts, delicious eats and a great Gift Guide for the whole family. PLUS these features:

- The gift of giving back
- Foster care or adoption: Know the answers
- Understanding autism: The truth might surprise you
- Health mythbusters: The 5-second rule & other things your mom said
- Hit the slopes: Learning to ski/snowboard

**Topics are subject to change*

APPROXIMATE PAY: Payment is negotiated per article and depends on the complexity of subject, the length of the article and the writer's level of professional experience and/or track record writing for us. For original articles, we generally pay $40-$200. For reprints, we generally pay $25-$40; however, authors willing to localize their reprints with interviews with local parents and experts can expect more. If your submission is accepted, you should submit an invoice (within an email is fine) that includes name, address, phone number, name of story and payment amount. Payment shall be due within 30 days after the print date of the publication.

AMERICAN BABY

New York, NY – monthly (2,000,000)
americanbaby.com
125 Park Avenue, 25th Floor
New York, NY 10017

GUIDELINES: *American Baby* is a monthly, national publication dedicated to being a knowledgeable guide for pregnant couples and new parents, particularly those having their first child or those whose child is birth to age Mothers are the primary readers, but fathers are involved also. Parenthood is a new and engrossing experience for our readers. They want to keep up with the latest issues affecting their new family, particularly health and medical news, but they don't have a lot of spare time to read. They are not interested in abstract or theoretical issues, or in subjects they can read about in general-interest magazines. We forgo the theoretical approach to offer quick-to-read, hands-on information that can be put to use immediately. And we present a balance view of some controversial issues, such as childhood immunizations, so the readers can make their own decision. Our readers want to feel connected to other parents, both to share experiences and to learn from one another. They want reassurance that the problems they are facing are solvable and not uncommon.

FULL-LENGTH ARTICLES: Submitted articles or query letters should offer helpful information on some aspect of pregnancy or child care; should cover a common problem of child-raising, along with solutions; or should give advice to parents on a psychological or practical subject. Articles about products, such as toys and nursery furniture, are not accepted as these areas are covered by staff members. Medical subjects are acceptable as long as at least two medical doctors or medical authorities are mentioned. A list of sources and contacts will be expected with submission of the article. Most feature articles run between 1,000 and 2,000 words. If practical, query first. Short items: We accept items of 50-350 words for Crib Notes (news and feature topics) and **HEALTH BRIEFS** (health and medicine). Items must appeal to a nationwide audience. Dated or seasonal material must be received at least three months in advance. If practical, query first. We do not accept fiction, fantasy pieces, dreamy musings, or poetry.

A simple, straightforward, clear approach is mandatory. We are an understanding shoulder to lean on, an experienced friend to lend a helping

hand. Articles can focus on the reality, the humor, and the delight of child-rearing, but not on its mystical or magical qualities. A preachy or know-it-all tone is unacceptable. Researched topics should include real-life anecdotes. Articles should contain approximately four to five subheads and a suggested headline. Articles submitted with sidebars and other short, additional elements are preferred. For query letters, include published clips, if available, and a brief outline/synopsis of the article idea. One article idea per query letter, please. Do not send queries by fax. Submit all queries and manuscripts with self-addressed, stamped envelopes to: Editor, *American Baby*, 375 Lexington Avenue, New York, NY 10017. Sample copy: For a sample copy of *American Baby* send a 9" x 12" self-addressed stamped envelope and $2 or equivalent postage to: *American Baby*, 375 Lexington Avenue, New York, NY 10017.
APPROXIMATE PAY: Between $800 and $1,000 for feature articles, depending on article length and whether the author has written for *American Baby* before, paid upon acceptance. First-person experiences pay $500 upon acceptance. Our kill fee is 25 percent of the stated payment.

ANN ARBOR FAMILY
FINDLAY FAMILY
TOLEDO AREA PARENT
Toledo, OH – monthly
toledoparent.com
cjacobs@toledocitypaper.com
nadine@adamsstreetpublishing.com
APPROXIMATE PAY: $35 per publication

ARIZONA PARENTING
Phoenix, AZ – monthly (70,000)
arizonaparenting.com
todd.fischer@azparenting.com
GUIDELINES: 600-1,600 words (columns, features and vignettes). Content includes Q&A with locally and/or nationally prominent people. Most articles require localized sidebars, as well. Art/photo needs: 300 dpi (original size) .jpg images. Submit as Microsoft Word attached, as well as in body of email.
APPROXIMATE PAY: $25-50 reprints. Payment for assigned features varies.

ATHENS-OCONEE PARENT
Watkinsville, GA – monthly
athensparent.com
editor@athensparent.com
GUIDELINES: We are always looking for well-written articles on subjects

such as health, teens, single parenting, dad's perspective, discipline and family life. Be sure to proof-read, spell check and check references. Include a small bio at the end of your story. Regular/semi-regular sections include: Health, Style, Education, A Reader Shares, Finances, Ages & Stages, Teen Talk, Eyes Wide Open, Grandparenting, Simple Living, Parenting 101, Product Reviews, Dad's Chair and Feature. *Athens Parent Magazine* reserves first-time rights to story. Editorial may also be published on the website. Writers will be assigned a story by the publisher or editor. Contract will include due date of story, topic and points to be covered.
APPROXIMATE PAY: $25 for reprints.

ATLANTA PARENT
ATLANTA BABY
JUST KIDS (Special Needs)
BIG BOOKS: Parties, Schools, Camp Guide
Atlanta, GA –monthly (120,000)/quarterly
atlantaparent.com
editor@atlantaparent.com
GUIDELINES: Submit seasonal material six months in advance. Authors should include name, address, phone number and email address at the top of the first page, along with the word count.
APPROXIMATE PAY: $35 for reprints.

AUBURN-OPELIKA PARENTS
auburnopelikaparents.com
EASTERN SHORE PARENTS
easternshoreparents.com
MOBILE BAY PARENTS
mobilebayparents.com
MONTGOMERY PARENTS
montgomeryparents.com
Auburn, AL
info@montgomeryparents.com
APPROXIMATE PAY: $20 for reprints. $10-15 if published online at *Eastern Shore Parents* plus $30-35 per article if also published in *Montgomery Parents*. Negotiate rates with editor up-front to find out what to charge and exactly which publications will feature your story.

AUGUSTA FAMIILY
Augusta, GA – monthly
augustafamily.com
kate.metts@augustamagazine.com
APPROXIMATE PAY: $25 for reprints.

AUSTIN FAMILY
Round Rock, TX – monthly (35,000)
austinfamily.com
editor2003@austinfamily.com
APPROXIMATE PAY: $25 for reprints.

BABBLE.COM
www.babble.com
submissions@babble.com
GUIDELINES: Use Babble search to see if your topic has been covered already. If not, indicate in the subject line of your email what section of Babble your piece would run: pregnancy, baby, toddler, kid, mom, celebrity, products, or food. Mom is the general category subsuming mom/parent identity, health, and relationship issues. Example subject line: Article for Mom: I Hate Going to the Park, Am I the Only One? As concisely as possible, indicate if you've written for Babble before (include links to articles) and include 2-3 links to other things you've written. If you've never been published, that's ok. Just let us know. Tell us the topic of your piece in 1-2 lines maximum. If you can't explain it easily, it's not ready to pitch. Then explain your angle — your new contribution to the topic, what's insightful/entertaining/counter-intuitive/poignant about your approach. For this, again, 1-2 lines maximum. Give us the first paragraph of the piece and then an outline of the rest. If it's a list, include a few sample entries. If the piece is already written, include it as an attachment. We are unable to accept articles that have been published elsewhere, including on personal blogs. Only submit a piece once and please don't follow up. Because of the volume of submissions, we can't respond to everyone who writes us. If you don't hear back, assume we decided not to accept it. Sorry about that.
APPROXIMATE PAY: $150 for an 800-1,000 word article.

BABY CORNER
thebabycorner.com
editor@thebabycorner.com
GUIDELINES: If you are interested in writing for the *Baby Corner*, there are two options. First, you can inquire about being added to our writers' pool. Should we accept your inquiry, we would then match your preferred writing topic with upcoming articles in that area. If we feel your interest, skills, and experience match what we are looking for, we will notify you of an assignment. Please see the topics we cover below. The second option available to writers interested in working with *Baby Corner*, is that of submitting a query letter. Perhaps you have a unique idea for an article that wouldn't ordinarily be seen. If so, you may want to submit a query letter to us. *Baby Corner* takes pride that all the information provided is written by

parents who have experience in the topics they write about. All articles are assigned with the writer's experiences, and stage of parenting in mind.

Topics We Cover

Fertility & Infertility	Pregnancy
Fertility Charting	Baby Showers
TTC Concerns	Pregnancy Checklists
Donor Insemination	Complications
General	General
Health	Health & Fitness
Testing Basics	Childbirth
	Maternity Fashion
	Nutrition
	Postpartum
	Signs & Symptoms

Babies	Toddler
Adoption	Health
Baby Care & Health	Parenting
Breastfeeding	Play Time
Bottle Feeding	Potty Training
Baby Development	Parenting
Newborns	Education
Parenting	
Safety	
Sleep	

Dads	Moms
Expecting Baby	Family Time
Parenting	Working Mom
Sex, Marriage & Relationships	Working at Home
Family Time	Stay at home moms
	Sex, Marriage & Relationships

Baby Corner's goal is provide a wide range of information for parents, and we seek out submissions that are informative and unique. We rely on the experience, research, and information of writers to publish articles that will appeal to our readers. However, we ask that our writers use the following guidelines of style when submitting an article: Please make sure your article is unique, and not currently published in print, or online. Never underestimate the power of spell checking. Try to keep the tone of your article upbeat, comical if appropriate, and unique. Do not use any special formats, colors, or fonts within your article. While it may look pleasing to the eye, it creates problems for us when placing your text into HTML format. If writing a feature article, please do not write in the first person. While we appreciate your personal experiences on the topic, most of our articles will be informational. Submissions written in the first will be considered personal essays. Please spell out abbreviations. This includes all numbers under 10, with the exception of weights and measures. Other instances where abbreviations should not be used include pounds, ounces, centimeters, etc. Be sure to fact check all your articles, and please provide your sources for medical information. Be sure to give credit where credit is due. If at all possible, use the name and general location of your source. If you need to change a name to provide anonymity to your source, please insert a disclaimer at the end of your work to reflect this. Direct quotes from doctors, nurses and other professionals are always a plus, especially if writing about medical topics. Please do not, in any way, change direct quotes. If you need to work around an error (grammar, usage, style, etc.), do so with the use of sub-text or paraphrasing. You may want to also consider asking your source for a re-quote or clarification. Please include a short bio at the end of your article, not to exceed three sentences. Please note that submitting either a query letter or an article for publication does not guarantee it will be used. We will do our best to respond to all queries. Should we express interest, we will notify you via e-mail. Either option is considered a freelance position, but you may have more opportunities, should you be added to the writers' pool. Either option requires that you submit an initial query letter. Query letters must contain the following: Tell us about yourself! (We like to get to know the writers we work with.); Topic(s) of Interest. (What do you feel most comfortable and experienced writing about? Why do you feel that you are experienced in this area?); Three samples of your writing. Please send only plain text documents in the body of your email. If you are submitting an article for consideration, please note whether or not it has been previously published.

BABYFIT

babyfit.com

rachel@babyfit.com

GUIDELINES: BabyFit.com is owned and operated by SparkPeople Inc., a leading online preventive health company. Our goal is to help as many people as possible reach their goals and lead meaningful lives. All of our programs are medically sound, completely free of charge, community-based and accessible. BabyFit.com specializes in the areas of fitness and nutrition within the context of pregnancy and parenting. Our members include women at different stages of family life—trying to conceive, pregnancy and parenting. BabyFit provides the information and encouragement that women need to enjoy healthy pregnancies and raise active families. BabyFit publishes weekly and daily e-newsletters, as well as articles and other content features that members can access through their Start page and Resource Center. As a small site with a focused mission, we have to be selective in choosing writers and articles that best fit our brand and help our members. Sample articles can be found in our Resource Center, and any potential writer should familiarize herself with the categories of our articles and topics that we have covered already.

Tone & Style

BabyFit articles are written by experts or well-researched writers. They should appeal to our average member, who is seeking healthy living, family-oriented information. The voice of BabyFit is helpful, encouraging, entertaining, easy to follow and/or relatable. Generally, articles are between 500 and 1,200 words in length.

Categories

BabyFit articles generally fall into the broad categories of Nutrition, Fitness, Pregnancy or Post-partum (parenting). To see the articles we have in each section of the site, use the following links.

Nutrition: Covers pregnancy-specific nutrition, family and child nutrition, food safety, eating away from home, healthy eating habits, meals and food choices, buzz-worthy research, quick and easy tips, seasonal and holiday tips, and special concerns.

Fitness: Pregnancy-specific exercise, safety, family and lifestyle, special concerns, tips and strategies for busy parents, and specialty workouts.

Pregnancy & Post-Partum: Motivation for healthy living, parenting & baby care, breastfeeding, and general pregnancy topics.

Freelancing Opportunities

The vast majority of BabyFit's content is created by our in-house staff of experts, but we do occasionally hire freelance writers who specialize in health topics related to pregnancy, parenting, nutrition and fitness. If we do not offer you a writing project, please understand that the decision is multifaceted, not a negative judgment of your skills. Each year, we receive numerous queries from people who want to contribute content to BabyFit. We produce a limited number of articles each week, and therefore, can only assign a small number of articles. If you are interested in writing for BabyFit.com, please send an email with attachments of your resume and an applicable writing sample(s) to Rachel@BabyFit.com.

APPROXIMATE PAY: As a free site, we try to keep our costs as low as possible. Freelancers are typically paid between $25 and $90 per piece, based on experience, credentials, and writing ability, and are required to carry their own professional liability insurance.

BABYTALK
babytalk.com
letters@babytalk.com
New York, NY – 10 times/year (2,000,000)
530 Fifth Avenue, 4th Floor
New York, NY 10036
Phone: 212-522-4327
GUIDELINES: *BabyTalk* is the one baby magazine that tells it like it is, helping women navigate the emotional roller coaster and practical realities of being a new mom. *BabyTalk* provides straight talk for new moms through three cornerstones:
1. Focus: on what she needs here and now
2. Practicality: emphasis on what really works for her life and her baby
3. Small Victories: helping her attain and celebrate those key milestones.

BabyTalk magazine serves as a manual for parents in their day-to-day experiences with new parenthood. Features cover marriage and sex, pregnancy, baby care basics, toddler/infant health, how-tos, growth and development, toys/equipment, and work/day cares. Query with clips. **APPROXIMATE PAY**: $150-2,500 for word count of 100-2,000 (appx. $1.50/word)

BALTIMORE'S CHILD (exclusive)
Baltimore, MD – monthly (48,000)
baltimoreschild.com
editor@baltimoreschild.com
GUIDELINES: We are looking for articles that emphasize positive, constructive, and practical advice that will help parents make informed choices. We seek stories with a local angle that offer specific resources and information. For example, an article on teaching children to swim should be accompanied by a list of places in the Baltimore area providing swim lessons. Feature-length articles run about 1,200 words long. Short features and columns generally run about 750 words. Articles are usually assigned three months or more in advance, but articles that are extremely timely will be considered as close to six weeks prior to publication. Queries should include the proposed subject, a description of the information the article will cover, and an indication of style. If this is a first letter of inquiry, samples of other published work should accompany the query. Unsolicited manuscripts, including articles submitted for reprint, are also considered. All manuscripts submitted for publication should be accurate and original. All sources of quotes and copied material must be noted and/or attributed within the article. We will not knowingly publish or accept responsibility for material that plagiarizes or infringes on existing copyrights. Unless otherwise stipulated, payment of articles is for first-time publishing rights in

the Baltimore area. Although writers are welcome to query other publications for reprint possibilities, we ask that you do not submit the same or similar manuscript to other local, competing publications. We ask that, where possible, writers ask for photos from the venues and/or people about which the article is being written. Photos should be sent by email, directly to the editor, at the same time the article is submitted. Also, each photo should be labeled with the name(s) of the subject(s). Every attempt is made to respect the integrity of the writer's material, but we reserve the right to edit the material as needed to fit the style, format, and philosophy of our publication. While we expect writers to double-check all facts, we may also check facts for accuracy. Writers will be given a deadline at the time the article is assigned. Should you have difficulty meeting a deadline for an assigned article, notify the editor as soon as possible. Failure to meet the deadline may cancel the contract, including payment. Also, it is unlikely that writers who miss deadlines without giving prior notification will be assigned further work. Style sheet is on the website.
APPROXIMATE PAY: Payment is made within 30 days of publication. Fees are competitive with other local publications. The amount of payment for each article is specified by the editor at the time the article is assigned.

BATON ROUGE PARENTS
Baton Rouge, LA – monthly (25,000)
brparents.com.com
amy@brparents.com
NORTHSHORE PARENTS
Baton Rouge, LA – monthly (25,000)
www.nsparents.com
nsparents@brparents.com
APPROXIMATE PAY: $25 for reprints or original articles.

BAY AREA PARENT
Silicon Valley, Peninsula/SF/Marin, East Bay editions – monthly
bayareaparent.com
jill.wolfson@parenthood.com

BAY STATE PARENT
Millbury, MA – monthly
baystateparent.com
editor@baystateparent.com
APPROXIMATE PAY: $25-35 reprints.

BC PARENT
Vancouver, British Columbia, Canada – 8 times per year (45,000)

www.bcparent.ca
info@bcparent.ca
APPROXIMATE PAY: $50 for reprints.

BIRMINGHAM PARENT

Pelham, AL – monthly (35,000)
birminghamparent.com
editor@birminghamparent.com
GUIDELINES: All articles are expected to carry a local slant. Therefore, the magazine usually prefers to work with local, established, professional writers. We occasionally use reprints. No "how to have fun this summer" pieces, etc. We rarely do columns from submissions from businesses; we prefer stories with numerous sources by local writers. Sometimes these are more advertising than informative. Local Features (1,000-2,500 words) cover topics that apply to parents and children in our area. These might include serious topics like education, health, family travel, nutrition, parenting and so on, or roundups of local parks, museums, etc. "Human Interest" stories are rare for us, but we do offer a local monthly column, "Community Heroes," that highlights someone making a difference in the community. We prefer to have photography/art with each story. Monthly columns include Family Travel, Parenting Solo (single parenting), Community Heroes, Family Feasts (restaurant review) and Our Home & Garden, along with Baby & Me, Birmingham Teens, Birmingham Senior, etc. Queries should explain the premise of your article, its structure and the sources you plan to quote, if you can supply photos, as well as your qualifications as a writer. Without clips or prior experience with our editor/publication, we may require the story on spec. Query at least three months in advance for timely material and expect us to take at least four weeks to respond. Query holiday-based articles four months in advance. *Birmingham Parent* can accept Microsoft Word files, .rtf and text files, or the article can be pasted into the email. Or, a CD or floppy can be mailed, but should be mailed early enough to arrive by the set deadline. A signed copy of the agreement and an invoice should accompany the submission. A one-time W-9 is required. Digital photos are preferred, and should be 300 dpi or greater, preferably .jpg format. Please do not send photographs that must be returned. Websites are not accepted as main sources of any story, except a story about a website or websites. Websites are not guaranteed accurate. Our niche/hook is that we are a local magazine—both for our readers and our advertisers. We need to have local people quoted and used as sources. If you are having difficulty finding local sources on a certain topic, get in touch with us as soon as possible, and we will try to help you locate someone appropriate. In addition, if you are quoting a website, you should quote the website and not a person speaking on the website as though you

have actually spoken with them, unless you have actually talked to that person. All stories need attribution. We don't want "written off the top of your head" stories unless you are writing a column for us or have expertise in a particular subject and we can point that out. Those of you who are columnists—this doesn't apply to you, of course. We are now using a writer's contract for all stories. It protects us all and makes clear what the assignment is. If you didn't get one, please remind me/let me know. (Again, columnists have a one-time contract.) Of course, photos are always appreciated if you have access to them. Remember to give yourself a tag line at the end of your story. I need an invoice for each story, and a one-time W-9 if you are a new writer. If your story doesn't match what we agree upon by contract, a 20% kill fee will be paid.

APPROXIMATE PAY: Fees are paid on a case-by-case basis, negotiated between writer and editor, by contract. Full payment is made upon publication, within 30 days. *Birmingham Parent* purchases First North American Serial Rights, and 10% of the fee paid goes toward electronic rights. Each writer signs a contract on a story-by-story basis, and writers are expected to fulfill the agreement in order for the story to be used and them to be paid. Fees range from $35-50 for a reprint or short "fast facts" piece, to $300 for a full-length, heavily researched feature.

BLACK HILLS PARENT

Rapid City, SD
blackhillsparent.com
editorial@blackhillsparent.com

GUIDELINES: *Black Hills Parent* magazine is looking for freelance writers who demonstrate a fresh, engaging writing style and a keen sense of the topics that matter to local parents. Before you pitch a story to us, we recommend you get a feel for the type of articles we value and promote. We are a free, full-color family and parenting magazine, published 4 times per year. As Black Hills' exclusive, all-in-one parenting resource, our readers include parents with children ages newborn through teens, as well as expectant moms, grandparents, and caregivers. We publish several stories in each issue, from articles on serious topics to pieces designed for fun and entertainment. Our writing tone is easy-to read and conversational, yet packed with plenty of impact. Through our pages, we want our readers to feel understood, supported and empowered to make healthy parenting and life choices. We suggest writers examine our Editorial Calendar (below) for information concerning the proposed features/focus of each publication. We also accept submissions on topics not included in the Editorial Calendar. Our ongoing editorial needs include topics relating to parenting and families, such as: health & wellness, education, pregnancy & babies, enrichment activities, holidays, sports & fitness, nutrition, technology, special needs, parties & celebrations, green living, family travel and all ages & stages (toddlers, preschoolers, school-age children, tweens & teens). We do not accept fiction, fantasy pieces, dreamy musings or poetry. We welcome story pitches, especially from local freelancers. You may send multiple queries. Your query should be no more than 4 paragraphs and include:

- What is the focus of the story? A brief summary written in the style of your proposed piece.
- What are some of the key points you will cover and the sources you will interview?
- Answer the "so what" question. Why is this story important to our readers? Why should you be the one to tell it?
- What is the anticipated word length? (In general, feature articles should be between 650 and 800 words in length. Other articles can range between 200-400 words.)
- If you have not written for us before, include 2-3 writing samples along with your query. Links to online stories are preferable, but PDFs are ok too.

Tips: Make your pitches detailed and concise. Pitch early. Be mindful that content for *Black Hills Parent* is determined months in advance. Therefore, story ideas should be pitched 2-4 months before the issue it would run. This is particularly important for seasonally anchored stories. We welcome unsolicited articles that meet our story requirements. Send the complete article and if we are interested in your article, we will contact you prior to publication to negotiate an acceptable rate, actual story length needed, and obtain permission for use. We do require market (Rapid City and the surrounding Black Hills communities) exclusivity. Due to the frequencies of all of our publications, our response time can take several weeks. Often we consider story ideas for several issues and may delay the publication of some stories for seasonal reasons. If your query/submission is accepted, we will email you an acceptance letter that specifies deadline, word count and writer's fee. With the exception of reprints, we purchase all rights to articles, including the option to republish articles in special editions or post them online at www.BlackHillsParent.com. Here is an Editorial Checklist. Please review your article with the following in mind:

- Did I include a proposed headline? (Subheads, stand first, and pull quotes are good, too.)
- Did I put my name directly below that?
- Did I write in third person, rather than first person? (If your article can only be written in first person, please refer to FIRST-PERSON SUBMISSIONS.)
- Did I interview local sources (experts, parents, kids)?

- Did I write in an easy-to-read, conversational style? Does the article sound informative but not authoritative (and certainly not lecturing!), while leaving the "voice of authority" to the experts?
- Did I write an interesting, compelling lead that grabs the reader? • Does my story include unpredictable details and fresh insights?
- Did I include a sidebar? (Most articles benefit from one or two sidebars, which might provide helpful tips, "how-to" steps, additional resources, or other information related to the subject.)
- Does each paragraph logically lead to the next paragraph? Are there transitions, subheads, etc., to guide the reader if these are necessary?
- Did I include the name and phone number of all the sources at the end of story (in case Black Hills Parent has any follow-up questions)?
- Are all sources, quotes or references accurate and used with permission of the source?

FIRST-PERSON SUBMISSIONS *Black Hills Parent* is currently accepting the following submissions, told in first-person:

Personal Essays: These essays share personal experiences that would appeal to our readers. We are looking for inspiring, thought-provoking and humorous essays that honestly portray life. Make us laugh. Make us cry. Show us the good, the bad or the downright ugly. What did you (the person in the article) learn and/or change? Did it turn out as expected? What did it all mean to them? The goal is to entertain, inform and to offer the wisdom gleaned from the experience.

Tips. Help make a parent's life easier by sharing creative ideas and solutions to everyday challenges, including (but not limited to): organization, scheduling, parenting, relationships, traveling, birthdays, holidays and more. These submissions should be between 300-700 words. Photographs grab readers' attention, and we include them whenever possible. If you have photos or leads for photos, please pass that information along as early in the writing process as possible. All submissions are subject to editorial review and approval by us and may be edited for grammar, clarity, brevity and tone. If major revisions are needed, you will be contacted. We reserve the right to reject an article at any stage before publication.

EDITORIAL CALENDAR

Appearing In Every Issue: Extensive Family Calendar, Spotlight Stories on a Local Family, Volunteers, Grandparents, Ages and Stages, Making an Impact, Youth-driven Success Stories, Family Wellness and Babies, Fun and Memories, Education, Home, You and Me

Fall: (Publishes Aug – Covers through Oct) The Back to School and Fall Fun Issue: Everything you need to know to help gear up for a great year—from health checkups to school success strategies and special education

programs. Also featuring • Family finance • Fall fun • Fitness & kids
Winter: (Publishes Nov – Covers through Jan) The Big Holiday Issue: Holiday planning, events and entertainment, Family Vehicle Review, toy and gift review. Also featuring • Youth-driven success stories • Volunteering, charity • winter family fun
Spring: (Publishes Feb. – Covers through Apr) The Resolutions and New Beginnings Issue: Everything babies, Summer camp guide, Family health, fitness and nutrition, family and relationships, home services, kids and the arts. Also featuring • Youth sports • Celebrate moms • Party planning
Summer: (Publishes May – Covers through July) The Family Summer Fun Issue: Activities, gear, advice/tips, summer attractions, programs and venues. Also featuring • Youth activities • Celebrate dads • Summer Fun
APPROXIMATE PAY: Payment is negotiated per article and depends on the complexity of subject, the length of the article, and the writer's level of professional experience. For original articles, we generally pay .05-.08 per word based on the previous qualifiers. For reprints, we generally pay .03-.05. If your submission is accepted, you should submit an invoice (within an email is fine) that includes name, address, phone number, name of story and payment amount. Payment shall be due within 30 days after the print date of the publication.

BOOM! 50+ POSITIVE AGING

riverregionboom.com
jim@riverregionboom.com
GUIDELINES: Needs grandparent articles, positive aging.
APPROXIMATE PAY: $25 reprints.

BOSTON PARENTS PAPER (locals only)

Norwood, MA – monthly
boston.parenthood.com
deirdre.wilson@parenthood.com
GUIDELINES: *The Boston Parents Paper* has no formal guidelines, but generally never works with writers who live outside of our region. Department length pieces should be no more than 1,000 words, while features should be no more than 1,600-1,800 words in most cases. We consider queries, but for the most part we do not accept reprints. We do usually require a Resource List (as a sidebar) at the end of any major department article or feature with books, websites and organizations readers can turn to for more information. We also like sidebars or boxes with bulleted tips offering parents real, actionable steps toward solving a particular problem or dealing with an issue.
APPROXIMATE PAY: We pay anywhere from $100-400.

BOYS' LIFE
boyslife.org
Only query by mail
GUIDELINES: *BOYS' LIFE* is a general-interest, four-color monthly, circulation 1.1 million, published by the Boy Scouts of America since 1911. We buy first-time rights for original, unpublished material.
NONFICTION
Major articles run 500-1,500 words; payment is $400-1,500. Subject matter is broad. We cover everything from professional sports to American history to how to pack a canoe. A look at a current list of the BSA's more than 100 merit badge pamphlets gives an idea of the wide range of subjects possible. Even better, look at a year's worth of recent issues. Find the magazine in libraries and in BSA council offices. Query Senior Editor Paula Murphey. Departments run up to 600 words; payment is $100-400. Department headings are science, nature, earth, health, sports, space and aviation, cars, computers, entertainment, pets, history, music—and others. Each issue uses seven departments, on average. We also have back-of-the-book how-to features. Query Associate Editor Clay Swartz.
FICTION
Our short stories are assignment-only. Please do not query or send manuscripts. Unsolicited manuscripts will be returned unread.
STYLE
All articles for *BOYS' LIFE* must interest and entertain boys ages 6 to 18. Write for a boy you know who is 12. Our readers demand crisp, punchy writing in relatively short, straightforward sentences. The editors demand well-reported articles that demonstrate high standards of journalism. We follow *The Associated Press Stylebook*. We receive approximately 40 queries and unsolicited nonfiction manuscripts per week. Because of our high standards, all of our articles are commissioned; thus, unsolicited nonfiction manuscripts rarely are appropriate for publication and regrettably must be returned unread. Please query by mail (with SASE), not by e-mail or phone.
APPROXIMATE PAY: $100-1,500.

BRAIN, CHILD
Lexington, VA – quarterly
brainchildmag.com
editor@brainchildmag.com
GUIDELINES: *Brain, Child* is an award-winning literary magazine for mothers. We publish 20-plus essays per month for our print, online and blog publications. Founded in 2000, our mission is to bring the voices of women of different backgrounds and circumstances together on the page, on our website, and on our blog. We are excited by great writing. It makes our day when we hear from an established writer or publish an author for

the first time. We believe our writers are the lifeblood of our publication and strive to publicize and promote our writers through our website, Facebook (100,000+ fans), and partnerships with Babble.com, The Huffington Post, Mothering.com and others. We respond within eight to ten weeks. We offer competitive pay rates. We welcome follow up emails if by chance you do not hear from us. For all submissions, please email the manuscript in the body of the email toeditorial@brainchildmag.com with "Submission" and the department (i.e., "Fiction" "Essay" "Feature Pitch") as the subject heading. Please don't send your submission as an attachment. We do not accept submissions through the mail, and we do not accept previously published pieces.

PERSONAL ESSAYS (800-4,000 words): These are the signature pieces of the magazine, the heart and soul of our endeavor. We're looking for essays that share certain qualities—specificity and insight primary among them. These pieces should employ illustrative anecdotes, vivid scenes, authentic dialogue, a strong personal voice, and a down-to-earth tone. Examples of recent essays include a woman searching for her egg donor on Facebook, a blind mother raising her sighted child, and a mother's fight to adopt her foster child. Please note that we don't publish how-to articles.

FEATURE (3,000-5,000 words): Each issue, we devote space to at least one traditional feature, a piece that relies more heavily on reporting than introspection. Examples of our feature stories include an in-depth look at home birthing, how to talk to children about sexual abuse, and an investigation into teens' overuse of performance enhancing and focus and productivity boosting drugs. We look for high-quality research and reporting that also incorporates a strong narrative. Please query with clips and a one-page story outline.

FICTION (1,500-4,000 words): We look for strongly developed characters, vivid scenes and authentic dialogue. Since much of Brain, Child is made up of personal essays, we prefer stories that aren't written from a first-person point of view.

POETRY Poetry submissions are closed as of November 1, 2014. Our poetry slots are full through 2015.

NUTSHELL (200-800 words): Nutshell is our news section, offering both stories you won't find in the mainstream media and unique perspectives on hot topics. Example stories include: a profile of pediatrician whose own children watched three hours of TV a day; a report on a new study of lesbian adoptive mothers; and an interview with a mother whose child left home for college at fourteen. Please query with clips and a pitch.

DEBATE Our section of friendly fire, where two writers square off on a topic of controversy. We're looking for concise, thoughtful words on issues such as sex education, letting kids quit, and whether sleeping with your children is okay: for the magazine, 750 words on a yes/no question; for the website, up to 1,000 words on a particular perspective. Brief anecdotes desirable; very strong opinion required. Please query with the issue you will address, clips and/or publication credits and the writer you will pair up with if you have one.

REVIEWS (200 words for mini-reviews; 700-2,500 for longer reviews): We review new and not-so-new books of parenting-related nonfiction, memoir, autobiography, and fiction as well as theme-based roundups (an example of this is a collection of stories that "Teach Tolerance" or books that encourage children to "Make the World a Better Place." Our short reviews focus on books dealing with family or parenting (no how-to or expert advice manuals). The longer review essays tackle several books on a distinct theme; these essays are thesis-driven rather than a serial review of the works at hand.

MOTHERWIT (800 words): This is our back page essay that relishes humor. We're open to a variety of forms (e.g., narrative, letter, quiz, etc.)—as long as it makes us laugh.

CALL FOR SUBMISSIONS

BRAIN, TEEN Accepting submissions ongoing.

BRAIN, MOTHER (500-1,200 words): This is our signature blog where we capture short essays that spur thinking and conversation. Recent posts include a mother teaching her children about discrimination, a mother deciding whether to medicate her daughter, and a mother's adoption of a foster child.

RIGHTS First North American Rights with exclusive for six months after publication and crediting/linking to *Brain, Child* as the original publisher if work is published after the exclusivity period.

BRONX FAMILY
BROOKLYN FAMILY
QUEENS FAMILY
BABYNEWYORK
NEW YORK SPECIAL CHILD

Brooklyn, NY – monthly (35,000)
yournabe.com
kbrown@cnglocal.com

GUIDELINES: A local angle is critical.

APPROXIMATE PAY: $35-75.

BROWARD FAMILY LIFE

Davie, FL – monthly
browardfamilylife.com
info@browardfamilylife.com

APPROXIMATE PAY: Yes, but not much!

CALGARY'S CHILD

Calgary, Alberta, Canada – bimonthly
calgaryschild.com
calgaryschild@shaw.ca

GUIDELINES: They will send an email to writers they've worked with before letting the writers know what the upcoming issue will be about and what kinds of articles they are looking for. If you already have something in our "article bank" that fits their needs, you can offer it to them. Otherwise, email them back quickly to let them know your ideas for writing a new piece for them.

APPROXIMATE PAY: $50 Canadian for originals or reprints; $25 if only online.

CAROLINA PARENT (exclusive)
CHARLOTTE PARENT
PIEDMONT PARENT

Durham, NC – monthly (100,000)
carolinaparent.com
editorial@carolinaparent.com

GUIDELINES: *Carolina Parent* provides parents and others who care for children in the greater Triangle area of North Carolina with current and useful information, news, advice and resources. Freelance writers provide articles for the following resources:

- Monthly magazine with a readership of more than 100,000 that includes feature articles and department columns written by freelance writers either on assignment or purchased as reprints.
- Annual guides with shorter feature articles.
- Website with articles that appeared in print and blogs.

Feature-length articles are 850-1,600 words. Departments are 650-1,200 words, with most around 850 words. These are best initial pieces for new writers. Regular departments with rotating writers include: Nesting (home), Ages/Stages (pregnancy, 0-5, 6-10, 11-18) and Family Fun (with a focus on local places and activities). Freelance assignments are made two to three months in advance for monthly magazine articles. For example, articles for an April issue usually are assigned during January and due Feb. 10-22, depending on the writer's experience and complexity of the article. Query three months before the issue date with ideas and/or available reprints. Submit reprints two to three months in advance of when they would be used. For example, reprints that fit our April theme should be submitted in January. Local writers also blog on our website. These bloggers are not paid, but affiliation with CarolinaParent.com provides exposure and recognition. If you would like to blog for CarolinaParent.com, contact Web Editor Odile Fredericks at ofredericks@carolinaparent.com. Send an e-mail query to the appropriate editor listed above that includes:

- Why the topic is of interest to *Carolina Parent* readers; include local relevance.
- Story outline with proposed headline, sections and overview of information.
- Potential local sources.

If you are new to *Carolina Parent*, also include:

- Writing experience and related background.
- Two or three writing samples (links or PDFs are fine).

Tip: Provide a hook. Tell us, clearly and succinctly, why this is a great idea for *Carolina Parent* and what it will look like. We receive many more article queries than we can respond to personally. However, if you are a local writer and have not heard back within two weeks, you may submit another query, repeating the details. Persistence often pays off. If your query is accepted, we email an outline that includes: due date, word count and rights purchased. During the writing process, please let us know if:

- New information will change the focus of the article
- Sources change or you need help finding sources
- You need help or guidance with organization, angle or focus
- Assigned article length is not sufficient; you estimate the piece needs to be longer or shorter than established word count
- You will not meet your deadline

We take deadlines seriously. However, we recognize that emergencies happen. Please let us know if you do not think you will be finished by the deadline, but do not make it a regular occurrence or your work will no longer be considered. Writers on assignment may contact us by e-mail or phone. It is better to ask for clarification and guidance than to rewrite an article after deadline. Writers with reprints available for purchase should send the complete article, or enough content to provide the tone, coverage and sourcing. Provide a list of articles available for reprint, organized by topic or type of piece. Send these quarterly or seasonally for best results. We will contact you prior to publication to negotiate an acceptable rate and obtain permission for use. Submit reprints in the body of an email and also as a Word attachment. Include a short intro paragraph explaining why this is important or helpful information for our readers. Include in the e-mail and in the document itself:

- Your byline as you want it to appear.
- Contact information, including e-mail, address and phone.
- Short biographical information at the end explaining any relevant tie to the topic and your writing interests.

Let us know if the pre-written article has not been printed elsewhere and you are willing to localize it for our market. Submitting contracted articles:

E-mail your article by 5 p.m. of the due date unless you have otherwise notified the assigning editor. Include in your article: a suggested headline and deck; subheads to break up the copy and make it easy for readers to follow; possible call-outs or quotes to highlight; bulleted items for lists, steps or examples (if appropriate); byline as you would like it to appear; bio line at the end

Other guidelines:

- Do not use any special formatting other than boldface. Left justify copy and use Times New Roman, 12-point font. Do not use page numbering or headers and footers.
- Use only one space after a period.
- Submit as a Word attachment, .doc, not .docx.
- Include sidebars at the end of the main article if they are short and limited (one or two). Longer or extra sidebars may be submitted as separate documents, but note them on the main article.
- Provide online URLs for resources for online linking at the end of the article or sidebars.
- Include list of sources as a separate document.
- Share relevant information in the body of the e-mail, such as: additional information for possible sidebar, photo availability, when to best contact you about editing process (i.e., if going out of town or are unavailable during certain times of the day).
- Include a separate invoice. (See payment section for details.)

Carolina Parent is owned by Carolina Parenting Inc., which also publishes *Charlotte Parent* and *Piedmont Parent.* Articles can be resold to these publications. Some articles are assigned and written for all three markets. Become familiar with *Carolina Parent* by reading a few issues and/or several articles online. Most of our articles are written in an easy-to-understand, helpful, relatively casual style. Think of yourself as a friend or advisor to our readers, who are informed parents of children birth through high school. Write in an objective, balanced style, with respect and regard for a varied audience with potentially different beliefs and parenting styles. Let your natural voice show through so your writing isn't stilted or overly formal, but don't insert yourself unnecessarily into the piece. (Most of our articles do not use first person except in limited situations where there is a direct tie to the topic or it is an essay.) Pay attention to subject/verb agreement. Use active, not passive, voice. The subject should "do" the action with sentence structure of subject then verb. Our goal is to provide balanced information in an easy-to-read format that helps parents make decisions that are best for them and their families. Most articles are reported pieces, using interviews from local experts and parents. Feature-length pieces require a minimum of three relevant sources. All assigned articles must have local sources and local relevance. Use experts who can provide factual, relatively unbiased information. Consider university professors, other educators and researchers, nonprofit and professional organization spokespeople, government sources, book authors, and those who do not monetarily benefit from a particular point of view. If you interview a source with a specific bias, include a source with an opposing view. Balance sources geographically in the readership area, which stretches from Durham to Clayton, including Chapel Hill, Carrboro, Cary/Apex, Holly Springs, Garner, Raleigh, Wake Forest, and points in between. To find parent sources, ask organization contacts or experts you talk with to recommendations or leads. Tap into parenting community groups and acquaintances of contacts. Interviews are best conducted in person. While that may not always be possible, a phone interview is the next best alternative. We strongly discourage e-mail as a way to gather information for an article with the exception of verifying information or getting additional background information after or prior to an interview. It is the writer's responsibility to be sure all facts are correct. Double-check all information before turning in a story. We do not have dedicated fact-checkers on staff. At a minimum, be sure to verify:

- Spelling of names and organizations
- Ages if appropriate
- Titles and/or related professional or educational experience
- Contact information such as phone numbers and websites

It is *Carolina Parent*'s policy not to provide copies of articles to sources to review prior to publication. To verify information in an article, you can read back what a source has said or summarize and ask if that is correct. If you are at all unclear or unsure about something a source has said, be sure to ask for clarification. Note: Writers are not allowed to accept gifts, tickets or gratuities in connection with an assignment for *Carolina Parent.* At a minimum, writers must turn in copy that is free of grammatical and spelling errors. Read your piece through for content, context and flow, and then read it again for spelling and grammar. Read it backwards to catch typos. Write clearly and concisely, without extraneous or duplicative information. Tip: Read the article out loud to see if it flows well and sounds natural. Except for a few minor exceptions, we follow the *Associated Press Stylebook* first and *Webster's New World Dictionary* second. AP style is what newspapers use; it is different from Chicago style or what you were taught in English class. Please look up how to reference names, addresses, ages, dates, professions and titles, composition titles and any other information you are unsure about. One exception to AP style is we use present tense for most attribution, i.e., Thomas Wilson says versus said. Note that the name comes before "says" except when identifying information needs to follow the name. We reserve the right to edit your work. If more than basic copy editing is required, we will share an edited version with you as time allows;

however, this is not always possible. We may not use your work in the future if excessive changes are necessary. Guide features range 650-1,300 words. Queries (article ideas) and reprints should be submitted four months in advance of publication date.
APPROXIMATE PAY: $15-35 for reprints for each publication. Feature rates start at $50 for first-time writers for 850-word original articles. We pay mid-month after publication and send a tear sheet. We normally purchase one-time print rights, exclusive to our geographic area, and online/digital use. We also purchase first-print rights for assigned pieces and do not allow these articles to be published by competitors.

CENTRAL CALIFORNIA PARENT
Fresno, CA
ccparent.com
ccparent@ccparent.com

CENTRAL PENN PARENT
Harrisburg, PA – monthly (38,000)
journalpub.com
editor@centralpennparent.com
GUIDELINES: We ask that all stories include a minimum of two local sources. We prefer a mix of experts and parents from different regions in our four-county market. The purchase of reprints is considered. The same should be included on any submitted attachments. All submitted copy must include clearly identified resources (names, phone numbers).
APPROXIMATE PAY: Fees for original articles start at $50 and max out at $125. Writers who work with us for an extended time and writers who work on unusually research-heavy pieces will be paid at the higher end of the scale. Our standard rate for reprints is $35. We will ask you to submit a writer's agreement specifying the negotiated rate. The agreement will also state that the writer retains ownership rights to the piece for future reprint (available after one month). The contracted rate includes the right for *Central Penn Parent* to reprint and archive said piece on centralpennparent.com.

CHARLOTTE PARENT (exclusive)
CAROLINA PARENT
PIEDMONT PARENT
Charlotte, NC – monthly (52,000)
charlotteparent.com
editor@charlotteparent.com
GUIDELINES: As Charlotte's leading parenting resource, our readers include parents, teachers, child-care providers and other advocates for

children ages newborn through teens. Each issue has a theme, regular features and departments. We seek new perspectives, voices and viewpoints from local parents about the issues that impact families. We welcome email submissions from freelance writers. Our policy is to buy one-time print rights with exclusivity within our region and the right to post the story on our website. Reprints of articles from publications outside our region are also considered. We run several feature articles on topics related to our monthly theme. Features require thorough research (citing a minimum of three reliable sources), knowledge of our audience and concise interviewing and writing skills. Articles on topics other than the issue's theme are also considered. We prefer articles and essays with local relevance. Word counts range from 500-1,200 words. Articles are accepted in Microsoft Word format and pasted into the body of the email, with author's name, address, phone number and word count on the first page of the story. The editorial department reserves the right to edit for clarity, length and style. If major revisions are needed, you will be contacted. Please remember that we receive many more submissions than we can use. We may not be able to respond personally to every query. Accompanying photographs, especially electronic art (300+dpi preferred), are welcome. We use the *Associated Press Stylebook* and *Webster's New World Dictionary*. Deadlines: two to three months before issue is printed.
APPROXIMATE PAY: $45 if localized. Fees vary depending on the length, depth and use of the story. Assigned articles generally pay $45-$125, and reprints pay $15-$35.

CHARLOTTESVILLE FAMILY

Charlottesville, VA – monthly
charlottesvillefamily.com
editor@ivypublications.com
GUIDELINES: Stories will likely get a local sidebar. Please email for current needs. Regular columns are 550 words, features run 100, 1,400 and 1,800 words. Submit as Microsoft Word document attached, as well as full story in body of email. Response time is one to two weeks. We want something fun and useful. Personal essays are particularly encouraged.
APPROXIMATE PAY: Varies from $15-65/piece.

CHESAPEAKE FAMILY

Annapolis MD – monthly (40,000)
chesapeakefamily.com
editor@chesapeakefamily.com
GUIDELINES: Send an introductory email to our editor and include two story ideas, a list of previously published work and one writing clip. We are looking for professional writers who are conscientious and fact check their

work. Our articles are short (about 1,000 words for a feature and 750 for a column), so pick your main theme and develop it well. Talk to three local sources considered authorities on the topic at hand. Perform all the legwork for the reader and list local resources, answering the obvious questions: Where? When? How much? Whom can I call? What's the number? We generally do not run first person or personal essays unless they are unusually compelling. Articles are due on the 15th of the month, two months before the publication issue, so articles for the July issue are due on May 15, for example. Please submit your article with a creative title/headline suggestion and brief bio to run at the end. Attach a separate invoice that includes your name, address, phone number, email address, Social Security number, the date, title of article and agreed-upon rate.

APPROXIMATE PAY: For assigned articles, we start at $75 and go up to $150. Articles that require more research can generate more. We pay around $35 for reprints but note that we try not to overlap coverage with the other parenting publications in the region: *Maryland Family*, *Baltimore's Child*, *Washington Family*, *Washington Parent* and *ParentLine*. We buy one-time print rights and web rights. We pay upon publication, and sometimes must hold articles over when space is shy. If we assign an article and do not run it for any reason, we will pay a kill fee of $25.

CHICAGO PARENT

Oak Park, IL – monthly
chicagoparent.com
chiparent@chicagoparent.com

GUIDELINES: We ask first-time writers to pitch us an idea. They may be asked to submit a full article on speculation, with no guarantee of publication. Reader Essays are a good way to get published. These parent essays, written on speculation, are told in first-person in 400-600 words, with a provided photograph. We receive about 15-20 essays a week so the essays selected usually have a lingering message, humor or other traits that set them apart. We ask writers to use the best experts on a subject—national and local, but almost every story should use local parent voices and children when possible. And we want a news peg—a reason for doing the story. Our regular columns are written by freelancers who have a long-standing relationship with *Chicago Parent*.

APPROXIMATE PAY: Short Stuff articles are 300-400 words in length, payment is $25-$50, depending on the reporting. Reader essays pay $100. The average feature story is 800-1,500 words in length. Payment varies depending on the writer's experience and the relationship with *Chicago Parent*, but begins at $100 for a one-page story of 800 words. We pay on publication. Checks are disbursed on the first day of the month of the publication. Invoices are necessary. We buy one-time print publication rights for *Chicago Parent* with exclusive first North American publishing rights as well as electronic rights allowing us to place the material on our website. If we reprint an article in our semi-annual *Chicago Baby* or quarterly *Going Places*, we will pay extra. For commissioned material; typically we pay 10% of the manuscript fee. There is no kill fee for first-time submissions, even when commissioned.

CHICKEN SOUP FOR THE SOUL

GUIDELINES: We have many *Chicken Soup for the Soul*® books in development and are adding new titles all of the time. We are always looking for new stories and poems. Take a look at the list of our future book topics to see if you have a story or poem on a subject we are looking for and then please submit it to us. If you have a great story or poem you want to submit but we are not collecting for that topic at this time, please save it and check back with us soon. Our list of Possible Books Topics (http://www.chickensoup.com/form.asp?cid=possible_books) is added to frequently and hopefully, in the near future, we will add a topic that will be a perfect fit for your story or poem. We prefer that you submit your stories only once, but if you believe your story fits in more than one book topic, please indicate which other topics you have submitted it for in the **Comments** line on the submission form (http://www.chickensoup.com/form.asp?cid=submit_story). More guidelines: http://www.chickensoup.com/cs.asp?cid=guidelines
APPROXIMATE PAY: $200 plus 10 free copies.

CHILD GUIDE

Hagerstown, MD
childguidemagazine.com
cis@childguidemagazine.com
APPROXIMATE PAY: $25 reprints.

CINCINNATI FAMILY
NORTHERN KENTUCKY FAMILY

Cincinnati, OH – monthly (30,000)
cincinnatifamilymagazine.com
chad@daycommedia.com
GUIDELINES: We adhere to the *Associated Press Stylebook*. Double space after each period in a sentence. Depending on the subject, features should run 1,300-2,000 words (decision made upon assignment). Sidebars are additional. Assignment letters are not provided unless stipulated by the editor-in-chief. It is the writer's responsibility to follow an agreed upon assignment and to contact the editor-in-chief or managing editor should there be questions/discrepancies/delays in procuring interviews, etc.

Assigned writers may be contracted for full rights (including Internet) in the terms of a standard "Work for Hire" agreement. Contracting is negotiable. Payment for accepted stories is made on the first day of the month following the month's publication in which your story appears i.e., 30 days. Fees are set at assignment of article and are based upon topic assigned. Fee paid also includes the right to post the assignment on the publication's website, parentworld.com.

APPROXIMATE PAY: $50 for reprints with exclusivity in Ohio. Fee includes both publications. Sometimes they might send your piece to WZPL.com (WZPL Family).

CINCINNATI PARENT (exclusive)
INDY'S CHILD
MIDWEST PARENTING PUBLICATIONS

Cincinnati, OH – monthly (37,000)
cincinnatiparent.com
editor@cincinnatiparent.com
Indianapolis, IN – monthly (42,000)
indyschild.com
editor@indyschild.com

GUIDELINES: We are currently and actively seeking reprint articles from freelance writers as well as local freelance writers who have had professional experience and may be interested in writing for our publication in the future. To keep everyone abreast of our guidelines we ask that you read this entire page then complete the writer's agreement (can be found on the website). Please note that you must follow these guidelines for every piece of editorial that is submitted to our office. Failure to do so may prevent us from using your editorial. Because we want you, the writer, to understand the process of our editorial structure we would like to give you some insight on how our process works. First, your article is sent to our general editorial e-mail. Your article is then organized by article type and for the specific month it will be considered for. Next, our Executive Editor will sit down with staff along with the list of editorial that have come in for a particular month and determine what articles are to run and what will be assigned. Once these decisions have been made you will be notified and we will then obtain your information for payment purposes. The final process is that the article will be edited by our copy-editor and then placed on our Web sites (CincinnatiParent.com and IndysChild.com) and in both publications, if applicable. Finally, you will be mailed payment for your article. Articles submitted should address current parenting issues with a Cincinnati and/or Indianapolis tie-in whenever possible. Strong emphasis is placed on how and where to find family-oriented events, as well as goods and services for children, in Cincinnati and Central Indiana. We are interested in well-researched, non-fiction articles on surviving the newborn, preschool, school age and adolescent years. Our readers want practical information on places to go and things to do in the Central Indiana and Cincinnati areas. They enjoy humorous articles about the trials and tribulations of parenthood as well as "how-to" articles (i.e., organizing a child's room, keeping your sanity while shopping with preschoolers, ideas for holidays and birthdays, etc.) Articles on making a working parent's life easier are of great interest as are articles written by fathers. We prefer a warm, conversational style of writing, however, we also prefer a well-balanced range of in-depth articles on challenging and hot topics.

Most *Cincinnati Parent Magazine* articles are purchased from freelance writers. In a typical issue, readers will find a variety of regular columns: Rave Reviews, Publisher's Note, Women's Health, Museum Note, Local Profiles, News You Can Use, Mayor's column and more. We also run two to three feature articles at 1,500 words per article and six-10 shorter articles at about 500-800 words per article which are reprints only. The topics must pertain to Indiana parents and families in general. Features consistently require in-depth research and interviews with sources in Cincinnati (or Indiana, Ohio for our sister publication). Because we take pride in the editorial that we publish for our readers, we will only continue using articles from writers who follow rules of grammar and publishing. Excessive grammar and punctuation errors will result in a disqualification from future publishing of articles as this is incredibly time consuming on our copy editor. Please note that if you send your article via e-mail that simple formatting is best. Fancy word-processing layouts only bog down our layout department, as your formatting has to be removed before we can place your work into our page formats. Also, when you type for publication, there should only be ONE SPACE after the period at the end of a sentence. Although that violates the rule you learned in typing class, when doing page layouts via computer, that extra space causes problems and each one has to be removed. Also, you should understand the differences between dashes, en dashes and em dashes as well as to put all quotation marks on the OUTSIDE of periods and commas. Also, we omit the last comma in a string of characters. (e.g., Shoes, socks, shirt and shorts rather than a comma before the and). We know this seems trivial but this saves us a great deal of time. If we get articles with these errors, our copy editor will notify you of your errors for correction in future issues. We reserve the right to edit your work if it does not comply with company policies or in the event of grammatical errors and if excessive changes need to be made we may refrain from using the article or your work at a future date. Your article will be scrupulously fact-checked before being published in our publications. Therefore, we require that your research be as current as possible. You should source actual published studies, not books in which the studies are quoted. The latter is called a secondary reference, and is not reliable. Your research should also be organized and readily available, so you will be able to respond to fact-checkers questions quickly and accurately. You will also be responsible for answering questions readers might have about your work so accuracy is imperative. When contacting sources, you may state that "I'm writing an article for Midwest Parenting Publications" if the article has been specifically assigned, in writing, by a managing editor of Midwest Parenting Publications. You may not represent yourself as anything other than an independent contractor on assignment for Midwest Parenting Publications. If you or a close relative or friend are related in any way (e.g., board memberships, employment, volunteer work) to a story you wish to work on, this relationship must be disclosed to the editor prior to accepting the assignment. Under no circumstances are writers allowed to accept gifts, gratuities, free tickets or other special privileges in connection with an assignment for *Cincinnati Parent Magazine* without permission first.

Your subject must have local scope or implications. For example, a story about how you handled a sibling rivalry in your family (aside from being first-person) might not be as appealing as a story with interviews of local therapists and parenting techniques to give readers a more in-depth answer to this issue. Reporting must be authoritative and original, based on interviews that you conduct yourself. Health articles, for example, should quote medical experts rather than simply relating a personal tale. Choose a topic that you care about deeply. If your story does not make you happy or sad, angry or elated, excited or curious, chances are that our readers won't care that much either. Because we must retain a high level of editorial professionalism we do not accept first person articles. We also do not accept fiction, nostalgia, poetry, cartoons, history, quizzes, puzzles, quotes, trivia, etc. We prefer that articles and stories are in-depth and specific to a particular topic and must be very thorough and use local subjects when at all possible. We will not run articles that have run in other local competing publications and for feature articles that we are purchasing first time rights for these articles may not be submitted to other local competitors. Articles must be submitted by the first of the month TWO MONTHS prior to the publication month. For example, because we begin publishing our May issue at the beginning of April we need your editorial by the first of March to begin the editorial process. If you are assigned an article as a feature (first-rights piece) and we do not receive your article by this deadline your article will not be considered. This same deadline applies for reprints. Writers MUST adhere to our guidelines in order to participate in order to keep our process as structured as possible. We welcome your queries but only full manuscripts will be considered. See query guidelines below. You will not receive a reply once you submit your editorial. We receive over 300 requests per day and it is absolutely impossible to reply to all individuals. If your editorial will be used, our accountant or editor will contact you. Please do not follow up on editorial pieces sent. Because of the sheer volume, we cannot address every submission. You are contacted only when your piece is considered or assigned. Do not send your editorial piece to multiple individuals within our publication. Doing so will not increase your odds of having your article published and may diminish your chances of getting published. You must submit your manuscripts in the following format. If these are not included this may cause delays in payment and usage.

1. Author byline for the end of the editorial piece. Who are you? What do you do for a living? Children, spouse, pets, hobbies, etc.?
2. Photos for the article if they apply. While most publications require photos to be submitted with the article we do not require them but do encourage them. Photos should be attached to the e-mail when the article is sent and must be 200 dpi in CMYK format as a .jpg, .tiff, .eps or .pdf
3. Photo of the author for use on our Web site. This is a must-have.
4. Author's complete name, phone number, email address and mailing address.

Please note that we will not return any work or photos submitted. We are not responsible for unsolicited materials. Do not send any valuable or irreplaceable items. When submitting your editorial via email, your SUBJECT LINE must include the following information. If you fail to follow these instructions this may result in loss of your submission. MANUSCRIPT: "TOPIC OF YOUR ARTICLE." Query letters should be one page and three or four paragraphs should be sufficient. IMPORTANT: Propose only ONE topic per query. If more than ONE query is sent per e-mail your e-mail cannot be sorted properly and poses a problem for our organizational methods. The query should include:

1. Your central theme or point in no more than a few sentences. If you cannot state the theme in this way, the article surely lacks focus.
2. Your sources on all sides of the issue. Whom will you interview?
3. The story's general trajectory. Briefly, how will you organize it?
4. A summary of your most important writing credits.
5. Attach one or two writing samples.

If your query is selected your article must be original and done on a first-time rights basis only, at which point we will contact you to begin the process. Do not send queries for articles that are already completed as these articles will need to be done using local references.

APPROXIMATE PAY: Midwest Parenting Publications pays 10 cents per word for first publication rights to an article and 15 cents per word if your work is used in both of our publications. Feature articles must be no less than 1,500-2,000 words. Reprint articles are paid $35 for articles under 500 words and $50 for articles up to 1,000 words. These fees include the rights to use your article for both *Cincinnati Parent Magazine* and *Indy's Child Parenting Magazine* in Indianapolis, IN, as well as for use on both CincinnatiParent.com and IndysChild.com once published. Payment will be made within 90 days of publication. (Kerrie says to also check out guidelines for *Indy's Child* because they are just a teeny bit different. The writer's agreement they email to you [not the one online] should clear everything up, but if not, just ask the editor!)

CLUBHOUSE
Colorado Springs, CO
clubhousemagazine.com
Address all submissions to:
Stephen O'Rear
Clubhouse Editorial Assistant
Focus on the Family
8605 Explorer Drive
Colorado Springs, CO 80920
GUIDELINES: Focus on the Family *Clubhouse* readers are 8- to 12-year-old boys and girls who desire to know more about God and the Bible. Their parents (who typically pay for the membership) want wholesome, educational material with Scriptural or moral insight. The kids want excitement, adventure, action, humor or mystery. Your job as a writer is to please both the parent and child with each article.
Fiction needs:

- Humor with a point (500 words)
- Historical fiction featuring great Christians or Christians who lived during great times (900 or 1,600 words depending on the depth of story)
- Contemporary, multicultural/exotic settings (1,600 words)
- Fantasy or Sci-Fi, avoiding graphic descriptions of evil creatures and sorcery (1,600 words)
- Mystery stories (1,600 words)
- Choose-your-own adventure stories (1,600-1,800 words)

Fiction flops:

- Contemporary, middle-class family settings (existing authors meet this need)
- Stories dealing with boy-girl relationships
- Preachy sounding stories where parents solve all the problems
- Poems (not printed)

Nonfiction needs (all nonfiction should fall between 400-500 or 800-1,000 words):

- Personality features of ordinary kids doing extraordinary things

- Activity theme pages with three-five fun things for kids to do
- Short, humorous how-to stories with a point (how to get good grades, how to be a good friend)
- Quizzes (multiple choice or true/false) that teach a biblical concept or character trait
- Fun-filled animal factoids
- Fact stories from a Christian worldview that talk about apologetics, biblical archeology or Christian value (i.e., the sanctity of life, living a moral life, etc.)
- Short craft or recipe ideas around a central theme or holiday
- Interviews with noteworthy Christians or Christians who experienced noteworthy events

Nonfiction flops:

- Bible stories—we only publish Truth Pursuer stories as of Jan. 2007
- Information-only science or educational articles without Christian insight
- Biographies told encyclopedia or textbook-style—need a kid angle

All manuscripts should be typed, double-spaced, on one-side only of 8 ½-by-11-inch paper. The author's name, address, phone number and an approximate word count should appear on the first page. We accept completed manuscripts only; no query letters. Material will not be returned unless a self-addressed envelope with adequate postage is included. Seasonal material should be sent at least eight months in advance.

APPROXIMATE PAY: Generally 15 to 25 cents a word. $200 on up for feature-length fiction stories. $150 on up for nonfiction stories.

CLUBHOUSE, JR.

clubhousejr.com
Address all submissions to
Stephen O'Rear
Clubhouse Jr. Editorial Assistant
8605 Explorer Drive
Colorado Springs, CO 80920.

GUIDELINES: Focus on the Family *Clubhouse Jr.* is a 32-page magazine designed to inspire, entertain and teach Christian values to children ages 3 to 7. With a circulation of approximately 60,000, the magazine reaches young readers and their parents all over the world.

FICTION

Fresh, inviting, creative fiction is the foundation of our magazine. The stories we publish explore a worthy theme. The characters should be well-developed, the story line fast-moving and interesting, and the prose descriptive and carefully constructed. Our stories are not always explicitly

Christian, but they should be built upon a foundation of Christian beliefs and family values. Humor and charm are key elements in a strong story. Length: For beginning readers 250-500 words; for parents to read aloud 500-800 words.

NONFICTION

Nonfiction articles should be concisely written in short caption-style format. Science and nature articles should be handled from a unique perspective, giving information that a child wouldn't find in a nature magazine. Articles about real children or adults with interesting experiences are also accepted. We love hearing about modern-day and historical heroes of the faith. The most successful articles are those that teach the audience in an amusing way and don't go over their heads with information. Length: No longer than 600 words.

BIBLE STORIES

Bible stories should be imaginative yet accurate retellings of Scripture. We generally favor the lesser-known stories from the Bible. The best styles are short captions, easy reader, poetic, rebus or comic-strip versions. A nonfiction sidebar highlighting accurate facts about the subject is a plus. Length: No longer than 600 words

REBUS STORIES

These picture-story pieces are written with the intent of encouraging parent/child interaction. Repetition of images, concise word choice and a humorous, insightful ending are the most important aspects of a successful rebus. Length: No longer than 350 words.

POETRY

Poems should reflect real-life experiences of young children. We generally publish humorous, descriptive poetry that tells a story and has a Christian-based message. Length: No longer than 250 words.

ACTIVITIES/CRAFTS

Activities and crafts should offer creative, fairly easy ideas for parents and children to accomplish together. Materials should consist primarily of common household items. Short crafts and activities or longer articles combining a number of activities and/or crafts on the same topic are accepted. Length: No longer than 500 words.

PUZZLES

Puzzles should be creative, fun and usually biblically based. Nearly all the puzzles published in the magazine are staff-written. Standard types, such as word searches and crossword puzzles, are not accepted. Length: One-page puzzles only.

All manuscripts should be typed or computer printed, double-spaced, on one side only of 8 1/2" by 11" paper. The author's name, address, phone number and an approximate word count should appear on the first page. We accept completed manuscripts only; no query letters, please.

Material will not be returned unless a self-addressed envelope with adequate postage is included. Seasonal material should be sent at least six months in advance. We do our best to respond to manuscripts within 8 weeks.

APPROXIMATE PAY: Unsolicited fiction, nonfiction and Bible stories pay $100-$200, depending on how much editing is required (and other factors). An average payment for poetry is $50-$100. Puzzles pay $30-$80, and rebus stories pay $75-$150. Contributors are paid on acceptance and receive three complimentary copies of the issue in which their work appears. We purchase first rights only, and simultaneous submissions are not accepted.

Assignment Writing: We generally begin to consider authors for assignment work after at least three unsolicited manuscripts have been purchased. We do not give assignments to writers who have never had a story published in our magazine.

COASTAL FAMILY (mostly nonpaying)

Savannah, GA – monthly (17,500)
coastalfamily.com
publisher@savdailynews.com

GUIDELINES: Accepts pieces on family health, ages and stages, education, etc. Likes local content. They usually don't pay for content, but they sometimes do.

COLORADO PARENT

Greenwood Village, CO – monthly (50,000)
coloradoparent.com
edit@coloradoparent.com

APPROXIMATE PAY: $35 reprints.

COLUMBUS PARENT (locals only)

Lewis Center, OH – monthly (58,500)
columbusparent.com
jhawes@columbusparent.com

GUIDELINES: *Columbus Parent Magazine* no longer accepts unsolicited materials for publication. If you are a freelance writer based in Central Ohio who is interested in being considered for assignments, please submit your resume and three writing samples which reflect our magazine's writing style and content to:

Editor
Columbus Parent Magazine
34 S. Third St.
Columbus, OH 43215

Please include headline suggestions, photos with cut lines and credits, and web exclusive material (if we discussed the web exclusive previously).

Suggest sidebar and pull quote materials to run alongside the story. Let your personality shine through in your writing. If you think something is interesting, there's a good chance that our readers will, too. The title of the article, the word count, and date of origin details are greatly appreciated in the subject line of your email. Please include a very brief summary and your bio in the body of your email.
APPROXIMATE PAY: Our stories are paid by the word and vary from writer to writer. (☺ Kerrie says: The editor told me over the phone that they pay 10 cents per word.)

CONNECTICUT PARENT
FAIRFIELD COUNTY PARENT

Branford, CT – monthly
ctparent.com
editorial@ctparent.com
GUIDELINES: We use an average of three to four articles each month from submissions of articles as reprints, typically from similar parenting publications. We require first rights in our market, Connecticut, which used to be a problem, but we've lost our competition in this market.
APPROXIMATE PAY: $40 per article on publication.

COULEE PARENTING CONNECTION

LaCross, WI – bimonthly
cpclax.com
cpclax@charter.net
GUIDELINES: We have never used writers outside of our region for first-time rights articles. We occasionally use reprints. We do consider writers in Wisconsin, Minnesota, and Iowa to be "regional" and like to consider their work over others, but we gladly consider any general, high-quality piece.
APPROXIMATE PAY: $10-50, but most often $35 for reprints.

CREATIVE CHILD

Henderson, NV — bimonthly
creativechild.com
editorial@creativechild.com
GUIDELINES: *Creative Child Magazine* is a national publication that provides parents with the latest information on how to nurture their child's creativity. With departments such as Kids at Play, Health and Safety, Discovering Creativity, Nurturing Talent and Tomorrow's Child—Investing for Your Child's Future, *Creative Child Magazine* is essential and the most complete parenting publication for raising well-balanced children.

CRICKET MAGAZINE GROUP (14 PUBLICATIONS)
Carus Publishing (different cities and different email addresses/mailing addresses)
cricketmag.com
GUIDELINES: We welcome submissions from writers of every level of experience, and we assure you that your manuscript will be read and reviewed when submitted. Unless otherwise noted, we consider all submissions for all our kids' magazines, so if you submitted an article for publication in SPIDER, we may deem it more suitable for LADYBUG, CRICKET, or another of our publications.

Submission Guidelines for BABYBUG magazine for babies ages 0-3
BABYBUG, a listening and looking magazine for infants and toddlers ages six months to two years, is published by Cricket Magazine Group. BABYBUG features simple stories, Mother Goose rhymes, short poems, words and concepts, illustrated in full color by the best children's artists from around the world. BABYBUG measures 6-1/4" x 7", contains 24 pages, and is printed in large (26-point) type on high-quality cardboard stock with rounded corners and no staples. The paper and colors are non-toxic. Published: monthly except for combined May/June, July/August, and November/December

Manuscripts
Stories: very simple and concrete; 4 to 6 short sentences maximum
Poems: rhythmic, rhyming; 8 lines maximum
Nonfiction: very basic words and concepts; 10 words maximum
Activities: finger plays, parent/child interaction; 8 lines maximum

Art

- By assignment only. Artists should submit review samples of artwork to be kept in our illustrator files. We prefer to see tear sheets or photoprints/photocopies of art.
- If you wish to send an original art portfolio for review, package it carefully, insure the package, and be sure to include return packing materials and postage.
- Author-illustrators may submit a complete manuscript with art samples. The manuscript will be evaluated for quality of concept and text before the art is considered.
- Rate: $500/spread ($250/page).
- We purchase all rights; physical art remains the property of the illustrator and may be used for artist's self-promotion.

Comments

- Before attempting to write for BABYBUG, be sure to familiarize yourself with this age group and read one or more past copies of the magazine.
- PLEASE DO NOT QUERY FIRST.

- We will consider any manuscripts or art samples sent on speculation and accompanied by a self-addressed, stamped envelope. Submissions without a SASE will be discarded.
- Response time: Please allow 6 months for manuscripts and 3 months for art samples.
- We do not distribute theme lists for upcoming editions.

BABYBUG normally purchases the following rights:

1. For previously unpublished stories and poems, BABYBUG purchases all rights.
2. For stories and poems previously published, BABYBUG purchases second North American publication rights. Fees vary, but are generally less than fees for first publication rights. Same applies to accompanying art.
3. For recurring features, BABYBUG purchases the material outright. The work becomes the property of BABYBUG and is copyrighted in the name of Carus Publishing Company. A flat fee per feature is usually negotiated.
4. For commissioned artwork, BABYBUG purchases all rights plus promotional rights (promotions, advertising, or in any other form not offered for sale to the general public without payment of an additional fee) subject to the terms outlined below:
    1. Physical art remains the property of the illustrator.
    2. Illustrator may use artwork for self-promotion.

Please address all MANUSCRIPT SUBMISSIONS to:
Submissions Editor, BABYBUG
Cricket Magazine Group
70 E. Lake St., Suite 300,
Chicago, IL 60601

Please address all PORTFOLIO SAMPLES to:
Art Submissions Coordinator
Carus Publishing
70 East Lake Street, Suite 300
Chicago, IL 60601

Direct inquiries regarding PERMISSIONS to:
Mary Ann Hocking, Rights and Permissions Manager
Carus Publishing
315 Fifth Street
Peru, IL 61354

Submission Guidelines for LADYBUG magazine for ages 3-6

LADYBUG, a reading and listening magazine for young children ages 3 to 6, is published by the Cricket Magazine Group of Carus Publishing. LADYBUG features original stories and poems written by the world's best children's authors, illustrated in full color by the best children's artists from around the world. LADYBUG measures 8" x 10", is full color, contains 36 pages plus a 4-page activity pullout, and is staple-bound. Published: monthly except for combined May/June, July/August, and November/December

Manuscripts

Fiction: read-aloud stories, picture stories, original retellings of folk and fairy tales, multicultural stories. Length: up to 800 words.

Action rhymes: energetic rhymes that call for physical movement. Length: up to 20 lines.

Nonfiction: nature, science, cultures, concepts, vocabulary, simple explanations of things in a young child's world. Length: up to 400 words. (Be prepared to send backup materials and photo references—where applicable—upon request.)

Poetry: rhythmic, rhyming; serious, humorous, active, from a child's perspective. Length: up to 20 lines.

Other: imaginative activities, games, crafts, songs, and finger games. See past copies for types, formats, and length.

An exact word count should be noted on each manuscript submitted. Word count includes every word, but does not include the title of the manuscript or the author's name.

Rates

Stories and articles: 25¢ per word; $25 minimum

Poems: $3.00 per line; $25 minimum

Art

- By assignment only. Artists should submit review samples of artwork to be kept in our illustrator files. We prefer to see tear sheets or photoprints/photocopies of art.
- If you wish to send an original art portfolio for review, package it carefully, insure the package, and include return packing materials and postage.
- Author-illustrators may submit a complete manuscript with art samples. The manuscript will be evaluated for quality of concept and text before the art is considered.
- Rates: $500/spread ($250/page)
- We purchase all rights; physical art remains the property of the illustrator and may be used for artist's self-promotion.

Comments

- Before attempting to write for LADYBUG, be sure to familiarize yourself with this age group, and read several past copies of the magazine.
- In evaluating manuscripts, we look for beauty of language, a sense of joy or wonder, and a genuine child point of view.
- PLEASE DO NOT QUERY FIRST.
- We will consider any manuscripts or art samples sent on speculation and accompanied by a self-addressed, stamped envelope. Submissions without a SASE will be discarded.
- Please allow 6 months for manuscripts and 3 months for art samples.
- We do not distribute theme lists for upcoming editions.

LADYBUG normally purchases the following rights:

1. For previously unpublished stories and poems, rights vary.
2. For stories and poems previously published, LADYBUG purchases second North American publication rights. Fees vary, but are generally less than fees for first publication rights. Same applies to accompanying art.
3. For recurring features, LADYBUG purchases the material outright. The work becomes the property of LADYBUG and is copyrighted in the name of Carus Publishing Company. A flat fee per feature is usually negotiated.
4. For commissioned artwork, LADYBUG purchases all rights plus promotional rights (promotions, advertising, or in any other form not offered for sale to the general public without payment of an additional fee) subject to the terms outlined below:
   (a) Physical art remains the property of the illustrator.
   (b) Illustrator may use artwork for self-promotion.

Please address all MANUSCRIPT SUBMISSIONS to:
Submissions Editor, LADYBUG
Carus Publishing
70 East Lake Street, Suite 300
Chicago, IL 60601

Please address all PORTFOLIO SAMPLES to:
Art Submissions Coordinator
Carus Publishing
70 East Lake Street, Suite 300
Chicago, IL 60601

Direct inquiries regarding PERMISSIONS to:
Mary Ann Hocking, Rights and Permissions Manager

Carus Publishing
30 Grove Street, Suite C
Peterborough, NH 03458

Submission Guidelines for SPIDER magazine for children ages 6-9
In January 1994, the Cricket Magazine Group of Carus Publishing Company launched SPIDER magazine, a literary and activity magazine for children ages 6 to 9. SPIDER publishes original stories, poems, and articles written by the world's best children's authors. Occasionally, SPIDER publishes reprints of high-quality selections. SPIDER is full color, 8" x 10", with 34 pages and a 4-page activity pullout. It features artwork by top-quality artists and illustrators. It is staple-bound. Published: monthly except for combined May/June, July/August, and November/December

Categories
Fiction: realistic fiction, easy-to-read stories, humorous tales, fantasy, folk and fairy tales, science fiction, fables, myths, and historical fiction.
Nonfiction: nature, animals, science, technology, environment, foreign culture, history, music, and art.
(A short bibliography is required for all retold folklore and nonfiction articles, and copies of research material will be required for all accepted articles. Be prepared to send other backup materials and photo references—where applicable—upon request.)
Poetry: serious, humorous, nonsense rhymes.
Other: recipes, crafts, puzzles, games, brainteasers, math and word activities.

Length
Stories: 300 to 1,000 words
Poems: no longer than 20 lines
Articles: 300 to 800 words
Puzzles/Activities/Games: 1 to 4 pages
An exact word count should be noted on each manuscript submitted. Word count includes every word, but does not include the title of the manuscript or the author's name.

Rates
Stories and articles: up to 25¢ per word (1,000 words maximum)
Poems: up to $3.00 per line

Themes
There is no theme list for upcoming editions. Submissions on all appropriate topics will be considered at any time during the year.

Art
For art samples, it is especially helpful to see pieces showing children, animals, action scenes, and several scenes from a narrative showing a character in different situations. SPIDER prefers to see tear sheets or

photoprints/photocopies of art. If you must send original art as part of a portfolio, package it carefully and insure the package. SPIDER will also consider submissions of photography, either in the form of photo essays or as illustrations for specific nonfiction articles. Photographs should accompany the manuscript. Color photography is preferred, but black-and-white submissions will be considered depending on subject matter. Photocopies or prints may be submitted with the manuscript, but original transparencies for color or good quality black-and-white prints (preferably glossy finish) must be available upon acceptance.

Comments

- SPIDER would like to reach as many children's authors and artists as possible for original contributions, but our standards are very high and we will accept only top-quality material.
- PLEASE DO NOT QUERY FIRST.
- SPIDER will consider any manuscripts or art samples sent on speculation and accompanied by a self-addressed, stamped envelope. Submissions without a SASE will be discarded.
- Response time: Please allow 6 months for manuscripts and 3 months for art samples.

SPIDER normally purchases the following rights:

1. For stories and poems previously unpublished, rights vary.
2. For stories and poems previously published, SPIDER purchases second North American publication rights. Fees vary, but are generally less than fees for first publication rights.
3. For recurring features, SPIDER purchases the material outright. The work becomes the property of SPIDER and is copyrighted in the name of Carus Publishing Company. A flat fee per feature is usually negotiated.
4. For commissioned artwork, SPIDER purchases all rights plus promotional rights (promotions, advertising, or in any other form not offered for sale to the general public without payment of an additional fee) subject to the terms outlined below:
   (a) Physical art remains the property of the illustrator.
   (b) Illustrator may use artwork for self-promotion.

Please address all MANUSCRIPT SUBMISSIONS to:
Submissions Editor, SPIDER
Carus Publishing
70 East Lake Street, Suite 300
Chicago, IL 60601

Please address all PORTFOLIO SAMPLES to:
Art Submissions Coordinator

Carus Publishing
70 East Lake Street, Suite 300
Chicago, IL 60601

Submission Guidelines for CRICKET magazine for ages 9-14
In September 1973, Open Court Publishing Company began publishing CRICKET magazine, a literary magazine for young readers. CRICKET, for readers ages 9 to 14, publishes original stories, poems, and articles written by the world's best authors for children and young adults. In some cases, CRICKET purchases rights for excerpts from books yet to be published. Each edition also includes several reprints of high-quality selections.
CRICKET measures 8" x 10", contains 48 pages, has a full-color cover, and is staple bound. Full-color and black-and-white illustrations of the highest quality appear throughout the magazine. Published: monthly except for combined May/June, July/August, and November/December
Categories
Fiction: realistic, contemporary, historical, humor, mysteries, fantasy, science fiction, folk tales, fairy tales, legends, myths
Nonfiction: biography, memoir, history, science, technology, natural history, social science, archeology, architecture, geography, foreign culture, travel, adventure, sports, music, dance, theatre
(A bibliography is required for all retold folktales and nonfiction articles. Be prepared to send other backup materials and photo references—where applicable—upon request.)
Poetry: serious, humorous, nonsense rhymes
Other: crossword puzzles, logic puzzles, math puzzles, crafts, recipes, science experiments, games and activities from other countries, plays, music, art
Length
Stories: 200 to 2,000 words (2 to 8 pages)
Articles: 200 to 1,500 words (2 to 6 pages)
Poems: no longer than 50 lines (1 page, 2 pages maximum)
An exact word count should be noted on each manuscript submitted. For poetry, indicate number of lines instead. Word count includes every word, but does not include the title of the manuscript or the author's name.
Rates
Stories and articles: up to 25¢ per word
Poems: up to $3.00 per line
Art
CRICKET commissions all art separately from the text. Any review samples of artwork will be considered. Samples of both color and black-and-white work (where applicable) are appreciated. It is especially helpful to see pieces showing young people, animals, action scenes, and several scenes

from a narrative (i.e., story) showing a character in different situations and emotional states. CRICKET accepts work in a number of different styles and media, including pencil, pen and ink, watercolor, acrylic, oil, pastels, scratchboard, and woodcut. While we need humorous illustration, we cannot use work that is overly caricatured or "cartoony." We are always looking for strong realism. Many assignments will require artist's research into a particular scientific field, world culture, or historical period.

Themes

CRICKET does not publish an advance list of themes. Submissions on all appropriate topics will be considered at any time during the year.

Comments

- CRICKET would like to reach as many illustrators and authors as possible for original contributions, but our standards are very high, and we will accept only top-quality material. Before attempting to write for CRICKET, be sure to familiarize yourself with this age group.
- PLEASE DO NOT QUERY FIRST.
- CRICKET will consider any manuscripts or art samples sent on speculation and accompanied by a self-addressed, stamped envelope. Submissions without a SASE will be discarded.
- For art, send tear sheets or photoprints/photocopies. PLEASE DO NOT send original artwork. Be sure that each sample is marked with your name, address, and phone number.
- Please allow 6 months for manuscripts and 3 months for art samples.

CRICKET normally purchases the following rights:

1. For stories and poems previously unpublished, rights vary.
2. For stories and poems previously published, CRICKET purchases second North American publication rights. Fees vary, but are generally less than fees for first publication rights.
3. For recurring features, CRICKET purchases the material outright. The work becomes the property of CRICKET, and it is copyrighted in the name of Carus Publishing Company. A flat fee per feature is usually negotiated.
4. For commissioned artwork, CRICKET purchases all rights plus promotional rights (promotions, advertising, or any other form not offered for sale) are subject to the terms outlined below:
   (a) Physical art remains the property of the illustrator.
   (b) Illustrator may use artwork for self-promotion.

Please address all MANUSCRIPT SUBMISSIONS to:
Submissions Editor
CRICKET
Carus Publishing

70 East Lake Street, Suite 300
Chicago, IL 60601

Please address all PORTFOLIO SAMPLES to:
Art Submissions Coordinator
Carus Publishing
70 East Lake Street, Suite 300
Chicago, IL 60601

Direct inquiries regarding PERMISSIONS to:
Mary Ann Hocking, Rights and Permissions Manager
Carus Publishing
30 Grove Street, Suite C
Peterborough, NH 03458

Submission Guidelines for CICADA magazine for teens ages 14+
CICADA is once again open for submissions. Please review the following guidelines before submitting. NOTE: We are now including a section on Current Needs. (Authors and artists ages 14-23, please see General Submissions at http://www.cicadamag.com/.) In September 1988, Carus Publishing Company began publishing CICADA magazine, a literary magazine for teen and young adult readers. CICADA is part of the Cricket Magazine Group that includes CRICKET magazine for children ages 9-14, SPIDER magazine for children ages 6-9, LADYBUG magazine for children ages 3-6, and a selection of other fine literary and nonfiction magazines. CICADA, for readers ages 14 and up, publishes original fiction, poetry, and first-person nonfiction by both adult and teen writers. In some cases, CICADA purchases rights for excerpts from books yet to be published. Each edition also includes reprints of high-quality selections. CICADA measures 8" x 10.5", contains 48 pages, has a full-color cover, and is staple bound. One-color and/or black-and-white illustrations of the highest quality appear throughout the magazine. Published: bimonthly (6 times a year)

Categories
Fiction: realistic, contemporary, historical, humor, mysteries, fantasy, science fiction
Nonfiction: first-person experiences of interest to teen and young adult readers
Poetry: serious, humorous, rhyming or free verse. Submissions on all appropriate topics will be considered at any time. Please keep in mind that CICADA's readers are intelligent and sophisticated and can handle complexity with respect to theme, characterization, and plotting. The

editors want to provide a balance of serious and humorous writing within each edition.

CURRENT NEEDS: While we are open to (and need) all genres, we are especially looking for HUMOR: satire, lighthearted romance, deadpan humor, black humor, screwball comedy, humor with heart, contemporary realism with absurdist overtones ... whatever makes you smile, even if it's through your tears. IMPORTANT: Please make sure the word HUMOR appears on the outside of your envelope.

Length

Fiction/Nonfiction: up to 5,000 words

Novella: up to 10,000 words (We run one novella per edition.)

Poems: no longer than 25 lines

An exact word count should be noted on each manuscript submitted. For poetry, indicate number of lines instead. Word count includes every word, but does not include the title of the manuscript or the author's name.

Rates

Rates and contract rights vary.

Art

CICADA commissions all art separately from the text. Any review samples of artwork will be considered. Samples of both color and black-and-white work are appreciated. It is very important that candidates review CICADA for level of sophistication, design, typography, and storytelling. CICADA's illustration ranges from a narrative mode for one story to abstract in another; we use inference, suggestion, and symbols in stories and poems. We are open to a wide variety of styles and media, and look for people who can provide compelling concepts as well as strong imagery. *Remember, this magazine is for high-school and college-age readers and* ***not*** *for grade-school children.* CICADA would like to reach as many authors and illustrators as possible, but our standards are very high, and we will accept only top-quality material. Before attempting to write for CICADA, be sure to familiarize yourself with this age group. PLEASE DO NOT QUERY FIRST. CICADA will consider any manuscripts sent on speculation and accompanied by a self-addressed, stamped envelope. Submissions without a SASE will be discarded. PLEASE DO NOT send original artwork, photocopies, books, or prints. Send us your samples via e-mail, according to the directions under **Artwork Submissions** below. Please allow 4 months for manuscripts. For artwork, we will keep your samples on file, and if we find an assignment that suits your style, we will contact you for further information.

CICADA normally purchases the following rights:

For stories and poems previously unpublished, rights vary. For stories and poems previously published, CICADA purchases second North American publication rights. Fees vary, but are generally less than fees for first

publication rights. Same applies to accompanying art. For recurring features, CICADA purchases the material outright. The work becomes the property of CICADA, and it is copyrighted in the name of Carus Publishing Company. A flat fee per feature is usually negotiated.
For commissioned artwork, CICADA purchases all rights plus promotional rights (promotions, advertising, or any other form not offered for sale) are subject to the terms outlined below:
(a) Physical art remains the property of the illustrator.
(b) Illustrator may use artwork for self-promotion.

Please address all MANUSCRIPT SUBMISSIONS to:
Deborah Vetter , Executive Editor,
CICADA
70 East Lake Street, Suite 300
Chicago, IL 60601

To send ARTWORK SUBMISSIONS: E-mail a link to your online portfolio to: mail@cicadamag.com

Make sure PORTFOLIO SAMPLES is the subject line of the e-mail. If you do not have an online portfolio, you may e-mail a sample. Please limit any e-mailed file to a maximum attachment size of 50 KB. We will keep your samples on file and contact you if we find an assignment that suits your style.

Direct inquiries regarding PERMISSIONS to:
Diane Sikora, Rights and Permissions Coordinator
Carus Publishing
30 Grove Street, Suite C
Peterborough, NH 03458

Submission Guidelines for CLICK magazine for children 3-6
The goal of CLICK is to allow young children access to the world of ideas and knowledge in an age-appropriate yet challenging way. It is often assumed that many areas of human endeavor and knowledge are uninteresting and beyond the understanding of young children. However, CLICK assumes otherwise and attempts to provide children with a clear and inviting introduction to many of the same phenomena and questions about the world that intrigue their adult counterparts. CLICK also attempts to introduce children to the processes of investigation and observation and encourages children to be active participants in the search for knowledge and understanding of their world. Each edition of CLICK is built around a central theme; CLICK themes introduce children to ideas and concepts

within the natural, physical, or social sciences; the arts; technology; math; and history. CLICK presents nonfiction concepts to young children through a variety of formats: stories, articles, poems, photo essays, and activities. CLICK seeks articles that explain the how and why of something in a friendly, engaging, perhaps humorous way. CLICK prefers a more informal, conversational style to a formal, textbook style. The best articles tackle one idea or concept in depth rather than several ideas superficially. CLICK also seeks stories that contain and explain nonfiction concepts within them. Since it is part of CLICK's mission to encourage children to question, observe, and explore, successful stories often show children engaged in finding out about their universe—with the help of supportive, but not all-knowing, adults. CLICK articles are usually between 200-400 words; stories are usually between 600-1,000 words. The best way for writers to understand what CLICK is looking for is to read the magazine. Writers are encouraged to examine several past copies before submitting an article or story. CLICK magazine is not accepting unsolicited manuscripts or queries at present. Experienced science writers who wish to be considered for commissions may send a resume and published clips to:

CLICK Submissions Editor
Carus Publishing
70 East Lake Street, Suite 300
Chicago, IL 60601

Submission Guidelines for ASK magazine for children ages 6-9
ASK is a nonfiction magazine for children 6-9 years old who are curious about science and the world they live in. Each edition of ASK is built around a central theme on some question or concept in the natural, physical, or social sciences, technology, mathematics, history, or the arts. ASK introduces kids to the joys of thinking, writing, and observing scientifically, and presumes them to be active participants in the ongoing search for better knowledge about the world. ASK articles should read as engaging nonfiction, not like school textbook or encyclopedia material. Intended to be accessible and appealing to newly independent readers (grades 2-5), the ideal ASK article should also be interesting to any general adult reader. ASK looks for articles that are concrete, specific, and relevant to this age group. They should tell a good story, with an emphasis on ideas rather than just facts. ASK encourages the use of humor as a teaching strategy, and believes that no topic is beyond the grasp of an intelligent young person if explained well in plain terms. ASK encourages writers to stretch the boundaries of topic themes and come up with interesting perspectives and unexpected connections. For example, for an edition on size, good articles topics might include "Why do we stop growing?" or

"How do clothing makers decide how many of each size pants to make?" But we would not be interested in a worlds-records style list of biggest and smallest insects, animals, etc., with no discussion of why they are that size. All articles in ASK are commissioned; ASK welcomes queries for articles for upcoming themes. Queries should give an overview of the proposed article, including scope and treatment, resources, and a draft opening paragraph. Writers new to ASK should also provide a resume and two writing samples, including at least 200 words of unedited copy on any nonfiction topic. Feature articles are usually 1,200-1,600 words, with sidebars. ASK also occasionally commissions photo essays (400-600 words), humor pieces (200-400 words), short profiles of people, inventions, events, or the arts (200-400 words), and theme-appropriate experiments. Authors are expected to ensure that all content is scientifically correct in both conception and detail, and drafts should include a full list of references and sources consulted. Authors wishing to write for ASK should consult any past copy to get a sense of the tone, style, and range of articles.

Queries and questions should be directed to:

Editor, ASK Magazine, ask@caruspub.com, subject=Submissions

Authors are also encouraged to check the ASK author's page at http://askauthorpage.blogspot.com/ for current edition status, needs, and updates from the editor. See website for theme lists and query due dates.

Submission Guidelines for MUSE magazine for children ages 9-14

MUSE magazine is not accepting unsolicited manuscripts or queries at present. Experienced science writers who wish to be considered for commissions may send a resume and published clips to:

Submissions Editor, MUSE
Carus Publishing
70 East Lake Street, Suite 300
Chicago, IL 60601

Submission Guidelines for APPLESEEDS magazine for ages 6-9

Following are writers' guidelines for APPLESEEDS, a 36-page, multidisciplinary, nonfiction social studies magazine for children ages 6 and up (primarily in grades 3 & 4). Writers are encouraged to study recent APPLESEEDS past copies for content and style. We are looking for articles that are lively, age-appropriate, and exhibit an original approach to the theme. Scientific and historical accuracy is extremely important. Authors are urged to use primary sources and up-to-date resources for their research. And remember, your article must stimulate the curiosity of a child. APPLESEEDS purchases all rights to material.

Feature articles: 1-4 pages, (Most editions contain about 10 feature articles.)

Includes: nonfiction, interviews, and how-to

Departments:

- Fun Stuff (games or activities relating to the theme, 2 pages)
- Reading Corner (literature piece, 2-4 pages)
- By the Numbers (math activities relating to the theme, 1 page)
- Where in the World (map activities, 2 pages)
- Your Turn (theme-related opportunities for children to take action, 1 page)
- Experts in Action (short profile of professional in field related to theme, 1 page)
- The Artist's Eye (fine or folk art relating to theme, 1 page)
- From the Source (age-appropriate primary source material, 1-2 pages)

Assume 150 words per page; payment approximately $50 per page

Query Guidelines

Writers may propose an article for any upcoming edition. The article idea must be closely related to the theme. Please include a completed query: write a brief description of your idea, including a list of sources you plan to use, your intended word length, and any unique angle or hook you think will make your piece irresistible to its intended audience (6- to 9-year-olds and their teachers and parents).

Please note that:

- Each query must be written separately, but you may email them together.
- Feel free to include copies of published writing samples with your query if you have not yet written for APPLESEEDS.
- After the deadline for query proposals has passed, the editors will review the suggestions and assign articles. This may take several months. We may suggest modifications to your original proposal or assign a new idea.

Please do not begin work until you've received a detailed assignment sheet from us!

Notes

- Email queries are required. To avoid problems in downloading attachments, always include your query in the body of the email. You may also include attachments if you wish.
- Queries may be submitted at any time before the deadline, but queries sent well in advance of deadline MAY NOT BE ANSWERED FOR SEVERAL MONTHS.
- Assignments are made about one month before manuscripts are due.
- Due to the large volume of queries we receive, we are no longer able to notify writers whose queries are not selected for assignment. If you

wish to check on the status of your query, please e-mail the editor no earlier than one month after the query due date.

- See website for theme list and query due dates.

Email queries to: susanbuckleynyc@gmail.com

Photo Guidelines

To be considered for publication, photographs must relate to a specific theme. Writers are encouraged to submit available photos with their query or article.

- Our fees for non-agency professional quality photographs range from $25-50/image.
- Cover fees are set on an individual basis for one-time use, plus promotional use.
- All cover images are color.
- Prices set by museums, societies, stock photography houses, etc., are paid or negotiated. Photographs that are promotional in nature (e.g., from tourist agencies, organizations, special events, etc.) are usually submitted at no charge.
- If you have photographs pertaining to any upcoming theme, please contact the editor by email. You may email low-resolution images for consideration, but please do not mail original non-digital images unless specifically requested to do so.

Submission Guidelines for CALLIOPE magazine for ages 9-14

CALLIOPE covers world history (East/West) and we are looking for lively, original approaches to the subject. Keep in mind that our magazine is aimed at youths from ages 9 to 14. Writers are encouraged to study recent past copies for content and style. All material must relate to the theme of a specific upcoming edition in order to be considered. CALLIOPE purchases all rights to material.

Procedure

In order for your idea to be considered, a query must accompany each individual idea (however, you can mail them all together) and must include the following:

1. a brief cover letter stating the subject and word length of the proposed article,
2. a detailed one-page outline explaining the information to be presented in the article,
3. an extensive bibliography of materials the author intends to use in preparing the article,
4. a self-addressed stamped envelope.

Authors are urged to use primary resources and up-to-date scholarly resources in their bibliography. Writers new to CALLIOPE should send a writing sample with the query. If you would like to know if your query has been received, please also include a stamped postcard that requests acknowledgment of receipt. In all correspondence, please include your complete address as well as a telephone number where you can be reached. A writer may send as many queries for one edition as he or she wishes, but each query must have a separate cover letter, outline, bibliography, and self-addressed stamped envelope. All queries must be typed.

Guidelines

Feature Articles:

- 700-800 words
- Includes: in-depth nonfiction, plays, and biographies

Supplemental Nonfiction: 300-600 words

Includes: subjects directly and indirectly related to the theme. Editors like little-known information but encourage writers not to overlook the obvious.

Fiction:

- Up to 800 words
- Includes: authentic historical and biographical fiction, adventure, retold legends, relating to the theme.

The above three pay 20 to 25 cents per printed word.

Activities: up to 700 words.

Includes: crafts, recipes, woodworking, or any other interesting projects that can be done either by children alone or with adult supervision. Sketches and description of how activity relates to theme should accompany queries.

Puzzles and Games: (please, no word finds). Crossword and other word puzzles using the vocabulary of the edition's theme. Mazes and picture puzzles that relate to the theme.

The above three pay on an individual basis.

Photo Guidelines

To be considered for publication, photographs must relate to a specific theme. Writers are encouraged to submit available photos with their query or article. We buy one-time use. Our suggested fee range for professional quality photographs* follows:

	¼ page		full page
b/w	$15	to	$100
color	$25	to	$100

* Please note that fees for non-professional quality photographs are negotiated.

- Cover fees are set on an individual basis for one-time use, plus promotional use. All cover images are color.
- Prices set by museums, societies, stock photography houses, etc., are paid or negotiated. Photographs that are promotional in nature (e.g.,

from tourist agencies, organizations, special events, etc.) are usually submitted at no charge.

- If you have photographs pertaining to any upcoming theme, please contact the editor by mail or fax, or send them with your query. You may also send images on speculation.
- See website for theme list and query due dates.

Note

Queries may be submitted at any time, but queries sent well in advance of deadline MAY NOT BE ANSWERED FOR SEVERAL MONTHS. Go-aheads requesting material proposed in queries are usually sent five months prior to publication date. Unused queries will be returned approximately three to four months prior to publication date. Hard copy queries ONLY, no email

Mail queries to:
Editorial Department
Cobblestone Publishing
Attn: Rosalie Baker
30 Grove Street, Suite C
Peterborough, NH 03458

Submission Guidelines for COBBLESTONE magazine for ages 9-14

COBBLESTONE is interested in articles of historical accuracy and lively, original approaches to the subject at hand. Do not forget that our magazine is aimed at youths from ages 8 to 14. Writers are encouraged to study recent past copies for content and style. All material must relate to the theme of a specific upcoming edition in order to be considered. COBBLESTONE purchases all rights to material.

Procedure

In order for your idea to be considered, a query must accompany each individual idea (however, you can mail them all together) and must include the following:

1. a brief cover letter stating the subject and word length of the proposed article,
2. a detailed one-page outline explaining the information to be presented in the article,
3. an extensive bibliography of materials the author intends to use in preparing the article,
4. a self-addressed stamped envelope.

Authors are urged to use primary resources and up-to-date scholarly resources in their bibliography. Writers new to COBBLESTONE should send a writing sample with the query. If you would like to know if your query has been received, please also include a stamped postcard that requests acknowledgment of receipt. In all correspondence, please include your complete address as well as a telephone number where you can be reached. A writer may send as many queries for one edition as he or she wishes, but each query must have a separate cover letter, outline, bibliography, and self-addressed stamped envelope. All queries must be typed. Please do not send unsolicited manuscripts - queries only!

Feature Articles: 700-800 words

Includes: in-depth nonfiction, plays, first-person accounts, and biographies

Supplemental Nonfiction: 300-600 words

Includes: subjects directly and indirectly related to the theme. Editors like little-known information but encourage writers not to overlook the obvious.

Fiction: up to 800 words

Includes: authentic historical and biographical fiction, adventure, retold legends, relating to the theme.

The above three pay 20 to 25 cents per printed word.

Activities: up to 700 words.

Includes: crafts, recipes, woodworking, or any other interesting projects that can be done either by children alone or with adult supervision. Sketches and description of how activity relates to theme should accompany queries.

Poetry: up to 100 lines. Clear, objective imagery. Serious and light verse considered. Must relate to theme.

Puzzles and Games: (please, no word finds). Crossword and other word puzzles using the vocabulary of the edition's theme. Mazes and picture puzzles that relate to the theme.

The above three pay on an individual basis.

Photo Guidelines

To be considered for publication, photographs must relate to a specific theme. Writers are encouraged to submit available photos with their query or article. We buy one-time use.

Our suggested fee range for professional quality photographs* follows:

	¼ page	to	full page
b/w	$15	to	$100
color	$25	to	$100

* Please note that fees for non-professional quality photographs are negotiated.

- Cover fees are set on an individual basis for one-time use, plus promotional use. All cover images are color.
- Prices set by museums, societies, stock photography houses, etc., are paid or negotiated. Photographs that are promotional in nature (e.g., from tourist agencies, organizations, special events, etc.) are usually submitted at no charge.

- If you have photographs pertaining to any upcoming theme, please contact the editor by mail or fax, or send them with your query. You may also send images on speculation.
- See website for theme list and query due dates.

Note

Queries may be submitted at any time, but queries sent well in advance of deadline MAY NOT BE ANSWERED FOR SEVERAL MONTHS. Go-aheads requesting material proposed in queries are usually sent five months prior to publication date. Due to the volume of submissions received, unused queries will no longer be returned.

Mail queries to:
Editorial Dept.
Cobblestone Publishing
Attn: Meg Chorlian
30 Grove Street, Suite C
Peterborough, NH 03458

Mail sample requests to:
Editorial Dept.
Cobblestone Publishing
Attn: Sample Requests
30 Grove Street, Suite C
Peterborough, NH 03458

Submission Guidelines for DIG magazine for children ages 9-14

DIG focuses on archaeology - recent discoveries, techniques used in the field and in the laboratory, archaeologists past and present, innovative 'dig' programs for our age audience (9- to 14-year-olds), rethinking of popular theories, and creative activities that entertain as well as inform. Accuracy is essential. Writers are encouraged to study recent past copies for content and style.

Procedure

In order for your idea to be considered, a query must accompany each individual idea (however, you can mail them all together) and must include the following:

1. a brief cover letter stating the subject and word length of the proposed article,
2. a detailed one-page outline explaining the information to be presented in the article,
3. an extensive bibliography of materials the author intends to use in preparing the article,
4. a self-addressed stamped envelope.

Authors are urged to use primary resources and up-to-date scholarly resources in their bibliography. Writers new to DIG should send a writing sample with the query. If you would like to know if your query has been received, please also include a stamped postcard that requests acknowledgment of receipt. In all correspondence, please include your complete address as well as a telephone number where you can be reached. A writer may send as many queries for one edition as he or she wishes, but each query must have a separate cover letter, outline, bibliography, and self-addressed stamped envelope. All queries must be typed.

Feature Articles: 700-800 words

Includes: in-depth nonfiction, plays, and biographies

Supplemental Nonfiction: 300-600 words

Includes: subjects directly and indirectly related to the theme. Editors like little-known information but encourage writers not to overlook the obvious.

Fiction: up to 800 words

Includes: authentic historical and biographical fiction, adventure, retold legends, relating to the theme.

The above three pay 20 to 25 cents per printed word.

Activities: up to 700 words.

Includes: crafts, recipes, woodworking, or any other interesting projects that can be done either by children alone or with adult supervision. Sketches and description of how activity relates to theme should accompany queries.

Puzzles and Games: (please, no word finds). Crossword and other word puzzles using the vocabulary of the edition's theme. Mazes and picture puzzles that relate to the theme.

The above three pay on an individual basis.

Photo Guidelines

To be considered for publication, photographs must relate to a specific theme. Writers are encouraged to submit available photos with their query or article. We buy one-time use.

Our suggested fee range for professional quality photographs* follows:

	¼ page	to	full page
b/w	$15	to	$100
color	$25	to	$100

* Please note that fees for non-professional quality photographs are negotiated.

- Cover fees are set on an individual basis for one-time use, plus promotional use. All cover images are color.
- Prices set by museums, societies, stock photography houses, etc., are paid or negotiated. Photographs that are promotional in nature (e.g., from tourist agencies, organizations, special events, etc.) are usually submitted at no charge.
- If you have photographs pertaining to any upcoming theme, please contact the editor by mail or fax, or send them with your query. You may also send images on speculation.
- See website for theme list and query due dates.

Note

Queries may be submitted at any time, but queries sent well in advance of deadline MAY NOT BE ANSWERED FOR SEVERAL MONTHS. Go-aheads requesting material proposed in queries are usually sent five months prior to publication date. Unused queries will be returned approximately three to four months prior to publication date. Hard copy queries ONLY, no email.

Mail queries to:
Editorial Dept.
Cobblestone Publishing
Attn: Rosalie Baker
30 Grove Street, Suite C
Peterborough, NH 03458

Mail sample requests to:
Editorial Dept.
Cobblestone Publishing
Attn: Sample Requests
30 Grove Street, Suite C
Peterborough, NH 03458

Submission Guidelines for FACES magazine for ages 9-14
Lively, original approaches to the subject are the primary concerns of the editors of FACES in choosing material. Writers are encouraged to study recent past copies for content and style. All material must relate to the theme of a specific upcoming edition in order to be considered (themes and deadlines given below). FACES purchases all rights to material.

Procedure
A query must consist of all of the following information to be considered (please use non-erasable paper):

1. a brief cover letter stating the subject and word length of the proposed article,
2. a detailed one-page outline explaining the information to be presented in the article,
3. an extensive bibliography of materials the author intends to use in preparing the article (if appropriate),
4. a self-addressed stamped envelope.

Writers new to FACES should send a writing sample with the query. If you would like to know if your query has been received, please also include a stamped postcard requesting acknowledgment of receipt. In all correspondence, please include your complete address as well as a telephone number where you can be reached. Manuscripts should be typed double-spaced and include final word count. Authors are requested to supply a 2- to 3-line biographical sketch.

Guidelines
Feature Articles: about 800 words
Includes: in-depth nonfiction highlighting an aspect of the featured culture, interviews, and personal accounts.
Supplemental Nonfiction: 300-600 words
Includes: subjects directly and indirectly related to the theme. Editors like

little-known information but encourage writers not to overlook the obvious.

Fiction: Up to 800 words

Includes: Retold legends, folktales, stories, and original plays from around the world, etc., relating to the theme.

The above three pay 20-25 cents per printed word.

Activities: Up to 700 words.

Includes: crafts, games, recipes, projects, etc., which children can do either alone or with adult supervision. Should be accompanied by sketches and description of how activity relates to theme.

Puzzles and Games: Crossword and other word puzzles using the vocabulary of the edition's theme. Mazes and picture puzzles that relate to the theme.

The above three pay on an individual basis.

Photo Guidelines

To be considered for publication, photographs must relate to a specific theme. Writers are encouraged to submit available photos with their query or article. We buy one-time use.

Our suggested fee range for professional quality photographs* follows:

	¼ page	to	full page
b/w	$15	to	$100
color	$25	to	$100

* Please note that fees for non-professional quality photographs are negotiated.

- Cover fees are set on an individual basis for one-time use, plus promotional use. All cover images are color.
- Prices set by museums, societies, stock photography houses, etc., are paid or negotiated. Photographs that are promotional in nature (e.g., from tourist agencies, organizations, special events, etc.) are usually submitted at no charge.
- If you have photographs pertaining to any upcoming theme, please contact the editor by mail or fax, or send them with your query. You may also send images on speculation.
- See website for theme list and query due dates.

Note

Queries may be submitted at any time before the deadline, but queries sent well in advance of deadline MAY NOT BE ANSWERED FOR SEVERAL MONTHS. Go-aheads requesting material proposed in queries are usually sent at least seven months prior to publication date. Unused queries will be returned if a SASE is supplied.

Mail queries to:
Editorial Department, Cobblestone Publishing
Attn: Elizabeth Crooker Carpentiere
30 Grove Street, Suite C
Peterborough, NH 03458

Submission Guidelines for ODYSSEY magazine for ages 9-14
ODYSSEY is interested in articles rich in scientific accuracy and lively approaches to the subject at hand. The inclusion of primary research (interviews with scientists focusing on current research) are of primary interest to the magazine. Keep in mind that this magazine is essentially written for 9- to 14- year-old children. Writers are encouraged to study recent past copies for content and style. All material must relate to the theme of a specific upcoming edition in order to be considered. ODYSSEY purchases all rights to material.

Procedure
A query must consist of all of the following information to be considered:

1. a brief cover letter stating the subject and word length of the proposed article,
2. a detailed one-page outline explaining the information to be presented in the article,
3. a bibliography of sources (including interviews) the author intends to use in preparing the article,
4. a self-addressed stamped envelope

Writers new to ODYSSEY should send a writing sample with the query. If you would like to know if your query has been received, please also include a stamped postcard that requests acknowledgement of receipt. In all correspondence, please include your complete address as well as a telephone number and / or email address where you can be reached. A writer may send as many queries for one edition as he or she wishes, but each query must have a separate outline, bibliography, and self-addressed stamped envelope. Telephone queries are not accepted unless the material is extremely time-sensitive to a specific edition. Please, type all queries. Articles should be submitted via email using a word processing program (preferably Microsoft Word - MAC). Text should be saved as ASCII text (in MS Word as "text only").

Guidelines

Feature Articles: 750-950 words
Includes: in-depth nonfiction articles. (An interactive approach is a definite plus!) Q & A interviews, plays, and biographies are of interest as well.

Supplemental Nonfiction: 200-500 words
Includes: subjects directly and indirectly related to the theme. Editors like little-known information but encourage writers not to overlook the

obvious.

Fiction: Up to 1,000 words

Includes: science-related stories, poems, science fiction, retold legends, etc., relating to the theme.

Department Features: 400-650 words

Includes: "Places, Media, People to Discover." Not a bad idea to consult past copies for direction on these departments that are also theme-related.

Activities: up to 750 words.

Includes: critical thinking activities, experiments, models, science fair projects, astrophotography projects, and any other science projects that can either be done by children alone, with adult supervision, or in a classroom setting. Query should be accompanied by sketches and description of how activity relates to theme.

The above five pay 20-25 cents per printed word.

Photo Guidelines

To be considered for publication, photographs must relate to a specific theme. Writers are encouraged to submit available photos with their query or article. We buy one-time use. Our suggested fee range for professional quality photographs* follows:

	¼ page	to	full page
b/w	$15	to	$100
color	$25	to	$100

* Please note that fees for non-professional quality photographs are negotiated.

- Cover fees are set on an individual basis for one-time use, plus promotional use. All cover images are color.
- Prices set by museums, societies, stock photography houses, etc., are paid or negotiated. Photographs that are promotional in nature (e.g., from tourist agencies, organizations, special events, etc.) are usually submitted at no charge.
- If you have photographs pertaining to any upcoming theme, please contact the editor by mail or fax, or send them with your query. You may also send images on speculation. Check website for theme list and query due dates.

Note

Queries may be submitted at any time, but queries sent well in advance of deadline MAY NOT BE ANSWERED FOR SEVERAL MONTHS. Go-aheads requesting material proposed in queries are usually sent four months prior to publication date. Unused queries will be returned approximately three to four months prior to publication date.

Mail queries to: **Mail sample requests to:**

Editorial Department
Cobblestone Publishing
Attn: Elizabeth Lindstrom
30 Grove Street, Suite C
Peterborough, NH 03458
Or email them to: blindstrom@caruspub.com

Editorial Department
Cobblestone Publishing
Attn: Sample Requests
30 Grove Street, Suite C
Peterborough, NH 03458

Cobblestone Publishing magazines select articles by detailed query letter and are also interested in *illustrators.*

CURIOUS PARENTS

Moorestown, NJ – monthly (110,000)
curiousparents.com
editor@curiousparents.com

GUIDELINES: If the article was published elsewhere, the date and publication name must be attached. Permission to reprint should be included. A 40-word bio with author photo should accompany articles. *Curious Parents* will make all attempts to contact the author prior to use. Submission of content constitutes permission to print text, photos, illustrations and any other content included in submissions. All submissions may be published in *Curious Parents* print, Internet, radio, TV and other media.

APPROXIMATE PAY: This one is tricky because their guidelines used to say they did not pay, but (1) I have a friend who got paid by them and (2) they wrote me once in response to a reprint asking me what the cost is.

THE DABBLING MUM

thedabblingmum.com
subs@thedabblingmum.com

GUIDELINES: Keep in mind that we do not want articles that are general in nature. We are looking for specifics. We want you to take a single idea and build upon that idea. Tell us how to take your idea and run with it; in other words, tell us how we can get from point A to point B. Don't leave us second-guessing or asking, "So what's the next step?"

FAMILY NIGHT WITH TEENS: Whether you set aside an evening a week or once a month, the important thing is that you're spending time with your children. Family nights offer you a chance to bond and laugh with your children. Through fun activities, your children learn to open up and share what's on their minds and in their hearts. Through these fun interactions, you'll get a true glimpse of who your child really is, and learn to enjoy life more. Please see similar stories and how-tos we've accepted online.

FIT FAMILIES: Physical activity doesn't have to cost a fortune. People have forgotten what it means to be active. We spend far too much time in front of the television set playing video games or watching movies and even more time in front of computer screens playing games, chatting, researching, reading, and watching. Add to that the fact that many modern conveniences make it much easier to "be lazy." We've lost sight of bonding through physical activities. What is the importance of getting fit physically? How does it help our mentality? How does it help our families? How does it help our job performances? How does it help end feelings of isolation and loneliness? And what types of activities can a family do without breaking the bank? Without having to go to the gym or buy expensive "toys"?

MARRIAGE SAVERS: Articles designed to save troubled marriages, build stronger marriages and make happy marriages happier. Articles about love, honor and respecting each other whether times are good or times are bad. Articles about compromise, give and take, forgiveness, and personal, spiritual and couple growth.

WRITING FOR THE WEB: Web publications differ dramatically from print publications in layout, design, and readability. Writers looking to pursue careers as content writers or copywriters for the Internet need to understand these differences. They need to know how to write with keywords and key phrases in mind. They need to write articles for easy scanning. They need to write articles that help sell products and services.

BUSINESS IDEAS: Pick a business idea from the list found online and write a how-to article. Write in a conversational style and avoid simple bullet-point lists. Don't just reiterate what's already been said online. We want fresh content. Add a new twist to an old idea.

Read our Writers Guidelines (below) very carefully and follow our instructions to the tee. And remember, we do not publish "duplicate" content so check out the center you're interested in writing for to make sure we haven't already accepted a similar idea.

SUBMISSION FORMS

If you want to donate an article, use thedabblingmum.com/writersdonate.htm

If you want payment use the format below:

Please answer all bullets in the body of an email. Make sure you use the same format listed below so we know you understand our terms.

- Your full name.
- Your email address.
- Your complete street address.
- How did you find us?
- Do you own the copyrights to submission, and can you legally sell it for publication?

- Do you agree to not resell to an online publication for a period of one month from date of publication?
- Do you understand that we archive online indefinitely and without further monetary compensation?
- Do you understand that we do not pay for articles you've distributed for free—past, present, or future?
- Is this article an original or reprint?
- If reprint, was it online or offline? Where and when? (if it's on your personal website, it's a reprint.)

Paste submission (no attachments) in the format below:

- What center or sub-center does your article fit in?
- Article Title.
- Body of Article (Either your prewritten article or a query with a sample to your writing).
- Your Byline (Name, two to three sentence description with mention of published book and website.)
- Headshot link or let us know you can get provide one on publication (.gif or .jpg). Headshot is needed for business, writing, and parenting centers. Headshot is not needed for recipe center.

Send your email to: subs@thedabblingmum.com with the subject line "Writers Submission." All attachments will be deleted without being read unless we specifically requested them from you. We do our best to respond with at least a form letter within eight-12 weeks of submission. Keep articles at 500-1,500 words or specified length for current topics being accepted. The theme of *The Dabbling Mum* is to show our experts as regular people. It makes us unique, more personable, and friendly. Therefore, we require headshots of our authors for articles placed online; except in our ezine and recipe center. We do not pay the expenses of a writer on assignment. We do not pay for long distance expenses should you choose to interview a source by phone. We purchase between four to eight articles per month or 48-96 submissions per year. Articles are published one to four weeks after acceptance notification, unless otherwise specified at time of acceptance. Articles are published throughout the month. We reserve the right to change the focus of this publication at any time. We reserve the right to edit for space, our publication's voice, style, grammar, punctuation, typos, etc. We reserve the right to change your article's title, condense your byline, and/or rearrange content to flow smoother. We reserve the right to ask for rewrites to make the piece its best. We reserve the right to refuse submissions at our discretion and to choose whether your piece will go into our ezine or be posted online. To better your chance of acceptance, provide original content. We don't want to read your article and think, "Did I read that somewhere before?" Articles should be entertaining, educational, informative, and actionable. Don't offer material that overlaps with an existing article. If you feel your article is better than one written on our website, or offers a fresh angle, don't hesitate to request a chance to prove it to us. Don't send us something that duplicates what is already on the site only written with a different voice. Be conversational. Write your piece with a conversational tone, but include more of a journalistic approach. Stay on topic. Write your articles on a single topic only. We don't like articles that barely scratch the surface by offering blurbs. Give details. Be as detailed as possible. Give us step-by-step instructions, take us from point A to point B; don't leave us guessing. Our readers don't want fluff; they want real substance. Be factual. There's a lot of misinformation on the Internet these days. We want to help our readers by providing true and accurate information. Don't be preachy. We're not interested in having you prove to us how wrong we are and how right you are. We're interested in learning and growing and forming our own decisions—educated and informed decisions. Include citations. When appropriate, use statistics, and information to back up or prove your point. If you are going to state a fact, statistic, or other figure in your piece, you must use the most recent data. Please do not use information that you researched a year (or more) ago. You must also give credit to your source. Include quotes and make them count. When appropriate, include Biblical quotes and references and use a combination of anecdotes, facts, and quotes. Quotes used must make your piece stronger. In other words, can the piece be written without the quotes and still make sense, or do the quotes help solidify the piece? We want new quotes from recent interviews and a minimum of two different experts. All expert quotes must be more than one-line sentences and used throughout your work; not just in one small section. We do not want a quote from an interview you did last year, and especially not one you did three years ago. We also do not want you taking quotes from other articles to be used in your article. You can use a quote from a book if you also reference the author's book as the source, but we will not pay the higher article fee for such quotes.

APPROXIMATE PAY: No kill fee paid. Article fee and publication rights are non-negotiable. Pays on acceptance. To receive payment, your article must never have been and/or never will be given away for free. Please understand no one wants to pay for an article that could have been received for free.

$15 ORIGINAL ARTICLE FEE

Unpublished article without expert quotes and sources. Buys first-time electronic (online) rights with one-month online exclusivity and indefinite non-exclusive online archival rights. Author may sell reprints to offline publishers immediately after publication.

$25 ORIGINAL ARTICLE FEE

Unpublished article with expert quotes and sources. Buys first-time electronic (online) rights with one-month online exclusivity and indefinite non-exclusive online archival rights. Author may sell reprints to offline publishers immediately after publication.

$120 YEAR-IN-ADVANCE COLUMNS FEE

Buys 12 original articles, 500 words each. Buys first-time electronic (online) rights with one-month online exclusivity and indefinite non-exclusive online archival rights. Author may sell reprints to offline publishers immediately after publication.

$5 REPRINT ARTICLE FEE

Reprints of 500 word articles that have also appeared online, but sparingly. Buys non-exclusive electronic (online) reprint rights with indefinite archival rights. Author may sell reprints to offline or online publishers immediately after publication.

$10 REPRINT ARTICLE FEE

Reprints of 500-1,500 word articles that have not appeared online. Buys non-exclusive electronic (online) reprint rights with indefinite archival rights. We don't want articles that have been heavily used on the Internet. Author may sell reprints to offline or online publishers immediately after publication.

$0 ARTICLE REPRINT FEE

Author donates article to publication and retains all rights. Publication buys no rights. Publication has permission to archive piece indefinitely. Donate articles if you've previously published your piece on a free content network, or given it away for free in the past or plan to distribute for free in the future.

$0 REVIEW REPRINT FEE

Author donates review to publication and retains all rights. Publication buys no rights. Publication has permission to archive piece indefinitely. Donate *original* reviews to Christian books or movies that fit into one of our review sections.

"Pays on acceptance" means when we receive the final draft of your article and approve it for publication. Payment is mailed within 32 days from the time we say your piece is ready for publication. Checks are written and mailed last day of each month. Payment: U.S. dollars in the form of a business check. You get a byline—under five sentences, including one web address and business name; 99 x 125 pixel .jpg headshot of author; an active link back to the author's website; and exposure for author's book/product—linked using our Amazon affiliate (as long as it's safe for children to read).

DALLAS CHILD (locals preferred)
FORT WORTH CHILD
NORTH TEXAS CHILD

Addison, TX – monthly (80,000)
dallaschild.com
editorial@dallaschild.com
GUIDELINES: The editors at *DallasChild, FortWorthChild* and *NorthTexasChild* strive to include fresh voices, ideas and perspectives in the magazines. We emphasize stories with a local focus and prefer to work with writers from the Metroplex area. They rarely run reprints.
APPROXIMATE PAY: $35-50 depending on length for reprints. We have used reprints for the web and will pay the same amount.

DAYTON PARENT

daytonparentmagazine.com
susan@daytonparentmagazine.com
Please send invoices to Roxanne@daytonparentmagazine.com.
GUIDELINES: *Dayton Parent* is always looking for talented, experienced freelance writers to enhance our magazine. Our general goal is to have a good mix of fun and substantive local stories of interest to local parents.

Story Pitches

We welcome queries and submissions, especially from local freelancers. Here are a few factors to consider before sending your pitch.

- Make it local. We're looking for stories and sources that reflect the communities we cover.
- Pitch early. Please be mindful that content for *Dayton Parent Magazine* is determined months in advance. Therefore, story ideas should be pitched a good two to three months before the month it would run. This is particularly important for seasonally-anchored stories.
- We may not respond. Because of the high volume of submissions and queries we receive, it is not always feasible to respond to each pitch. If you do not hear from us within a month of your submission, it is safe to assume that we have decided to pass.

Story Requirements

In general, we expect freelancers to use good journalism and solid writing in their articles. Here are some specific requirements we ask of our freelancers:

- Multiple sources. A minimum of two sources. A 1,000-word story should have no fewer than three sources; a 2,000-word story should have no fewer than four sources.
- Diverse sources. *Dayton Parent Magazine* will have a broad circulation throughout Dayton, so it's important to us that our sources reflect our readership. Freelancers don't have to hit every city we cover, but they should have sources from more than one. And the more cities covered, the better.

- Sidebars. Any story 1,000 words or more should have at least one sidebar. Sometimes it's an info box referring readers to more information from a local organization. Sometimes it's a list of tips related to the story's subject. Readers like having information broken up for them and they enjoy multiple points of entry into a story, so we value freelancers who are mindful of that.

APPROXIMATELY PAY: Payment structure varies based on each assignment. Susan Bryant will discuss payment structure with you. Payment is upon publication. Checks are usually sent out within the first week of the month of publication. Freelancers should submit an invoice (within an email is fine) that includes name, address, phone number, Social Security Number, name of story and payment amount. Please email invoice within a week of submitting story.

DURHAM PARENT
Ontario, Canada
durhamparent.com
editorialinquiries@gmail.com

FAITH AND FAMILY
North Haven, CT – bimonthly
faithandfamily.com
editor@faithandfamilymag.com
GUIDELINES: We prefer proposals to unsolicited manuscripts. The proposal should give a good idea of the angle and content of the prospective article or column and, where applicable, prospective sources should be identified. The proposal should target a specific section of *Faith and Family* and reflect good familiarity with both that section and the publication in general. Your proposal should include your relevant qualifications, and you should send samples of your published writings.
FAMILY & PARENTING (special supplement to *Owatonna People's Press*)
Owatonna, MN
owatonna.com
rensley@owatonna.com

FAMILY AND FAITH
familyandfaithmagazine.com
familyandfaithmagazine@gmail.com

FAMILY AUSTRALIA
familyaustraliamagazine.com
editor@familyaustraliamagazine.com

FAMILY CIRCLE

familycircle.com

GUIDELINES: If you would like to submit a story idea for consideration, please look over recent issues to get an idea of our format, columns and topics we have covered in the past. When submitting, please send a double-spaced, typed query along with clips (including one from a national magazine), bio, and a self-addressed stamped envelope. Due to the large quantity of submissions we receive, we cannot personally respond to, be responsible for, nor return any unsolicited material. And please, no e-mails or calls.

Submissions can be sent to:
Family Circle Magazine
Articles Department
375 Lexington Avenue, 9th Floor
New York, NY 10017

FAMILY LIVING

floridafamilyliving.com
beth@floridafamilyliving.com

FAMILY TIMES

Syracuse, NY
familytimes.biz
editorial@familytimes.biz

FAMILYFUN

Northampton, MA – 10 times/year (1,850,000)
familyfun.com
firstinitial.lastname@meredith.com
ATTN: [editor or department]
FamilyFun
47 Pleasant Street
Northampton, MA 01060
Phone: 413-585-0444

GUIDELINES: Founded in 1991, *FamilyFun* is the country's number one magazine for families with children ages three to 12, with more than 2 million subscribers. On every page, *FamilyFun* gives parents the information and inspiration they need to create unforgettable family moments. We are the trusted experts on family cooking, vacations, parties, holidays, crafts, and learning—all the essentials that enrich the precious time families share. *FamilyFun* is unique in the marketplace, delivering real ideas for—and from—real families. Our readers see the magazine as a reflection of their own lives and priorities, a place where they can find a community of like-minded parents and discover ideas for building strong, healthy families. Please familiarize yourself with the magazine before submitting a query. Our heavy emphasis on activities and ideas distinguishes us from other parenting and family magazines. We do not publish child development articles, fiction, or poetry. We are always looking for professional freelancers who are experts in the art of being a fun-loving, creative parent. Our criteria for content are simple: the activities must be fun, family-tested, affordable, and easy to do. We strive to entertain and inform with a writing style that is direct, upbeat, and personal. Our highly visual layouts dictate brevity. Articles are scheduled and assigned at least five months in advance of publication. Please send manuscripts and queries by email or standard mail only—not by telephone or fax. We do not accept unsolicited manuscripts for feature stories; we do accept unsolicited manuscripts for the following departments:

- Family Getaways
- Family Traditions
- Creative Solutions (see details below)

Queries should describe the content, structure, and tone of the proposed article. We receive many queries on the same topics, so please be as specific as possible about what makes your idea unique and why you are qualified to write about it. If appropriate, include photographs or sketches of the finished project, food, or craft. Due to the large volume of submissions, allow six to eight weeks for a response. Supporting materials, such as photographs and clips, will be returned if accompanied by a self-addressed, stamped envelope with correct postage. Please note: Editorial responses to submissions will be sent via email, so please provide an address for our reply. Our features present activities that are entertaining for the whole family, relatively inexpensive, and easy to do. Specific topics include food, crafts, parties, holiday celebrations, sports, games, creative solutions to common household problems and family challenges, educational projects, and home organizing and decorating. Travel features highlight moderately priced U.S. destinations that offer an exceptional value and specifically cater to the needs of families. Similarly, food features present recipes that have a track record with families, dishes that are fun both to make and to eat. Length: 850-3,000 words. Compensation: $1.25 per word upon acceptance. Submissions: Queries only; direct to Features Editor, Food Editor, or Travel Editor

DEPARTMENTS

- **EVERYDAY FUN** offers simple, fun, practical, and inexpensive ideas and projects, including crafts, games, nature activities, learning activities, kid-friendly recipes, outings, and so on. Length: N/A; please send ideas only (no finished manuscripts). Compensation: $200 for each idea. Submissions: Queries only; direct to Deborah Way, Senior Editor.

- **FAMILY GETAWAYS** offers two mid-length (600-1,000 words) articles every issue, some process-oriented, some destination-specific. Most are first-person. Each article is highly formatted and presents a family travel topic such as a road trip, insider's city weekend, or themed roundup of attractions or destinations. The department ends with a reader-recommended destination or tourist attraction that is "Worth the Trip." Because we are budget-conscious, we rarely cover international travel or expensive American resorts or programs. Compensation: $1.25 per word upon acceptance ($100 for the idea if we opt to use a staff writer). Submissions: Manuscripts and queries; direct to Becky Karush, Associate Editor.
- **FAMILY TRADITIONS** is a first-person, Q&A-style, one-page department that highlights one family's favorite or most meaningful tradition, such as a Saturday-morning ritual or a neat way to mark milestones. The topics vary but are often seasonal and usually focus on some way in which the tradition has helped shape that family's identity or brought them closer together. Each tradition should be inspiring, but also practical and universal enough that readers can adapt the idea for themselves. Each article is accompanied by a photograph of the writer and their family. Length: 500-600 words. Compensation: $1.25 per word upon acceptance. Submissions: Manuscripts and queries; direct to Amy Brown, Assistant Editor.
- **CREATIVE SOLUTIONS** showcases a practical, innovative idea that the writer used to solve a problem common among families: a game or homemade chart that got the kids excited about doing chores, for instance, or a trick that persuaded reluctant letter writers to keep up their correspondence with Grandpa. Each essay tells the story of how this Creative Solution changed or inspired the family. Length: 800-1,000 words. Compensation: $1,250 upon acceptance. Submissions: Queries accepted, manuscripts preferred; direct to Debra Immergut, Senior Editor.
- **MY GREAT IDEA** showcases simple, clever ideas that solve common household problems, but in the form of brief letters from readers. Length: 50-200 words. Compensation: $100 upon publication. Submissions: Letters only; direct to Amy Brown, Assistant Editor.
- **HEALTHY FUN** features a collection of refreshingly practical strategies and creative ideas for staying active, eating well, and feeling great. It offers timely updates on health issues that are relevant to kids and parents, as well as humorous, knowing, and down-to-earth suggestions for working healthy habits and exercise into family life. Health-related products and websites geared toward families are also covered. The

light approach and conversational tone underscore the fundamental challenge: sure, you know your kids should eat more veggies and get moving, but how do you really entice them? How do you make it fun for you and them? We're looking for real-world solutions to the health challenges today's families face. Length: 100-300 words. Compensation: $1.25 per word upon acceptance; $200 for the idea if we opt to use a staff writer. Submissions: Queries only; direct to Jodi Butler, Contributor.

- **FAMILY HOME** features creative and useful ideas for the home, yard, and garden. We look for practical solutions for staying organized, new products, and easy, unique ways to decorate. The ideas must be affordable and realistic, such as those in the "success stories" (sent in by families around the country) that we regularly run. The column is usually written by a select group of contributing editors, but we do buy individual ideas. Length: 1,000 words. Compensation: $100-200 per idea; $1,250 for writing. Submissions: Queries only, photos are appreciated but cannot be returned; direct to Debra Immergut, Senior Editor.
- **OUR FAVORITE THINGS** features parent-recommended family entertainment products and gear, such as toys, books, DVDs, video games, music, and more. Length: 50-200 words. Compensation: $1.25 a word. Submissions: Queries only; direct to Ellen Wall, Senior Associate Editor

APPROXIMATE PAY: See above.

FAMILY MAGAZINES OF MICHIANA
THE FAMILY MAGAZINE
BOOM
SASSY

Elkhart, IN – monthly
michianafamilymagazine.com
jessy@michianafamilymagazine.com

GUIDELINES: As a FAMILY publication, our mission is to provide relevant information that both serves and entertains Michiana families. We look for writers who share our vision and demonstrate a fresh, engaging writing style, and have a keen sense of our readers' interests. Our writers appropriately research their selected topic to provide factual information using the highest journalistic standards and focus specifically on topics that matter to mothers in our local community.

THE FAMILY MAGAZINE SUBMISSIONS:

The Family Magazine celebrates today's family and champions the women at its center. Every page provides smart, practical solutions to help moms of young children (typically ten and under) to raise happy, healthy families.

With a particular emphasis on the concerns and issues faced by all mothers today, *The Family Magazine* fills a need as the only family-focused magazine in the four-county Michiana area and targets a mom with kids ages ten and under. *Family Magazine* delivers essential advice for tough parenting challenges; provides fun suggestions for family activities; offers healthy resources; and showcases projects to create a well-rounded family. *The Family Magazine* helps moms look and feel their best by delivering the latest health, diet and fitness news, and beauty and fashion tips as well as parenting.

SASSY MAGAZINE SUBMISSIONS:

Sassy Magazine celebrates today's career-driven woman and champions the quest for work, life and balance with integrity. *Sassy Magazine* provides resources for women to live their best lives in the areas of health, wellness, business, style, home life and career. With a distribution focus on the four-county Michiana area, *Sassy Magazine* strives to give back to the community through charity-driven promotions and support. *Sassy Magazine* is focused on the career-driven Michiana businesswoman who does it all – with style! Topics include (but are not limited to) fashion, health, business, work-life balance, charity, relationships, finances and home décor. *The Sassy Magazine* reader target is a working, professional woman between the ages of 25-54.

BOOM MAGAZINE SUBMISSIONS:

Boom Magazine celebrates today's active baby boomer and champions their quest to live the best years of their lives. It has a focus on active men and women between the ages of 51 and 74. We are looking for local authors that fall within this age range to write for this magazine in particular. Main themes in *Boom Magazine* include (but are not limited to): travel, retirement, business, health, activities, giving back to the community, marriage/remarriage, grandkids, arts, gardening and other hobbies.

Local Experts

We ask writers to interview local experts who are authorities in their field. To ensure we remain family-focused, every article should include a local family or parent voice. We also publish profiles of outstanding families and family organizations, interviews with local family parenting experts, reviews of family books and relevant snapshots of local families. We incorporate photography to accompany articles as well. If you are interested in submitting a story or photograph, we ask that you examine our previous issues and familiarize yourself with the subject matter and tone of our magazines.

Inquiries and Proposals for Articles, Columns and Photography

We are happy to consider any story idea or photograph that reflects the values and mission of the magazine (see individual magazine descriptions at top). Please keep in mind that submissions are accepted on an individual basis, and consideration concerning appropriate articles is subject to the focus of the current issue, relevance to the publication and space available.

Submission Guidelines

Submissions will not be accepted without a query. Simultaneous queries are okay. We may not respond unless we wish to publish. Articles should be written in AP style and submitted electronically as Word documents. Keep attachments to a minimum. Also, please include your name, address, phone fax and email. Do not cut and paste or type into the body of an email. Submissions must be single-spaced, aligned left, with no indent at the beginning of paragraphs and a hard return at the end of paragraphs. Remove all hyperlinks, bold, italics and underline and type in 12-point font. No article will be accepted outside of these parameters.

Payment

Payment is based on writer experience. We strongly encourage writers to write original, unpublished work. Payment will also include web rights.

Lead Time

We require that any inquiries concerning future article topics be submitted AT LEAST TWO MONTHS prior to the intended publication of the article. We suggest writers examine our editorial calendar for information concerning the proposed focus of each month's publication. Please visit our website for more information.

Length

The average story should range from 600-800 words. If a writer is contracted to write a feature, the length can be upwards of 1,000 words.

Head Shot and Bio

We always appreciate a personal touch, which is why we ask writers to include a head shot along with a 30-word bio to accompany their submission. In the bio, please include your field of expertise or occupation, your connection with the area and something about your family. We do not allow emails in the bio or personal contact information. When submitting a head shot or any other photograph, please ensure that the picture is taken vertically and is of good professional quality. All photos should be submitted as high-resolution .jpg files.

We rarely accept article submissions that have been printed in other publications, exceptions occasionally being articles that have been printed outside our market. Therefore, an author's work should be original as we do require market exclusivity. Reprint payment is $15 including web rights. If The FAMILY Magazines publishes your submission, we also retain web rights. You may feel free to submit photos along with your article as long as they are in high resolution .jpg format. Photos may or may not be used at the discretion of the graphic designer. All submissions are subject to editorial review and approval by The FAMILY Magazines and may be edited for grammar, content and length.

Research and References

All articles are held to the highest of standards. Therefore, all submitted editorial content must be factual, unbiased and supported by expert opinions and research from multiple sources and references. We also ask writers to provide a list of references used at the end of the article. When it is appropriate to the content of the article, writers must make every effort to contact our advertisers to give a reference or quote when it pertains to their area of expertise. Be sure to ask the editor for a list of appropriate references for a given article if you are unsure. When a writer cites information of more than a few lines, whether from online research or other articles and books, writers must not only attribute the information to the original author but must also receive permission from the original source to use the information. Writers must also take care to accurately attribute information from an outside source within the actual text of the article. When a writer takes any quote, statistic or idea from an outside source, he or she must make clear within the article itself where this information came from. A list of references and/or links to websites should also be provided at the end of the article so the editor can easily locate the original source of the information.

FAMILY TIME

Frankfort, IL – monthly (65,000)
familytimemagazine.com
carrie@familytimemagazine.com

APPROXIMATE PAY: Payment for agreed-upon articles is as follows: 1,300+ words pays $70; 850 words pays $50; 450 words pays $25. Payment occurs upon publication within 30-60 days of publication with submitted invoice.

FIRST COAST PARENT (mostly locals)

Ponte Vedra Beach, FL
firstcoastparent.com
editorial@firstcoastparent.com

APPROXIMATE PAY: We do occasionally need a last minute space filler when on deadline. $30 is a palatable reprint cost but free is better.

FIT PREGNANCY

Woodland Hills, CA – bimonthly
fitpregnancy.com
Please send your queries to:
Sharon Cohen, Executive Editor

21100 Erwin St.
Woodland Hills, CA 91367
Phone: 818-884-6800

GUIDELINES: *Fit Pregnancy* is a bimonthly magazine covering health, nutrition, exercise, psychology, food, fashion and beauty issues related to pregnancy. It also includes editorial for parents of babies up to two years of age. Queries should be specific. Read the magazine and be clear whether you are presenting an idea for a feature or a specific column.

FEATURES (1,000-1,800 words) cover broad, timely topics. Features for which we accept freelance writing include:

- Prenatal Fitness: Pregnancy-safe workout programs
- You and Your Baby: A feature story about postpartum issues
- A postpartum exercise story (often includes weight loss)
- A story pertaining to breastfeeding issues
- Baby Pages (baby-care issues, with emphasis on the first six weeks)
- Nutrition and Food: Prenatal nutrition stories, often with a meal plan and recipes
- Psychology/Health: Topics relating to prenatal or postpartum issues

COLUMNS (550-1,000 words) for which we accept freelance writing include:

- Birth of a Father: A short personal essay, with a service angle, to other dads about fathering
- Your Family: Parenting issues as they relate to the new family, sex and relationships, family and financial issues
- Health: Health issues for the pregnant woman
- Healthy Baby: Health issues for the new baby
- Insight: Psychological issues relating to pregnancy or parenting
- Labor & Delivery: Emphasis on hard news, scientific breakthroughs, practical tips and hard news
- Nutrition: Prenatal-nutrition issues
- Small Packages: A section of short, newsy items on all topics covered in the magazine
- Time Out (550 words): A funny or poignant personal essay

Queries should be no more than one page in length. Tell us why your idea is new or particularly important to our readership. Please include experts you might interview, any expertise you may have in this area, other magazines you've written for and recent clips.

FLAGLER PARENT
flaglerparent.com
ST. JOHN'S PARENT
stjohnsparent.com

VOLUSIA PARENT
volusiaparent.com
charlie@bradymediainc.com

FREDERICKSBURG PARENT AND FAMILY
Fredericksburg, VA – monthly
fredericksburgparent.net
editor@fredericksburgparent.net
APPROXIMATE PAY: $25-35 reprints.

FUN FOR KIDZ
BOYS' QUEST
HOPSCOTCH
funforkidzmagazines.com
submissions@funforkidz.com
GUIDELINES: Head to the site for themes for all 3 magazines. Every *Fun For Kidz* contributor must remember we publish only six issues a year, which means our editorial needs are extremely limited. It is obvious that we must reject far more contributions than we accept, no matter how outstanding they may seem to you or to us. With that said, we would point out that *Fun For Kidz* is a magazine created for boys and girls from 6 to 13 years, with youngsters 8, 9, and 10 the specific target age. The magazine is designed as an activity publication to be enjoyed by both boys and girls on the alternate months of Hopscotch and Boys' Quest magazines. Our point of view is that every child deserves the right to be a child for a number of years before he or she becomes a young adult. As a result, *Fun For Kidz* looks for activities that deal with timeless topics, such as pets, nature, hobbies, science, games, sports, careers, simple cooking, and anything else likely to interest a child. Each issue revolves around a theme. We are looking for lively writing that involves an activity that is both wholesome and unusual. We are looking for articles around 500 words as well as puzzles, poems, cooking, carpentry projects, jokes, riddles, crafts, and other activities that complement the theme. Articles that are accompanied by good photos are far more likely to be accepted than those that need illustrations. We will entertain simultaneous submissions as long as that fact is noted on the manuscript. Submissions should be double-spaced. We use a number of photos printed in black and white, inside the magazine. These photos support the articles. Payment is $5 per photo. Most art will be by assignment, in support of features used. We are anxious to find artists capable of illustrating stories and features. We welcome copies of sample work, which will remain on file. Our inside art is pen and ink. We pay $35 for a full page and $25 for a partial page. *Fun For Kidz* is a fairly new publication. It is the companion to Boys' Quest, and Hopscotch. Like

Hopscotch and Boys' Quest, the issues each revolve around a theme. We often choose new themes as the result of a submission on a topic we haven't covered. We work far into the future. If you don't receive a quick response on your submission, we are holding it and giving it serious consideration. We strive to treat all of our contributors and their work with respect and fairness. It is important to include in the subject and body of the e-mail message which of the open issues your story is intended for.
APPROXIMATE PAY: We pay a minimum of five cents a word for both fiction and nonfiction, with additional payment given if the piece is accompanied by appropriate photos or art. We pay a minimum of $10 per poem or puzzle, with variable rates offered for games, carpentry projects, etc. *Fun For Kidz* buys first American serial rights and pays upon publication. It welcomes the contributions of both published and unpublished writers. We reserve the right to publish all material from the magazine on our website as a sample of the magazine. This is for display only on a limited time basis. Contributors will be compensated whenever their work is published to generate revenue and not strictly for exposure.

Boys' Quest Submission Guidelines

Every *BOYS' QUEST* contributor must remember we publish only six issues a year, which means our editorial needs are extremely limited. It is obvious that we must reject far more contributions that we accept, no matter how outstanding they may seem to you or to us. With that said, we would point out that *BOYS' QUEST* is a magazine created for boys from 6 to 13 years, with youngsters 8, 9, and 10 the specific target age. Our point of view is that every young boy deserves the right to be a young boy for a number of years before he becomes a young adult. As a result, *BOYS' QUEST* looks for articles, fiction, nonfiction, and poetry that deal with timeless topics, such as pets, nature, hobbies, science, games, sports, careers, simple cooking, and anything else likely to interest a 10-year-old boy. Each issue revolves around a theme. We are looking for lively writing, most of it from a 10-year-old boy's point of view, with the boy or boys directly involved in an activity that is both wholesome and unusual. We need nonfiction with photos and fiction stories around 500 words, as well as puzzles, poems, cooking, carpentry projects, jokes, and riddles. Nonfiction pieces that are accompanied by clear photos with high resolution are far more likely to be accepted than those that need illustrations. The ideal length of a *BOYS' QUEST* piece, for nonfiction or fiction, is 500 words. We will entertain simultaneous submissions as long as that fact is noted on the manuscript. Submissions should be double-spaced. We will pay a minimum of five cents a word for both fiction and nonfiction, with additional payment given if the piece is accompanied by appropriate photos or art. We will pay a minimum of $10 per poem or

puzzle, with variable rates offered for games, carpentry projects, etc. *BOYS' QUEST* buys first American serial rights and pays upon publication. It welcomes the contributions of both published and unpublished writers. We reserve the right to publish all material from the magazine on our website as a sample of the magazine. This is for display only on a limited time basis. Contributors will be compensated whenever their work is published to generate revenue and not strictly for exposure. A complimentary copy will be sent to each writer who has contributed to a given issue. We use a number of photos, printed in black and white, inside the magazine. These photos support the articles. Payment is $5 per photo. Most art will be by assignment, in support of features used. The magazine is anxious to find artists capable of illustrating stories and features and welcomes copies of sample work, which will remain on file. Our work inside is pen and ink. We pay $35 for a full page and $25 for a partial page. We are no longer accepting submissions by e-mail. Please mail submissions to:
Fun For Kidz Magazines
PO Box 227
Bluffton, OH 45817
When we review manuscripts, we automatically consider them for any of our three magazines, so it is not necessary for you to submit the same manuscripts more than once. All submissions need the following to be considered for publication:

- Self-Addressed Stamped Envelope (SASE) for acceptance/rejection letter
- Contact info including e-mail address, phone number, and mailing address
- Notation of which upcoming theme your content should be considered for

***Hopscotch* Submission Guidelines**

Every *HOPSCOTCH* contributor must remember we publish only six issues a year, which means our editorial needs are extremely limited. An annual total, for instance, will include some 30 to 36 nonfiction pieces, 9 or 10 short stories, 18 or so poems, six cover illustrations, and a smattering of puzzles, crafts, and the like. It is obvious that we must reject far more contributions than we accept, no matter how outstanding they may seem to you or to us. With that said, we would point out that *HOPSCOTCH* is a magazine created for girls from 6-13 years, with girls 8, 9, and 10 the specific target age. Our point of view is that every young girl deserves the right to be a young girl for a number of years before she becomes a young adult. As a result, *HOPSCOTCH* looks for articles, fiction, nonfiction, and poetry that deal with timeless topics, such as pets, nature, hobbies, science, games, sports, careers, simple cooking, and anything else likely to interest a

young girl. We leave dating, romance, human sexuality, cosmetics, fashion, and the like to other publications. Each issue revolves around a theme. We are looking for lively writing, most of it from a young girl's point of view, with the girl or girls directly involved in an activity that is both wholesome and unusual. Examples have included girls in a sheep to shawl contest, girls raising puppies that are destined to guide the blind and girls who take summer ballet lessons from members of the New York City Ballet. While on the subject of nonfiction, remembering that we use it 3 to 1 over fiction, those pieces that are accompanied by clear photos with high resolution are far more likely to be accepted than those that need illustrations. The ideal length of a *HOPSCOTCH* nonfiction piece is 500 words or less, although we are not about to turn down a truly exceptional piece if it is slightly longer than the ideal. We prefer fiction to not run over 1000 words. We will entertain simultaneous submissions as long as that fact is noted on the manuscript. Submissions should be double-spaced. We use a number of photos, printed in black and white, inside the magazine. These photos support the articles. Payment is $5 per photo. Most art will be by assignment, in support of features used. The magazine is anxious to find artists capable of illustrating stories and features and welcomes copies of sample work, which will remain on file. Payment is $35 for full-page illustrations and $25 for partial-page illustrations. Although we are working far into the future, we occasionally have room for one or two pages. We are always in need of cute and clever recipes, well-written and illustrated crafts, riddles, and jokes. It is important to include in the subject and body of the e-mail message which of the open issues your story is intended for.
APPROXIMATE PAY: We will pay a minimum of 5 cents a word for both fiction and nonfiction, with additional payment given if the piece is accompanied by appropriate photos or art. We will pay a minimum of $10 per poem or puzzle, with variable rates offered for games, crafts, cartoons, and the like. *HOPSCOTCH* buys first American serial rights and pays upon publication. It welcomes the contributions of both published and unpublished writers. We reserve the right to publish all material from the magazine on our website as a sample of the magazine. This is for display only on a limited time basis. Contributors will be compensated whenever their work is published to generate revenue and not strictly for exposure.

GEORGIA FAMILY

Macon, GA – monthly (20,000)
georgiafamily.com
olyafessard@gmail.com
GUIDELINES: We prefer articles which can be localized to parenting in Central Georgia; however, we do consider general articles which relate to the family. Material previously published outside Central Georgia is

welcome. We do not buy work from writers who are published by our competitors. For reprint offers, let us know where the material has already appeared.
APPROXIMATE PAY: $10 up to 500 words; $20 up to 1,000 words; $30 over 1,000 words.

GIGGLE

Newberry, FL
gigglemag.com
giggle@irvingpublications.com

GIRLS' LIFE

girlslife.com
katiea@girlslife.com
GUIDELINES: *Girls' Life* accepts unsolicited manuscripts on a speculative basis only. First, send an e-mail or letter query with detailed story idea(s). Please familiarize yourself with the voice and content of *Girls' Life* before submitting. *Girls' Life* magazine does not accept poetry submissions. Every story should have a title, blurb and byline. Author's complete name, address, phone number and e-mail address must be provided on submission. Referrals for art sources are appreciated, if applicable. *Girls' Life* conforms to *The Associated Press Stylebook and Libel Manual.* Manuscripts can be e-mailed in Microsoft Word. Documents should be double-spaced in 12-point Verdana font. All research must rely on primary sources. Manuscripts must be accompanied by a complete list of sources, telephone numbers and reference materials, if applicable. E-mail queries are responded to within 90 days. Unless submission is stated to be a possible work for hire, submission will be considered property of *Girls' Life* magazine. A memorandum of agreement is to be executed by both parties before payment is made. Head to the website for info on how to pitch to them.

GOOD HOUSEKEEPING

New York, NY – monthly (5,000,000)
goodhousekeeping.com
Article Submissions
300 W 57th Street, 28th Floor
New York, NY 10019
GUIDELINES: *Good Housekeeping* addresses 25 million women. Most are married with children (anywhere from newborn to college age, but predominantly in the 6-12 age group) and work outside the home. Submissions will be reviewed for the Blessings column on the back page. Submissions should be 500 words, about a person or event that proved to be a blessing in your life. We will also review health narratives—stories of

women (or a family member) who've overcome a significant medical problem, undergone a medical "first" or had a dramatic rescue. It's best to familiarize yourself with the tone and content of *Good Housekeeping* before you query us. (Back issues will likely be available at your local library.) The most successful queries or manuscripts are those that are timely, appropriately researched, engagingly written, freshly angled and tailored to *Good Housekeeping* readers in particular. Queries should be typed, and when possible, should have clips of previously published articles attached. You must include an SASE to receive a reply. Please allow two to three months for a response, due to the large volume of unsolicited queries we receive. Submissions in categories other than those listed above will not receive responses.

APPROXIMATE PAY: $1 per word for columns and departments for items 300-600 words.

GOOD LIFE FAMILY

Dallas, TX
goodlifefamilymag.com
sheryl@slpcompany.com

GOOD LIVING

Tampa Bay, FL
goodlivingmagazine.com
pam@goodlivingmag.com

THE GREEN PARENT

East Hoathly, Lewes, United Kingdom – bi-monthly (100,000 international)
thegreenparent.co.uk
features@thegreenparent.co.uk

GUIDELINES: We regularly cover the following subject areas:

- Pregnancy and conscious birth
- Breastfeeding
- Family life
- Alternative education
- Natural health and beauty
- Food and drink
- Eco-house and garden
- Green travel
- Ethical fashion

Length of features is between 1,500-2,000 words. We appreciate your interest in writing for *The Green Parent*. We welcome unsolicited articles from regular readers, or those who are at least familiar with the topics covered and the ethos of the magazine. Our main objective is to provide information that empowers our readers to make changes and supports them in being their own experts. We like articles that have a strong point of view and come from the heart. Our choice of articles depends on the other material we have published on the subject, how new the topic is to us, and how unique the presentation is. It helps if you include photos. Familiarise yourself with *The Green Parent.* We are more likely to publish your article if you are a *Green Parent* reader and are familiar with the issues we discuss. Think about the subjects you know well and those that are under covered. Please submit your article as a Word document and email it as an attachment. Please double-space your manuscript. But do not format in any other way. Include contact details (name, address, telephone number and email address) within your email and all subsequent correspondence. Please include a brief biographical sketch at the end of your submission so that we can print it if you article is used. Please do not send us an article that you have already submitted elsewhere unless you have had the article returned or have heard that it is not going to be used. Your contribution is for the use of your article for publishing in a particular edition. Articles will be used in the magazine and possibly on our Web site. Contribution of your article is deemed as agreement to these conditions. We request that your article is not published elsewhere for at least six months from the date of publication in *The Green Parent* and that republished articles carry the following: This article was first published in *The Green Parent* magazine, issue number __, date, including our Web address: www.thegreenparent.co.uk. Our procedure is to read and respond to articles within two months of receiving them. This can be a long time to wait, especially if you are eager for a reply. Please be patient. Contact us via email if you wish to inquire about your manuscript before hearing from us. Once an article is received and we retain it, we may want to keep it for several issues; we plan quite a bit in advance and may have already selected articles for upcoming issues before we receive your article. Even when an article is selected for an issue, it may be pulled for lack of space. These uncertainties make it difficult for us to be as specific in our acceptance as we would like; we appreciate your understanding of this creative process. We try not to keep an article longer than six months to a year because, although we may like it, we feel it should have a chance in another market. Our hardest task is returning articles that we cannot use. We try to be honest in our replies, but it is not always possible to provide in-depth feedback. We evaluate all articles in light of the other articles we have on hand, when last we covered the subject, and our readers' interest in the subject matter. We retain only a small percentage of the articles we receive. Returning a manuscript is not a personal rejection; it is a practical consideration. We encourage you to submit your manuscript elsewhere if we cannot accept it. We accept articles on a speculative basis so even if we have expressed an interest in, or given you the go-ahead on, a proposed article, we cannot guarantee its publication. Expenses are not usually paid, except in exceptional circumstances, and then only by prior arrangement. *The Green Parent* is an editorially-led magazine with a self-imposed ceiling of 25 percent advertising as well as self-imposed advertiser criteria (advertisers must reflect the values of *The Green Parent*—no disposable nappies, no formula milks or products that undermine breastfeeding, no electronic or plastic toys, no TV- or related-branded products, no products tested on animals, etc.). It is unusual for a magazine such as ours to pay for articles, but we feel that it is important to ensure the high level of journalism that our readers have come to expect, and we are also keen to support those writers who are stay-at-home parents. Enjoy your writing journey!

APPROXIMATE PAY: We pay £75 per 1,000 words [Kerrie says this is about $120, which fluctuates]. Payment is made on publication. In addition to payment, all authors receive a free copy of *The Green Parent.*

GROWING UP CHICO

Butte County, CA
growingupchico.com
marne@growingupchico.com

GROWING UP IN THE VALLEY

Roanoke, VA
growingupinthevalley.com
josh@growingupinthevalley.com

GULF COAST PARENTS & KIDS

Jackson, MS
parents-kids.com
magazine@parents-kids.com

GUIDELINES: In addition to the topics below, we also accept seasonal submissions. So we are always interested in a Valentine's story for our January/February issue. Notice our double issues (listed below) and submit seasonal things well in advance. Our tone is conversational. Write as if you were telling a neighbor all about the topic of the article. Avoid "personal essays." Our columnists write from a first person viewpoint—our feature articles should almost always be third person. Thus, do not write about your own experience, but interview other people who can tell the story. If there's a mix, call me and let's discuss it. I can almost always find ways to get other people quoted as well as the authorial voice. Decide on your point of view before the article. Simply start the story. Articles must be very tight—never to exceed 1,000 words, but 700 is even better. To increase your chances of acceptance, think in terms of your topic and our readers—what are the local implications for parents sending their children to day care, school, summer camp? What local programs or assistance can make life better? What does the average area parent need to know on this topic? Always put your byline just beneath the title of every article you write. But you think, "Of course Gretchen knows my name. Besides, it's on the email I attached the file to." I assign many articles, sometimes on related topics, such as "money" or "women's health." Also, your attached file is immediately removed from your email message. Thus, five days or five hours later when I open your file, I have no idea who wrote it without going back to my very full email folder. At the end of your article, please put a one-line bio. "Bella Cook is a Jackson, MS, miniature rat terrier who enjoys eating." If you are a parent, please say so. This is required. I favor stories with a local slant (quote local experts, local kids, local parents). Have I mentioned this before? Please do not send in your article until you have verified the following:

- Did I include a proposed headline or title? (Subheads are good, too.)
- Did I put my name directly below that?
- Did I include a one-line bio at the end of the article?
- Did I keep my article to less than 1,000 words? (700 is better, unless instructed otherwise.)
- Did I write in third person, rather than first person? (If your article can only be written in first person, please call me and discuss it before submitting it.)
- Did I interview at least three people? Local experts, parents, kids?
- Did I include at least one recommendation for the "More Information" section? A book, a business, a website, etc. Readers should know where to find out more.
- Does each paragraph logically lead to the next paragraph? Are there transitions, sub-heads, etc. to guide the reader if these are necessary?

Other hints: Single space. Do not indent, instead do a double hard return to indicate new paragraph. Sidebars are always welcome and a good way to save space with tight writing.

APPROXIMATE PAY: $25 for reprints. Pays upon publication plus 30 days.

HAMILTON COUNTY FAMILY

Indianapolis, IN
hamiltoncountyfamily.com
susan@hamiltoncountyfamily.com

GUIDELINES: *Hamilton County Family* is always looking for talented, experienced freelance writers to enhance our magazine. Our goal is to have a good mix of fun and substantive local stories of interest to area parents. We are a bi-monthly, full color, glossy parenting magazine. Over 25,000 copies are printed each issue. We welcome queries and submissions, especially from local freelancers. Here are a few factors to consider before sending your pitch.

- **Make it local.** We're looking for stories and sources that reflect the communities we cover: Carmel, Fishers, Noblesville, Westfield, Cicero, Sheridan, Arcadia and Atlanta. Therefore, Hamilton County ideas and sources are preferred.
- **Pitch early.** Please be mindful that content for Hamilton County Family is determined months in advance. Therefore, story ideas should be pitched two to three months before the month it would run. This is particularly important for seasonally-anchored stories.
- **We may not respond.** Because of the high volume of submissions and queries we receive, it is not always feasible to respond to each pitch. If you do not hear from us within a month of your submission, it is safe to assume that we have decided to pass.

HAWAII PARENT (mostly local)

www.hawaii-parent.com
hpks@hawaii.rr.com

APPROXIMATE PAY: They pay 15 cents a word on publication. Most articles they assign are between 800 and 1,200 words.

HELLO, DARLING (MOPS International)

mops.org
content@mops.org

GUIDELINES: *Hello, Darling* is a movement of women raising the world together. We celebrate the uniqueness of every woman's journey. In every way we connect our community through our quarterly print magazine, blog and social media outlets—we seek to inspire each mom as a whole woman knowing she is a past, present and future, a set of hopes and fears uniquely hers, a wife and sister, daughter and friend, as well as a nurturer of little people. We strive to make sure every mom knows she's welcome here, knowing the thing connecting us is the desire to be the best moms possible. As the group of women collectively raising the next generation of the world, we want to be a part of honest conversation, a chorus of voices seeking each other as we walk boldly toward hard questions, finding restoration and seeking hope. *Hello, Darling* lives under the wing of MOPS International, an organization creating communities of moms, because moms are world influencers. What qualities guide our material?

Honest

In everything we publish, we seek to inspire moms. We want to be willing to say, "this is the way things really are," "these are my honest questions," "here are the things in my life that seem bigger than me," knowing it is in the vulnerable conversations that we can make the most progress toward restoring the future for the next generation.

Welcoming
We are a community of moms from every corner of the country, and more than 30 other countries around the world. Our community spans every socioeconomic, marital status, origin of mothering, race, religious, denominational, age and lifestyle spectrum because we believe we mother best when we mother together. Every woman's story is valuable, and we seek to make *Hello, Darling* a safe place by acknowledging that one choice doesn't change the value or validity of another.
Family provides roots
Every act of mothering is significant because family is where children build the foundation for their futures. In every way possible we seek to provide practical resources for moms, and a safe place to fail because we know from experience motherhood includes both triumphs and failures, and both are required for moms to expand to their potential. And we believe all of it is worth it, because each child is a gift.
There is a woman inside the mother
Before motherhood, each woman was uniquely created with a past, present and future story, passions and gifts given to her to give the world, and a personality all her own. When she became a mother, this added to the shape of her story, coloring it with new extensions of herself. In everything we write, we aim to nurture the woman who still exists inside the mother.
There is hope in the story
Every sojourn involves struggle, setback and tragedy because this is the plight of life on Earth. We believe in the midst of every epic exists hope and redemption, and we seek to find them at every opportunity.
Types of published material
Calls for submission: We will post calls for submissions on our blog in the "we love" section. We will do a call for submissions every month based on the upcoming theme for the blog. And we'll do a call for submissions quarterly based on the needs of the magazine. The easiest way to access them will be through the tag: writers needed.
Regular types of material needed
On the blog:

- Recipes (with step-by-step photos)
- Practical home ideas
- DIY (with photos)
- Play ideas
- Parenting experts
- Make-up/fashion/beauty tips
- And, of course, stories about parenting, mothering and woman-related issues. And we're always up for a good tear-jerker or something to get us laughing.

We do not publish fiction, individual reviews on divisive issues (including doctrinal or political issues), devotions or Bible studies, book or product reviews. Just so you know, all articles are received on speculation. We will respond to all submissions when they are received to confirm submission and obtain submission agreement. If your article is selected for publishing, we will email you in advance with the date we will be publishing and the permalink. Please submit a complete article in an attached Word document or in the body of the email. Please include an article title, authors name, email address and two-sentence bio.

And Since You Always Ask

Yes, you may send material that has been previously published. Just make sure it meets our editorial needs first. Because, again, we take those writer's guidelines pretty seriously.

HIGHLIGHTS FOR CHILDREN

Honesdale, PA – monthly (2,000,000)
highlightskids.com
Manuscript Submissions
803 Church Street
Honesdale, PA 18431-1824

GUIDELINES: *Highlights for Children* is a general-interest, advertising-free magazine for children up to age 12. We encourage writers to read several recent copies of *Highlights* before submitting work. A sample copy will be sent on request. We do not accept submissions by email or fax. We pay for all material on acceptance. We buy all rights, including copyright, and do not consider previously published material. Generally we prefer to see a manuscript rather than a query. However, we will review queries regarding nonfiction. We accept material at any time of the year, including seasonal material. Each submission must include a self-addressed stamped envelope. We do not pay writers younger than 16 years old for their work. Guidelines for young writers will be sent on request. To find a listing of our current needs, guidelines for illustrators, and Fiction Contest guidelines, please scroll down to the bottom of the page.

FICTION should have an engaging plot, strong characterization, a specific setting, and lively language. No series or continuing stories. Stories for younger readers (ages three to seven) should have 500 words or fewer and should not seem babyish to older readers. Stories for older readers (ages eight to 12) should have 800 words or fewer and should be appealing to younger readers if read aloud. Frequent needs include humor, mystery, sports, holiday and adventure stories; retellings of traditional tales; stories with urban settings; and stories that feature world cultures. For stories that require research, such as historical fiction, please send photocopies of key pages in references and of any correspondence with experts. We prefer characters that set a positive example. We avoid stories that preach. We avoid suggestions of crime and violence. We seldom buy rhyming stories. Payment: $150 and up.

REBUS STORIES geared toward beginning readers should feature a variety of familiar words that can easily be shown as pictures. Rebuses should have 120 words or fewer. Rebuses with a surprise or twist at the end often work best. Payment: $100 and up.

VERSE, which is purchased sparingly, is rarely longer than sixteen lines and should be meaningful for young readers. Payment: $25 and up.

NONFICTION includes science, arts, biography, autobiography, sports, world cultures, economics, service/self-help, careers, adventure, and history. All articles should have 800 words or fewer. Nonfiction articles geared to our younger readers (ages three to seven) are especially welcome. These should not exceed 500 words. Articles with a tight focus are most successful. We prefer research based on firsthand experience, consultation with experts, or primary sources. Articles about cultural traditions and ways of life should reflect a deep understanding of the subject.

BIOGRAPHIES of individuals who have made significant artistic, scientific, or humanitarian contributions are strengthened by the inclusion of formative childhood experiences. We prefer biographies that are rich in quotes and anecdotes and that place the subject in a historical and cultural context. Complete bibliographies and photocopies of key pages in references must be included. Color 35mm slides, photos, or art-reference materials are helpful and sometimes crucial in evaluating submissions. Digital images should be no less than 300 dpi. We encourage authors to have their articles reviewed by an expert before submission. Please include the expert's response. Payment: $150 and up.

FINGER PLAYS and **ACTION RHYMES** should have plenty of action and minimal text. They must be easy for very young children to act out, step by step. Include directions for hand, finger, or body movements. Payment: $25 and up.

PUZZLES should not require readers to write in the magazine; therefore, no crosswords, word searches, and so on. We welcome visual puzzles, math puzzles, and code activities. Payment: $25 and up.

GALLANT KIDS articles should have 400 words or fewer. They should focus on children who are serving others through unique, interesting, kid-generated projects. Payment: $150 and up.

PICTURE PUZZLER ideas should be primarily visual and include little text. These puzzles, featured on the inside back cover of the magazine, can include photos, drawings, or detailed art suggestions for a full-page illustration. Original board games that can be played on the page are welcome. Picture Puzzlers should not require readers to write in the magazine. Ideas should be original and should appeal to boys and girls of a wide age range. Payment: $50 and up. For more tips and information of interest to writers, visit HighlightsFoundation.org. Writers may also find it helpful to search the magazine index or peruse the Fun Finder at HighlightsKids.com.

HOME EDUCATION MAGAZINE

Tonasket, WA – bimonthly (32,000)
homeedmag.com
editor@homeedmag.com

GUIDELINES: We publish stories and articles from families who empower their children and teens to live a life rich with self-directed experimentation, thought and action. Whether you are new to this lifestyle or experienced, whether your child/teen chooses to play all day or attend school (yes! self-directed people sometimes choose school!), we would love to read your story. We are also interested in stories of parents in such families who are learning, reinventing and unschooling themselves in the midst of family life. We welcome a diverse range of people, families and experiences. If you have a story to tell that is not within the suggested list below, send us an email with your idea. We'd love to hear about it. We will pay you for each article/story we print and for each of your photos we use. See our writer's guidelines for more submission information and payment rates. We are currently in search of your experience, insight and wisdom in the following areas:

We want to hear about the fresh, bright ways your family is learning and exploring the world together. Tell us about the ways you have successfully dealt with challenges in your family, ranging from divorce and illness, sibling or familial conflict, boredom, learning challenges, nay saying friends and relatives and more.

- Tell us how you have learned to maneuver the challenges of letting go of control and honor your child's inner compass.
- How do you live harmoniously with video games and television?
- Tell us about your special child or teen, or ask them to tell us: how have their unique drives, passions and interests led them to something exciting, revolutionary, inventive… earth-shattering in some way?
- Do you have an unschooled child or teen who has chosen to attend school? Tell us about the journey.
- Has your child or teen left a school environment and become an unschooler? Tell us about the transition.
- Has your child or teen (or your family) started a business that has been an extraordinary experience?
- Are you a grandparent who is unschooling or homeschooling your grandchild(ren)? Tell us about it!

- Are you a teen or young adult who has chosen to continue self-educating and not attend or aspire to college?
- Do you have an unschooled teen who chose college?
- What have you learned from your child or teen as they have blossomed and taken charge of their education, their world?

Writer Guidelines for *Home Education Magazine*

Home Education Magazine is an award-winning publication for unschooling families, or for anyone who enjoys living and learning. If you're not familiar with unschooling, please read some of the Featured Articles available on our website, unschooling.com.

Deadlines, editorial calendar

Please feel free to submit an article at any time, and we'll schedule it appropriately. Please note that articles are often selected four to six months ahead of our current issue. We do not publish or conform to an editorial calendar, preferring to select the best articles submitted at any given time. Replies to queries and submissions will be made as soon as possible but can take several weeks.

Submission Guidelines

Submissions via email are the preferred format; please send to editor-at-homeedmag.com, or use our Contact Form. Please include the article in the body of your email and, if possible, also attach the article as an RTF file, along with your name, postal mailing address (where we can send payment and a copy of the magazine if your article is accepted), phone number, and a short bio. We will also accept pen names if your subject matter is intimate, deeply personal or will otherwise compromise your comfort level. General article length is 2,000 words, but we do occasionally accept longer or shorter articles. We welcome articles from inexperienced writers, especially mothers with unschooling experience. Regardless of what you were taught in high school English classes, writing is nothing particularly mysterious. It's only another form of communication. If you can clearly explain your ideas to a friend, you can write a good article for our magazine. Our voice is from unschoolers to unschoolers, so you don't need to be an education expert or an English major to write for us. We can also assist you with your writing if we love the topic you are wanting to write about. If your article is not accepted, don't take it personally. We have many reasons why we can't take every article. Try submitting to us again with another article.

Photos

We always need sharp, clear photos for inside editorial use. Regular color or B/W print sizes work fine for inside use(images are printed at 300 dpi). Covers (300 dpi) require a very sharp, clear image. Color enlargements are best (8" x 10" minimum), but please send an image for review first. We prefer photos showing children and families doing everyday things, not posed educational-type shots. We advise studying our magazine before attempting photo submissions. Please include information about the photo, including names of anyone in the pictures, and the name of the photographer for credit. Electronic submissions of photos are recommended. Please arrange to send low resolution (72 dpi) for review. If your low resolution image is accepted, you can send the full-sized version at the resolutions noted above for inside and cover photos. For more information write to Mark Hegener at publisher-at-homeedmag.com, or use or Contact Form.

Rights

Home Education Magazine buys First North American Serial Rights (print and electronic) to all original and unpublished articles, columns, artwork and photos, and we make our content available to our partner sites (American Homeschool Association, Unschooling.com, and others), with your byline included and with credit to HEM for reprints (i.e., "Originally published in Home Education Magazine, month/year"). We upload selected articles and columns from each issue to our website. Rights purchased include our right to reproduce your work, in whole or in part, in CD-ROM format as well as in any other formats of Home Education Magazine in which your work appears, or in an anthology or collection of articles, columns, artwork and photos which have appeared in Home Education Magazine. All material purchased become the sole property of Home Education Magazine to be used as indicated here.

APPROXIMATE PAY: We pay $100 each for feature articles. For photos for inside use, we pay $10 each. For cover color photos, we pay $100 each. Contributors receive one free copy of the issue in which their article appears.

HOMESCHOOLING TODAY

Abingdon, VA – bimonthly
homeschoolingtoday.com
management@homeschooltoday.com

GUIDELINES: *Homeschooling Today* magazine is one of the most comprehensive home education magazines available, with a special focus on literature, fine arts, and Christian living. Our mission is to encourage, challenge, and support homeschooling families. We believe that as we obediently train and educate our own children and equip them with a Christian worldview, we will see families strengthened and future generations prepared for the task of reforming the church and changing society. While we understand that it will not always be possible (or preferable) for every article to fit into our issue theme, our readers have shown an interest in this format. Therefore, please browse our theme list for ideas and inspiration. Each theme includes a submission deadline which you will also want to take into consideration. You will find our Themes and

Deadlines on the *Homeschooling Today* website under Contact Us/Write for *HST*: homeschooltoday.com/write.

ARTICLE TYPES

We currently have four main types of articles in our magazine:

- Columns (written by our regular columnists)
- Feature Articles (1,300-2,000 words)
- Departments (500-875 words)
- Reviews (150-475 words or 150 words per product for multiple products in one review)

We also have a monthly email newsletter, *Homeschooling Helper* (900-1,100 words), which is intended for inspirational rather than how-to topics. Consider the category for your article when submitting it. Feature articles are more likely to be used when they relate to the magazine theme. We do not accept reprints at this time, and we no longer accept queries. We accept unsolicited articles submitted as Microsoft Word document attachments to an email or, if you are unable to submit an attachment, on CD mailed to the attention of the Editor-in-Chief of *Homeschooling Today* magazine. If you use Macintosh, please convert the file for us. Send articles with the words "Article Submission" in the email subject line. It is helpful if you include the issue date/theme as well, if you are submitting for a particular issue. Articles cannot be returned. Submission does not guarantee publication. Unsolicited articles should arrive at least six months prior to the issue date for which the article is intended (for example, March for the September/October issue). We receive a large number of unsolicited articles, so we appreciate your patience as we review submissions for possible publication. If you have not heard from us within six months, you may assume that we will not use your article. We do not send notification if we decide not to publish a submission. If your article is chosen for inclusion, we will notify you and will email a contract for you to sign and fax or mail to us.

FEATURE ARTICLES

Good feature articles include information on a topic, unit studies, encouragement, challenge, or an interview. Feature article word count is 1,400-1,650 words. This may take the form of one 1,400-1,650-word article or as a 1,250-word article with a 400-word sidebar. Final published word count, which is the basis for payment to the author, includes the text of the edited and published article and any resource list. It does not include the author's personal information on the first page, the title or byline of the article, or the bio of the author; it will likely differ from the word count of the article as originally submitted.

DEPARTMENTS

Not all departments are included in every issue. Word count for articles in the various departments is 500-875 words. Again, final published word count, which is the basis for payment to the author, includes the text of the edited and published article and any resource list. It does not include the author's personal information on the first page, the title or byline of the article, or the bio of the author; it will likely differ from the word count of the article as originally submitted.

We currently have regular writers for the following departments:

- UNDERSTANDING THE ARTS: Emily Cottrill, regularly writes an article to accompany a pull-out art print for each issue.
- LIVING LITERATURE: Emily Adams regularly writes for this department. We do accept additional article submissions in this category. Contact Kara Murphy if you would like to write for this department (kara@homeschooltoday.com).

In addition to the above bimonthly departments, we include several articles in each issue from the following departments which do not have regular writers or accept additional submissions. Not all departments are included in each issue:

- In the Word (Bible study) – 875 words
- Living Literature 1 (book studies appropriate for middle students, ages 8-12) – 500 words
- Living Literature 2 (for older students, 13 years old and older) – 500 words
- Living Literature 3 (for children ages 6-10) – 500 words
- Unit Study – 1500 words
- Bringing History to Life – 875 words
- Nature in Life (Nature Study) – 875 words
- Focus on Writing – 875 words
- Language Learning (English and Foreign Languages) – 875 words
- The Abacus (Mathematics) – 875 words
- Music Through the Centuries (History) – 875 words
- Making Melody (Musical Instruction/Enjoyment) – 875 words
- The Home Team (Physical Education) – 875 words
- Thinking (Logic, Biblical Thinking) – 875 words
- Homeschooling Around the World – 875 words
- The Art of Homemaking – 875 words
- Teach Them The Good Way (Training Methodology) – 875 words

HOMESCHOOLING HELPER

Homeschooling Today's online newsletter, Homeschooling Helper, is sent monthly to a free subscription-based email list. An inspirational article (900-1,100 words) is meant to encourage and refresh homeschooling parents in their day-to-day journey through homeschooling.

REVIEWS

Since thousands of homeschoolers are counting on our reviewers when making book and curriculum decisions, reviewers should remember that different families have different standards. They should warn parents of any objectionable, unpleasant, or secular content. Always focus on the good in a product while warning about the negative. Reviews of books, curriculum, and media/computer programs will appear in our Bookshelf and Beyond department. We accept suggestions for materials to review. Contact reviews@HomeschoolToday.com with ideas. (Check the site for their writer's guidelines and editorial calendar, which got too out of hand for me to paste here! They generally follow *The Chicago Manual of Style, 15th Edition.*)

APPROXIMATE PAY: We pay for published articles in one of the following ways:

- Ten cents per *published* word for original, unpublished works in print publications.
- Eight cents per published word for original, unpublished works in online media.
- Ten cents per published word for reviews in Bookshelf and Beyond plus five dollars to cover return postage for the book/product. Reviewers should read the specific Reviewers section (above) as well as the general guidelines.
- $50 flat rate, regardless of length, for reprints (when they are accepted for a rare reason) of previously published works (with proof—email or statement in some form from the original publication—that author owns copyright for reprint), or appropriate word rate, whichever is less.

HONOLULU FAMILY
Honolulu, HI
honolulufamily.com
christiy@honolulufamily.com

'HOOD
thehoodmagazine.com
hannah@thehoodmagazine.com
HOUSTON FAMILY
HOUSTON BABY GUIDE
Houston, TX – monthly (60,000)
houstonfamilymagazine.com
editor@houstonfamilymagazine.com
APPROXIMATE PAY: $20-25 reprints.

HUDSON VALLEY PARENT (exclusive)
Newburgh, NY – monthly (35,000)
hvparent.com
editor@excitingread.com
GUIDELINES: We typically run two to three feature articles in each

publication every month (700-1,200 words) on a variety of topics. First-person accounts are preferred, as our research has shown that our readers want to read about other people and their experiences. Articles are due at least four months prior to publication. We accept Windows-based Word documents as attachments, or you can embed your article into the email. We ask that you only submit articles that have not previously run in our territory. Include your name, phone number and best time to reach you. Also attach sample writings you have done so our editor can review your style of writing. You should also include topics which you enjoy writing about. Although most stories are assigned, feel free to submit queries with a few ideas you think might interest our readers. Describe any preliminary research you will complete and list other sources you plan to consult. Sell your story idea to us; tell us why we should publish it. If you don't believe in the topic (or can't effectively tell us why we should), how can we? We prefer articles with local information using local sources. We rarely run stories on specific organizations or events (e.g., a feature on one art school, one social service agency) and prefer stories on issues of concern to parents (e.g., art classes for kids, how to become a foster parent) or the active adult market. In many cases, the editor can assist with finding appropriate contact sources. Please do not use tab settings or other indentation markings to indicate the beginning of a new paragraph in your manuscripts sent via email. Do not use more than one space after a period. When possible send digital (jpg) photographs that are applicable to the piece. If you are able to send the photographs electronically, our graphic designers will provide electronic guidelines. Your article should contain at least one sidebar related to the article. This may be a list of helpful websites, local groups or places, contact information or information from the article that can stand alone. Include your name, address, phone number, email address, Social Security number and approximate word count at the beginning of your manuscript. A brief one- or two-line bio at the end of your manuscript should also be included.

APPROXIMATE PAY: $60 for locally-slanted, assigned one-page story of 700-800 words, $80-120 for 1,200-word or more features. Reprints are between $25-35 depending on the word count. Any unsolicited, non-locally-slanted feature is treated as a reprint; payment will be made based on the word count above. We purchase first-time rights for assigned features or other assigned articles. We also purchase online rights for local articles.

HYBRID MOM

Commack, NY
hybridmom.com
beth@hybridmom.com
allison@hybridmom.com

GUIDELINES: Readers of HybridMom.com and *Hybrid Mom* magazine are women who are leading double lives … and loving it. Blending a commitment to at-home parenting with other demanding roles means that their days are crazy; they crave a support group that is there when they have time for it, to make them laugh and feel good about the path they have chosen. These women are no longer choosing between a successful career or a successful family life, but rather integrating their many aspirations for the purpose of achieving a balanced life. *Hybrid Mom*'s editorial content reflects a voice of friendship, rather than an expert and focuses on the "real world" of this new generation of Moms. *Hybrid Mom* provides insight and intelligence, practical tools and strategies to guide today's Moms in their quest to work, play and live without sacrificing their families. We share secrets, stories, photos and wisdom gleaned from experience, but we don't tell readers how to be a better mother, housewife and person. We celebrate and commiserate rather than lecture. Our readers are more than mothers. They are wives and daughters and human beings with brains and dreams and a yearning for a community that fits all of their identities. Our readers are educated, determined and at times, frustrated. They are also very busy, so get to the point fast. Entertain them with stories about people like them. Educate them with information they need in the easiest-to-digest format possible. Most important, have fun. Find new and creative ways to reach the heart and mind of our readers. This is the next generation of "reality magazines." A good trick is to read the story out loud to a friend before you send it in. If it doesn't sound natural, try again. Read the stories on our site. Once you understand where *Hybrid Mom*'s readers are coming from, you will understand how to write for them. We are excited to hear your stories and ideas! Here are just some of the topics which need your voice. We do not pay for articles published on our website, but we do pay $150 for columns and $300 for features for published submissions. We pay for Personal Essays/Opinion (800-1,200 words); News/Informational (600-1,200 words); Humor (400-600 words); Reviews (200 words for mini-reviews; 600-1200 for longer reviews).

WITHIN OUR WORK CATEGORY

All content here will support and be relevant to how a Hybrid Mom "works." Categories include: career, continuing education, business technology tips, entrepreneurs, to work or not to work, volunteering.

WITHIN OUR PLAY CATEGORY

All content here will support and be relevant to how a Hybrid Mom integrates work, and however she defines it, within her every day. Categories include: body, entertainment, family, humor, mind, reviews, technology.

WITHIN OUR LIVE CATEGORY

All content here will support and be relevant to how a Hybrid Mom integrates these subcategories into living! Categories include: entertaining, friendship, marriage, money, parenting. To submit any content to be published on HybridMom.com please submit an article via email to Allison Rubin, Managing Editor or Beth Smith for publication in *Hybrid Mom* magazine. By submitting a piece, you grant us your consent to publish it on Hybridmom.com. You will retain all rights, and are free to publish the piece anywhere else as long as you put forth your best effort to make sure that "Originally published on Hybridmom.com" with a back link to us. By submitting a piece, you are acknowledging that you solely own the copyright and agree to the above guidelines. We will become the top online and offline destination for Hybrid Moms, with you, our readers and writers, sharing your experiences, your voice and your sense of humor!

IPARENT
Katy, TX
iparentmagazine.com
dbourgeois@iparentmagazine.com

THE IMPERFECT PARENT
imperfectparent.com
prescott@imperfectparent.com
Only use online form to submit
GUIDELINES: (☺ Kerrie says: Often you'll try to submit using the online form and it will say they are backlogged and to check back later. I just make a note on my calendar to try again in a few weeks.) We do not mind simultaneous submissions to other website/publications, but simply ask that you notify us immediately if your piece is accepted elsewhere. Please do not send us multiple submissions in a row. *The Imperfect Parent* does modestly compensate its writers, see further below for payment information. The main focus of *The Imperfect Parent* is to provide a world view from a parent's perspective. Our main criteria are that the writing either makes people think, laugh, or both. Our objective is to get parents to think about social, political and parenting methods in a way that seeks to inform and educate on issues that affect our children and us, as parents. Anecdotal stories are fine, but they need to have a point beyond "parenting is hard." You may be sentient of your navel, just don't have a staring contest with it. Submissions should generally fit into these main categories: Articles about alternative parenting methods in a newspaper/Associated Press format. These articles will inform parents of what certain parenting practice methods are, the organizations promoting them, if any, and what kind of impact it may have on our society. The most engaging writing on this subject will be from a neutral ground, or from the side of opposition, avoiding propaganda and jargon. Alternatively, personal essays regarding

why a parenting choice was made, and why it was right for you—avoid being preachy or judgmental of those who may have made an opposite decision. Topic examples: Formula Feeding, breastfeeding, attachment parenting, Taking Children Seriously (TCS), natural parenting, mainstream parenting, discipline methods, circumcision, child-centered parenting, authoritative parenting, etc. Writings about political and social issues from counter-culture or mainstream perspectives as a parent and how they relate to the child raising experience. It is important to us to provide a platform for parents that might not hold popular views. While we will certainly reject any content that contains overtly offensive material, we support political viewpoints on all sides. Our mission is to "preserve the balance" and give parents an opportunity to voice their opinion in a non-hostile environment. Editorializing is allowed in these pieces (but avoid overtly pushing a personal agenda), as long as it specifically relates back to your parenting goals or its effects on your children. Topic examples: global warming, the war, conservative values, liberal values, libertarian ideals, Bush Administration, the Middle-east, international issues, religion, civil rights, environmentalism, economics, feminism, abortion, justice system, etc. Anything that deals with any aspect of the lighter side of parenting—parody, satire, a funny anecdote, an "open letter", take your pick. And if you are questioning if your humor crosses the line, then definitely send it in—we don't want "safe". We are a gloriously independent site that doesn't answer to a board of directors or a huge corporate sponsorship. Use that to your advantage. We certainly aren't afraid of offending some people, and you shouldn't be, either. The feature articles we look for cover timely topics and issues relating to parents and families in a traditional magazine feature format. For example, an in-depth profile of a person/organization, or a detailed look at a current event. These articles would utilize interviews and quotes from experts and outside sources. We are not looking for straightforward "how to" or advice articles, but pieces with more human-interest. Content based on personal experience would be acceptable, but these pieces should not be heavily autobiographical. Features are generally assigned, but we will most certainly consider submissions—please send a query of your story idea and clips to our editor. Short (approximately 200-400 words) reviews of any book that may be of interest to parents (including children's books). To avoid multiple review submissions for the same book, please send a query to our editor with the title you are interested in reviewing. All that being said, we can say with one word what we're not looking for: poetry. Anything else is fair game. We place more weight on entertaining and engaging writing above any certain topic. Queries are only necessary for features and book reviews. Everything else, we don't really care about what aspect of parenting you're writing about as much as how well you write about it. If it has anything that may be remotely interesting to parents, we're interested (we are parents, after all). Rough general guidelines would be articles/essays: 800-1,000 words, humor: 600-800 words, book reviews: 200-400 words. Assigned features: 1,000-3,000 words. These are not absolute numbers—fortunately we do not have the restrictions of the print world, so we do not edit for length. If you can get your message across in a few paragraphs, go ahead. If it takes you five pages, that's great. Just make sure your piece is succinct and to the point, and try to keep it slightly shorter than a John Grisham novel. Besides preferring non-published material, we've found most blog entries submitted were written to a familiar audience, and not suitable for reprint. We are developing an area on our site dedicated to highlighting exceptional blogs and posts, where this would be appropriate. Send a note to blog@imperfectparent.com if you would like us to consider adding you to our daily reads. Here's our lawyer chiming in: All editing decisions will be solely at the discretion of *The Imperfect Parent* editors and management. Given that the volume of submissions is ever increasing but our editorial staff is not, you generally will hear back from us within three to four weeks. We do try to make a point of responding to every submission, so please refrain from sending follow-up inquiries.

APPROXIMATE PAY: Payment is contingent upon the quality and type of written work submitted. Book reviews pay $10. Original articles/essays pay $25. Payment for assigned features varies depending on the writer's experience and relationship with The Imperfect Parent, but begins at $50 for a 1,000-word piece. Checks are disbursed by the 15th of the month following publication. Unless an arrangement to the contrary is made, *The Imperfect Parent* is purchasing first exclusive electronic rights. We do not, in general, purchase works that have already appeared elsewhere, especially on the web. We also require a non-exclusive right to keep your piece available in our online archives. If *The Imperfect Parent* secures any reprints, we will pay half of the reprint earnings to the writer. Writers are free to sell their work after we publish it. Every writer receives full credit for their work, and every feature/essay writer has the opportunity to submit a brief bio that will be included at the end of the piece. This bio may contain a brief description about yourself, along with a link to your own website and email address, if so desired. We also feature the most current articles on our homepage.

inBETWEEN
inbetween.ca
rachel@inbetween.ca

INLAND EMPIRE FAMILY
OC FAMILY
Newport Beach, CA – monthly

inlandempirefamily.com
ocfamily.com
iemail@iemag.bz
GUIDELINES: Submit one-page queries in writing, accompanied by resume and clips to Editorial Department, email above.
APPROXIMATE PAY: $35 reprints.

IRVING PARENT
SUBURBAN PARENT

Irving, TX – monthly
irvingparent.com
suburbanparent.com
editor@irvingparent.com
editor@suburbanparent.com
APPROXIMATE PAY: $20 per publication (2).

ISLAND PARENT

Vancouver, Canada
islandparent.ca
Partners with kidsinvictoria.com
editor@islandparent.ca
GUIDELINES: *Island Parent Magazine* targets Vancouver Island parents with children aged newborn to 18 years. Our editorial philosophy is based on the belief that parents need encouragement and useful information, not negative messages or guilt trips. Our publication includes a wide range of topics of interest to parents. We encourage writers to cover topics that are of interest to them or that reflect their own experience. We're looking for a variety of perspectives, experiences and beliefs. Please keep in mind that our aim is to help our readers feel valued, supported and respected. Ideally, we can raise the profile of parenting and help create a community of healthy, happy families. If an article provides a welcome idea, pertinent information, a laugh or a poignant moment for our readers, we're achieving our goal. Up to half of the articles in any given issue of *Island Parent Magazine* are unsolicited manuscripts. We provide a vehicle on Vancouver Island for Canadian writers of varying degrees of ability and professional experience. Most of the articles published in our magazine are written by Vancouver Island writers. Readers appreciate learning about resources in their community so, when relevant, please include book titles, services or contact information pertinent to the topic. Our average article length is 1,000 words (three columns) or 700 words (two columns). If submitting a photo, cut the length by at least 100 words. We pay an honorarium for first-time North American rights for use in *Island Parent Magazine*, both in print form and in .pdf format on our website (we also post a selection of articles

in the Archives section of our website). We have partnered with the Kids in Victoria website as it shares our dedication to support parents in our region. A selection of articles will be posted on kidsinvictoria.com each month before being archived on islandparent.ca. At the editor's discretion, there will be no remuneration for articles that will benefit, even indirectly, the author's service or business. Manuscripts must be typed, double spaced, and must include the word count, writer's name, address and daytime phone number on the first page. Please include a one-sentence bio that tells our readers who you are and, if relevant, how they can contact you. The editor will respond to submissions within six weeks of receipt. **APPROXIMATE PAY**: $35 for original articles for publication in *Island Parent* (both the magazine and the website). An additional $25 will be paid for those articles posted on kidsinvictoria.com.

ITHACA CHILD, ITHACA PARENT & TEEN, ITHACA BABY BOOK

Etna, NY – bimonthly
ithacachild.net
jgraney@twcny.rr.com
APPROXIMATE PAY: $25 for smaller articles and reprints; up to $50 for longer.

JERSEY SHORE FAMILY

New Jersey – bimonthly
jerseyshorefamily.com
pam@jerseyshorefamily.com
APPROXIMATE PAY: Hopes to pay in the future.

KANSAS CITY PARENT, KANSAS CITY BABY (mostly locals)

Overland Park, KS – monthly/quarterly
kcparent.com
editor@kcparent.com
GUIDELINES: We feature many articles, many of which relate to our monthly themes. In addition, we run monthly columns including Teacher Talk, Healthy Kids, A Word from Dad, Media Review, Women's Health, and more. To be considered, submitted articles need to establish local relevance with three to five localized points of reference. Our editorial staff works 60-150 days ahead, so please keep this in mind when you are submitting articles which tie in with our editorial calendar. Articles should be submitted via email, preferably as a Microsoft Word document with a word count of 300-1,100 words.
APPROXIMATE PAY: $25 originals or reprints.

KERN COUNTY FAMILY
Bakersfield, CA – monthly (30,000)
kerncountyfamily.com
kerncountyfamily@earthlink.net
APPROXIMATE PAY: $25 and up.

KID STUFF (locals only; New Hampshire and Vermont)
Hanover, NH – 5 times per year
kidstuff.com
laurajean@uvkidstuff.com

KIDS ON THE COAST
Australia
kidsonthecoast.com.au
editor@mothergoosemedia.com.au

KIDS' PAGES (online only, exclusive)
Arvada, CO – monthly
kidspages.org
ellen@kidspages.org
GUIDELINES: *Kids' Pages* welcomes submissions from freelance writers. We emphasize stories with a local focus and prefer to work with local established writers. We occasionally use reprints of articles from publications outside our region. We run several monthly feature articles on a wide range of family-related topics. Features require thorough research, knowledge of our audience and concise interviewing and writing skills. We ask writers to use the best experts on a subject—national and local. We prefer articles that are positive and upbeat with local relevancy. Word counts for articles vary from 500-1,000 words. We love to do local sidebars to articles. For example, if we get an article on great camping advice, we do a sidebar on where to camp locally, the costs and kids' programs. Articles should be emailed, preferably as a Microsoft Word document. Manuscripts should include the author's name, address, email and daytime phone number on the first page of the story. Include the word count with the article.. Reprints of articles from publications outside our region are also considered.
APPROXIMATE PAY: We usually buy one-time print rights with exclusivity within Colorado for one year.

KIDS VERMONT (locals only, exclusive)
Shelburne, VT – 10 times per year (20,000)
kidsvt.com
megan@kidsvt.com

GUIDELINES: Articles should be anywhere from 500-1,500 words. They do not have another "parenting publication" they compete with, but there is the daily paper. *The Burlington Free Press,* and many town papers. They ask that you do not sell the same piece to any other Vermont paper or magazine. You can submit it, but their feeling is that the first one to print or buy it gets it. If another area paper has already published it, please do not submit it to us. A well-written local piece is preferred. The author can talk to parents and s/he knows the great "kid-friendly" shops, great places to have a party, etc.
APPROXIMATE PAY: If it's a humor or filler article, it's worth less ($20).

KIWI
New York, NY
kiwimagonline.com
sarahsmith@maymediagroup.com
Parents trust KIWI to help them raise their children and enjoy their lives in the healthiest way possible. They also know that KIWI is ahead of the curve when it comes to a green and organic lifestyle, so they can count on our trusted brand and initiatives to sift through and provide only the best news, advice, and products. KIWI understands that achieving the right balance between the ideal world and the real world can be difficult, so readers never feel scolded, only supported. KIWI helps parents make the best choices about health, food, home life, and more, so they can feel good about their families and the future.
KIWI says…

- Whatever you can do to support health—whether in yourself, your family, your community, or the planet—is better than nothing.
- Buy organic foods as often as you can, but when you can't, choose locally grown produce in season and natural brands.
- With busy schedules, we know every meal may not be healthy, so make as many balanced and nutritious meals as you can, and pat yourself on the back for each and every one.
- It's not easy to control everything your kids eat. Allow them to try out new foods when they go to friends' houses, and remember what they eat may be up to their friends' parents!
- Be more eco-friendly by recycling, walking, or taking public transit instead of driving. Use air conditioning or heat more sparingly and turn off lights when you leave a room. Over time, little bits add up to a lot.
- Show your children how to appreciate what they have compared to others. Volunteering or sponsoring a child through World Vision is a great start. Our goal of developing kind, caring children who will turn into kind, caring adults may be a long-term one, but starting now will get them there faster.

KRAZY COUPON LADY

thekrazycouponlady.com

contributors@thekrazycouponlady.com

GUIDELINES: The KCL contributor network is a new way for stay-at-home moms, working women and men-who-are-in-touch-with-their-money-saving-side to share their expertise with KCL's audience of millions. Earn money by submitting original, engaging content that helps others learn to save money!

1. Choose your topic. Select an area of expertise and write an article about how to save money relating to one of the following topics:
   a. Style/Fashion
   b. Home/Gardening
   c. Travel/Entertainment
   d. Family/Parenting
   e. Extreme Couponing
   f. Finance
2. Create a Title. Make a title that grabs the reader's attention. Look at the engaging titles you see on sites like Yahoo, and create a title that makes even a hurried reader pause with interest.
3. Write your Article. Compose your article for the busy woman (or man) who loves a deal almost more than her own mother! Keep in mind, all articles must be original and NOT previously published.
   - Choose a narrow focus. We are more likely to accept articles that share in-depth money saving strategies on a narrow topic, as opposed to shallow tips on a broad topic. Examples: Instead of an article about how to save on planning a wedding, write about how to save on fresh flowers for the wedding or how to get a state license, which allows you to shop at a wholesaler and DIY arrangement suggestions. Or, instead of an article about how to save on your wardrobe, write about how to save on wardrobe by using price adjustments and give lots of detail and specifics.
   - Make it fresh and new. Avoid redundant tips and information we've all heard before. Tell the reader something she didn't know so that she's left wanting to 'share this with a friend!' We want unique, innovative, out-of-the-ordinary ideas!
   - Write concise paragraphs. Use bullets and avoid lengthy paragraphs. The goal is for a reader to be able to get an overall feel for your entire article in about 5-10 seconds. Keep articles between 200-800 words in length. Articles with excessive grammatical, spelling and/or punctuation errors will not be accepted.
   - Infuse your article with wit and personality. Be corny, stay relatable, make it personal. Write in the "I" form. Include a catchy

introduction, some funny sarcasm, and loads of creativity to set you apart.
  - Give specifics. Wherever possible, share specific examples: past deals, where to find a product (with hyperlink), coupon codes to use online, and any other strategy to purchase products mentioned in the article at a discount.
4. Select an Image. Choose an image from iStockPhoto.com or upload your own. No need to purchase the photo from iStock; simply include a link to the image in your submission.
5. Submit the article to Contributors@TheKrazyCouponLady.com where it will be considered for publication. We prefer that you simply paste your article into the body of your email rather than send an attachment. You will receive a response within 7 days. Include your first name, and city/state so we can include it at the bottom of your post!

APPROXIMATE PAY: Upon acceptance, receive up to $50 payment via PayPal! Do not submit time-sensitive posts including: coupon deals at grocery or drugstores, free samples, printable coupons, or any other deal that may be unavailable within 72 hours of post-submission.

LA PARENT CITY EDITION/VALLEY EDITION (mostly locals)
EXPECTING LA (2 issues)

Burbank, CA – monthly
losangeles.parenthood.com
christina.elston@parenthood.com

GUIDELINES: We keep our features on the shorter side (1,200-1,500 words). We also prefer to work with Southern California writers. We cover L.A. county up north through Ventura, West Los Angeles, and Long Beach and the South Bay, but not the Inland Empire or Orange County. Please send all queries via email with the subject line "Query." We do not accept simultaneous submissions. We prefer articles that are 800-1,500 words in length and rarely run anything longer. Our readers tend to be highly involved parents with children in infancy through the pre-teen years. Child development, education and family health are a few of our more serious topics, but we're also delighted to receive articles about fun things to do (especially things we don't already know about) with kids. No matter the topic, the piece should be directly relevant to parents in Southern California, with the voices of local parents and/or other sources. Articles should not only give readers information, but tell them how they can use it. Make sure information is thoroughly researched and backed up with quotes from experts in the field. You get bonus points for compelling sidebars, info-graphics, and photographs that we can publish. (If you provide photos, we'll need model releases for everyone pictured.)

APPROXIMATE PAY: We do not pay for online-only articles or personal essays. We somctimes pay for feature articles that are used in print. Rate varies depending on length and type of article.

LADIES' HOME JOURNAL
www.lhj.com
lhj@mdp.com
GUIDELINES: While we do not have specific guidelines about subject matter or writing style, we do offer these suggestions. Read back issues. We do not publish an editorial calendar, so familiarizing yourself with our editorial content and style will help you decide if your work fits our needs. We have a fourth-month lead time and seasonal material is usually assigned six months in advance. Submit queries rather than manuscripts. Keep your query brief-one to two pages-citing your lead and describing how you will research and develop your story. Be specific, and always direct your query to the appropriate editor, as listed on the masthead of the magazine. If you have been published before, send clips, your credits and a resume.

LOWCOUNTRY PARENT
South Carolina
lowcountryparent.com
cfossi@postandcourier.com

MAHONING VALLEY PARENT
Youngstown, OH – monthly (44,000)
forparentsonline.com
editor@mvparentmagazine.com
GUIDELINES: Our audience of parents is mostly women ages 20-45 with children younger than 12 years old. We accept article/column queries on any topic of interest to this audience, but prefer well written and researched pieces. We use first-person essays sparingly and prefer more personality profiles and newsy items.
APPROXIMATE PAY: $35 reprints upon publication.

MAIN LINE PARENT (original pieces only)
(sister publication to *Philadelphia Family*)
Ardmore, PA
www.mainlineparent.com
melissa@familyfocusmedia.com
GUIDELINES: We're looking to publish works from moms (and dads, too!) across the Greater Philadelphia area, as well as local experts in pertinent fields of study. We're eager to receive your submissions for consideration! Because ours is a regional publication, we look for stories that will interest and inform parents in the Greater Philadelphia area. We feature timely

topics for local families, including issues relating to childcare and health, balancing work and family, and managing the everyday demands of raising children of all ages. We are pleased to be able to offer honoraria for published works on a sliding scale based on content, length, and research involved.

MOM-TO-MOM (OR DAD-TO-DAD!) ADVICE: We're interested in everything from beauty and fashion tips to healthy living, eating right, and learning to love your after-baby body.

DETAILED PRODUCT REVIEW OR LOCAL SHOP SPOTLIGHT: Provide us with an in-depth review of a product for moms, dads, babies, or families, or a detailed spotlight of a local family-friendly place. In addition to your own experience, these might include the history of a product or company, interviews, and/or testimonials from other parents.

PERSONAL ESSAY: We love to feature pieces with an emotional spin, inspired by moms' and dads' personal experiences. How can we support our growing community through our own tales and travails of parenting our children? If you've raised children who are now adults, or if you've got grandchildren of your own, our readers with infants, toddlers, 'tweens, and teens will appreciate your wisdom.

EXPERT ADVICE: If you are a local expert in anything related to childcare, family health, education, parenting, etc., we would be thrilled to consider your submission and feature your expertise at *Main Line Parent*!

Use an active voice and a personal tone, striking a balance between formal and conversational. Remember who your audience is. We recommend that submitted articles be between 400-800 words in length. Longer, researched articles can run up to 1,200 words (or more, where appropriate). Include data on the latest trends and statistics applicable to your particular topic. All minors are referred to by first initials only at *Main Line Parent.* The inclusion of visual elements is strongly encouraged, but not required. Please seek permission to use others' photographs for your article (including those found on websites, and especially those taken by professional photographers), and indicate "Photo Courtesy Of" where necessary. Lead photos (an article's header image) for the web should be sized at a width of 595px to fit our content slider. Please submit full drafts only to our ePublisher, Sarah Bond at sarah.bond@familyfocusmedia.com. Submissions should be sent as separate Word documents. Please include your 30-40 word biography and accompanying photograph. Writers must also submit a signed contract with the first of their approved submissions, granting *Main Line Parent* exclusive printing rights of published articles unless otherwise discussed.

APPROXIMATE PAY: Could not get a number, but they do pay.

MELBOURNE'S CHILD

Victoria, Australia – monthly
melbourneschild.com.au
editorial@melbourneschild.com.au

SYDNEY'S CHILD

Adelaide, Brisbane, Canberra, Perth and Newcastle's Child

New South Wales, Australia
editorial@sydneyschild.com.au

GUIDELINES: We are looking for writing that will provoke, entertain and enlighten our readership of parents and others involved in the care of children aged 0-16. When we review articles for publication, we ask ourselves three questions: Is this compelling? Does this reflect the experience of modern parenting? Does this offer something unique? We publish personal pieces on the experience of parenting (Your Stories), and researched pieces that cast new light on a topic, provoke thought and inspire parents and other carers to further investigate an issue (Feature Stories). We are not interested in material that tells parents what to do or how to do it. We prefer not to include 'top tips' or 'how to' boxes. We prefer submissions by email in Microsoft Word, without design elements. Story length ranges from 600-1,500 words, and payment is negotiated on acceptance. Please be patient: a response time of eight to 12 weeks is usual. With your submission, please include references for any claims made in your article and contact details for people quoted in it (please ensure that references can be attributed to real people).

MEMPHIS PARENT

Memphis, TN – monthly (39,500)
memphisparent.com
janes@contemporary-media.com

APPROXIMATE PAY: $50 reprints.

METRO PARENT/METRO BABY

Ferndale, MI – monthly (80,000)
metroparent.com
jelliott@metroparent.com

GUIDELINES: Parent Pipeline pieces are short pieces on trends, local people, products, etc. of interest to parents/kids: 300-600 words. Family Travelogue: travel article on family fun destination. 700-800 words plus ratings sidebar. Feature articles: 1,000-3,000 words. Department columns: 600-700 words.

DEPARTMENT COLUMNS

- Along the Way (personal essays)
- Dr. Mom's Health Notes (health issues)
- Fatherhood (essays, information, news pertaining to fathers or of interest to fathers)

- Ages & Stages (column on child development age or stage)
- Teens & Tweens (column on tween/teen issues)
- Family Finance (family money topics)
- Parenting Solo (column on single parenting issues)

Metro Baby magazine (prenatal to infant magazine that publishes in May and November); Dr. Mom (family health magazine that publishes in March and October); Going Places (guide to family activities that publishes in April and October); Party Book advertorial supplement (publishes in May and November), and MetroParent.com (our online presence is an extension of our print publications. It includes articles from previous issues in addition to web extras and online-only articles). Simultaneous submissions are okay. Make sure they are marked as such, and please notify us if the submission has been accepted by another publication. We require a minimum of two sources. A 1,000-word story should have no fewer than three sources; a 2,000-word story should have no fewer than four sources. Occasionally, some short Pipeline pieces have just one source, but that is rare. Bottom line: Do thorough reporting. *Metro Parent* magazine has a broad circulation throughout southeast Michigan. We have distribution locations in Oakland, Wayne, Macomb, Livingston and Washtenaw counties, so it's important to us that our sources reflect our diverse readership. Freelancers don't have to hit every county we cover, but they should have sources from more than one. And the more counties covered, the better. Any story 1,000 words or more should have at least one sidebar. Sometimes it's an info box referring readers to more information from a local organization. Sometimes it's a list of tips related to the story's subject. Readers like having information broken up for them, and they enjoy multiple points of entry into a story, so we value freelancers who are mindful of that. We largely subscribe to *Associated Press* style. Freelancers should follow AP style when writing their stories for us. We will make any slight adjustments in the few areas we deviate from AP style, if it is necessary. Do not indent for new paragraphs. Include your byline plus preferred tagline (e.g., Fran Walker is a mother of two from Westland.) Font should be Times Roman, 14 pt. Include a suggested headline and/or dek. Subheads are strongly encouraged for stories 1,000 words or more. We prefer stories to be sent as a Microsoft Word attachment. For those who don't have Word, please send the story within the body of an email. Include the name and phone number of sources at the end of story, in case we have follow-up questions.

APPROXIMATE PAY: Features 1,000-3,000 words: $100-350. Department columns: $65-100. Parent Pipeline pieces: $50-75. Reprints: $35. Payment is upon publication. Freelancers should submit an invoice (within an email is fine) that includes name, address, phone number, Social Security number, name of story and payment amount.

METRO PARENT

Portland, OR – monthly
metro-parent.com
editor@metro-parent.com
APPROXIMATE PAY: Varies greatly. Columns/personal essays around $150, and it goes up from there.

METROFAMILY

Edmond, OK – monthly (35,000)
metrofamilymagazine.com
editor@metrofamilymagazine.com
GUIDELINES: Features rarely run over 1,000 words, including sidebars. We purchase one-time print rights and web rights. We work two to three months in advance. Send articles in the body of your email. Bring on the humor. Try to put a surprise into every piece you write. Startle readers with an unexpected statistic or raise eyebrows with a surprising outcome.
APPROXIMATE PAY: $25 up to 400 words; $35-50 up to 900 words, paid upon publication.

METROKIDS (exclusive)

(editions in PA, south NJ and DE)
Philadelphia, PA – monthly
metrokids.com
editor@metrokids.com
GUIDELINES: We will consider general topics, especially if they can be localized with sidebars. Feature articles usually run 800-1,100 words; articles for one of our departments are usually 550-700 words. Reprints are acceptable. Articles that appear in *MetroKids* may not be sold to other parenting publications that primarily circulate in southeastern Pennsylvania, southern New Jersey or Delaware. Please let us know if you also write for another parenting publication that is local to us. That doesn't mean we won't use your articles, but we might ask you to write under a different name. Spell check and fact check your article, and let us know that you have done so at the top of the article. Sidebars: phone number style (215-291-5560) and URL style (metrokids.com). Don't interrupt the article with this information; put them in a sidebar. Submit your article as an email attachment, formatted as plain text or Word document, rather than including it in the body of an email message.
APPROXIMATE PAY: Compensation will be negotiated when we accept or assign an article. Payment will occur upon publication. $35 reprints.

METROPARENT

Waukesha, WI – monthly

metroparentmagazine.com
epaulsen@jrn.com
APPROXIMATE PAY: $50 reprints.

MIDWESTERN FAMILY (prefers local writers)
Peoria, IL – bimonthly
midwesternfamily.com
jrudd@midwesternfamily.com
APPROXIMATE PAY: Not specified; pays locals.

MINNESOTA PARENT
minnesotaparent.com
editor@mnparent.com
GUIDELINES: Send your resume and five previously published work samples (web links or attached files)—ideally pieces that exemplify the kind of work you'd like to do for us. Our freelance writers typically have some kind of journalism background. They know how to do research and interviews with outside sources and then synthesize everything they've learned into stories that delight, inspire and help Minnesota moms and dads. Though being a parent isn't a requirement for our writers, we find having a parent perspective—and connections in the parenting community—helps with ideation, sourcing and voice. If you want to pitch a story, first check out our back issues and our editorial calendar, and keep in mind we're always planning and assigning far in advance of publication. We're looking for lively, on-trend stories packed with relevant information for passionate, involved parents. We cover maternity, childbirth, health and development, childcare, education, toys and technology. But we're also seeking fresh places-to-go, things-to-do stories to inspire parents to get out and have fun with their kids—ideally for free—in the great state of Minnesota. We're talking travel and outdoor activities, near and far. And don't forget summer camps: We're a top source for planning a kid-friendly summer, including day camps and overnight camps, too.
Bloggers
If your experience is more in blogging or first-person writing, send links to your five best blog posts and your resume to editor@mnparent.com. We're currently looking to create partnerships with Minnesota bloggers.
APPROXIMATE PAY: We pay writers a per-story rate (based on experience and the type of story) within 30 days of publication. Stories are typically 500-1,500 words.

MOMMYTHINK
mommythink.com
writers@mommythink.com

GUIDELINES: Consider joining *MommyThink* as a contributor or regional editor! If you write about attachment parenting or natural mothering and would like to submit a relevant article to this site, we'd love to see what you have! Specific subject areas include pregnancy, natural childbirth, midwifery, home birth, breastfeeding, natural baby care, cosleeping, baby wearing, gentle discipline and other natural family living subjects. Yes, all articles on our website are special, but we mean an article that contains some kind of "scoop" or a super fresh look at a particular subject. Articles which require in-depth research would fit into this category. We expect to publish about one or two of these "exclusive" articles per quarter. In addition to our fairly modest compensation, we would be happy to publish your article or story with a bio that links to your website or provides further information about any services or products that you offer. No affiliate links, please. We like personal stories, a bit of humor and good references. Articles should be 750-2,500 words in length (though this is a flexible guideline). Email your material in the body of an email. Please include a short author's bio with any relevant links to your work, products or services. We will notify you within four weeks (sometimes sooner) if we plan to publish your article. If you do not hear from us, that means we cannot publish your article at this time. One of the most frequent reasons, at this time, for not publishing material is that it is not appropriate for our website. We are a niche website and we ask you to be familiar with the subject matter and style of this website in order to be sure that your submission would be relevant to our readers. If we decide to publish your piece, we will request either 30 or 90 day exclusive electronic rights and permanent internet archiving rights. In plain English, this means that this work cannot have been published before and you may not submit your work to any other website or electronic media outlet for 30 or 90 days (depending on agreed upon terms). It also means we may permanently keep your article in our archives (though you may sell it elsewhere).
APPROXIMATE PAY: For most articles, we pay $25 per article, for 30 day exclusive electronic rights, or $50 for 90-day exclusive electronic rights. We may pay up to 10 cents per word for extra special articles.

MONTANA PARENT (exclusive)

Bozeman, MT – 10 times per year
mtparent.com
leigh@mtparent.com
GUIDELINES: Columns range from 700-900 words; feature pieces 1,000-1,300 words. Deadline is by the 1st of the month, preceding the next month's issue. For questions on style, please refer to the *Chicago Manual of Style*. Photos can be submitted with the piece, digital or otherwise. If there is an extra fee for photos, please notify the editor first. The publisher must be

notified first regarding any other expenses related to writing the piece. Include word count, address, phone number, Social Security number and a one-sentence byline.
APPROXIMATE PAY: Fees vary based upon length, depth of piece and whether it's an original manuscript, submitted, assigned, or a reprint. Writers are paid upon publication, by the end of the month. In purchasing or assigning a story, we understand we will receive market exclusivity. We follow the National Writers Union's recommendation to compensate writers an additional 10% for electronic rights when the piece is placed on our site. $35 reprints.

MONTREAL FAMILIES

Montreal, Quebec Canada – monthly
montrealfamilies.ca
editorial@montrealfamilies.ca
GUIDELINES: Stories usually run about 800 words (one page), although sometimes we allocate a page and half (1,200 words) for a large feature. Please do not research and write a story and then send it to us hoping for publication. We prefer to discuss assignments in advance with writers. Stories should be timely, but not necessarily linked to a specific event (we do hold stories sometimes). Stories must also be local (greater Montreal region) and feature local families and experts. We love to publish humor pieces and personal essays. However, keep in mind that many people make a living out of writing personal essays on parenting. It's a popular topic so you have to work hard to find a fresh perspective and an interesting take on this universal experience. We don't run essays longer than 800-900 words. We don't usually assign personal essays unless we've been working with a writer for a long time. Contrary to our approach with features, please send in the finished essay for consideration. We occasionally publish travel articles, with most of them focusing on family travel to areas within a few hours' drive of Montreal. We will consider pieces on other regions of Canada and the world on a case by case basis. Our book review column is not open to freelance submissions. To make writing for *MF* a viable proposition for writers, I try to provide as many contacts as possible, as well as strong editorial direction so writers know exactly what is expected for a particular article. Writers sometimes worry that publications will "steal" their ideas if they make a pitch. Please be aware that we have a long list of story ideas that we consult each month. Your "idea" may very well be on that list, in another form (e.g., making a decision about buying your kid a cell phone). We will consider previously published material, but do let us know in advance where it was printed. If you have a story that you think is right for the publication, please email with a pitch. Tell us what the story is about, how you would approach it and any special perspective you bring to

the story. Please keep in mind that we assign stories several months in advance of their publication date. Please take the time to read at least two or three issues of the paper to get a sense of our style. We're looking for clarity in all pieces—tight organization of facts and a compelling lead. When working on an article, please carefully fact-check your work. We do not have the resources to hire a fulltime fact checker. Please always verify the spelling of people's names, their titles, the names of organizations, professional societies, etc. We will provide you with a style guide that covers matters of spelling, use of numbers, etc. Articles can be written from either a journalist slant or a more personal take, but stories must almost always include the voices of at least one local family or parent, as well as local experts. Writers should send the associate editor a list of the organizations and people they expect to contact for the story as soon as possible. I try to cut and re-jig with a light touch, but it does happen that your 800-word piece may end up being published as 500 words.

APPROXIMATE PAY: Discuss payment amounts with our associate editor. We ask for one-time publication rights and use of the story on our website.

MY CHILD MAGAZINE

Camperdown, Australia – quarterly
mychildmagazine.com.au
editorial@poppetgroup.com.au

APPROXIMATE PAY: Original articles pay 50 cents AU per word. Reprints pay half rate of 25 cents AU per word. Paid six months after publication.

NCW KID CONNECT

Cashmere, WA
ncwkidconnect.com
nikki@ncwkidconnect.com

NASHVILLE PARENT
RUTHERFORD PARENT
SUMNER PARENT
WILLIAMSON PARENT

Nashville, TN – monthly (50,000)
nashvilleparent.com
chad@daycommedia.com

APPROXIMATE PAY: $50 for a reprint in all four publications.

NEAPOLITAN FAMILY

Naples, FL – monthly (10,000)
neafamily.com
andrea@neafamily.com

GUIDELINES: Word counts 500-1,400, features written in third person,

humorous about trials and tribulations and how-to welcome.
APPROXIMATE PAY: $20 reprints.

NEW JERSEY FAMILY
RAISING TEENS
Mountainside, NJ – monthly
njfamily.com
njfamilyeditor@njfamily.com
GUIDELINES: The focus of any article should be: here are the facts, and here's what you can do for your child to prevent, promote, manage, help, teach, etc. in any given situation. In other words, every article should answer the question: what can parents in north and central New Jersey do to help their children? The most important piece of advice for any freelancer is this: know your audience. *Family Magazine*'s audience is the parents of children living in north and central New Jersey. Our articles cover topics that range from universal parenting concerns (health, education, development) to specific how-to and where-to-go information. For queries and submissions, please contact our editorial offices via email. If we agree to look at a manuscript based on a query, that does not mean we will accept the manuscript for publication. If we ultimately reject an assigned manuscript for any reason, we pay writers a kill fee of half our agreed-upon amount. We pay after print publication. Most articles are about 650-1,200 words. We like sidebars, so try to separate out something that can run on its own. We also love it when writers deliver an entire "package," including a short and/or clever headline and subheads to break up the text. We do not need photographs. Please submit your query or manuscript electronically. Please be sure to include your name, address, phone number, and email address on your manuscript and in your email. We prefer that you paste your article directly in the body of an email; we may not open attachments. Being a parent makes you an automatic expert on parenting issues. If you have other expertise, you're a step ahead of other freelancers. Please be creative and practical at the same time.
APPROXIMATE PAY: $35 for reprints.

NEW YORK FAMILY
newyorkfamily.com
emessinger@manhattanmedia.com

NOLA BABY & FAMILY
New Orleans, LA
nolababy.com
editor@nolababy.com

GUIDELINES: *nola baby & family* is always interested in hearing from freelance writers—those with experience, or just starting out. You do not need to be a parent to write for our publication. If you're interested in writing for us, please send an introductory e-mail to our editor, Leslie Penkunas detailing any relevant experience. Please also include one or two writing clips. Most of our freelance articles are on a topic assigned by us; however, if you have a story idea that you think would be of great interest to our readers, please feel free to pitch us on it. Our editorial calendar is set at least three months—and sometimes up to a year—in advance. Holiday- or seasonally themed article ideas should be submitted at least six months in advance. *Please note: we rarely accept first-person essays, and are not currently looking for any contributing columnists.* All of our feature stories should include a local focus, and require, at a minimum, three interviews with local experts and/or parents (in person or over the phone; sometimes when working with complicated medical topics, email correspondence with doctors is acceptable). We have received the gold award for overall writing from the Parenting Publications of America, and take pride in our editorial content and style. For pay ranges, please contact the editor. Payment is made upon publication, and covers all online rights unless we arrive at another agreement. We pay a kill fee of $25 for stories cut due to space requirements; stories cut because they do not meet *nola baby & family's* standards will receive no compensation. Should a story not meet the editor's satisfaction, though, she will do her best to work with you to make the story acceptable for inclusion. Stories moved to online-only status due to space will receive their full payment. *nola baby & family* buys one-time print rights and exclusive online rights for six months. At *nola baby & family magazine*, we strive to sound informative, but not authoritative (and certainly not lecturing!). We leave the "voice of authority" to the experts we interview for our various articles. We do like to strike a conversational tone at times:

- The first-person plural ("we") is okay to use on occasion to keep things friendly and familiar.
- The second person plural ("you") is fine to use as well.
- Please do <u>not</u> use the first person singular ("I") in your article, ever, unless you are contributing a column (This is to protect you, as well the magazine, from being cited as an expert by a reader).
- When quoting directly, please use the present tense. "We laughed all afternoon," *says* Sarah.

Sources: Unless otherwise noted, all articles should include:

- Quotes from at least one expert (i.e., Ob/Gyns or pediatricians for medical-related articles; financial planners for a financial planning article, etc.).

- At least two moms, moms-to-be, or dads who have experience in what the article addresses.

nola baby & family magazine has relationships with local area doctors, and will provide you with medical expert resources with your assignment. This is to facilitate your work, as they have been vetted by us and have agreed to be available to our writers. If you have a particular doctor you'd like to use as a source, please run his or her name by us first. How to reference sources: For the first reference of an expert, identify by full name, title, and hospital affiliation or private practice (e.g., Al Robichaux, M.D., Chairman of the Department of Obstetrics/Gynecology at Ochsner Health System). After that, use proper prefix and last name (Dr. Robichaux). For the first reference of moms, etc., identify by full name, where in town they live (e.g., Uptown), and, if applicable, number of children and their ages. After that, just their first name is okay, unless other sources have same name; then use first and last name again.

Abbreviations & misc.:

- New Orleans: you can abbreviate as NO (no periods), NOLA, or as the City.
- A note on hyphens: A one year old doesn't get hyphenated. But a one-year-old child does.
- Numbers: spell out one through nine; use numerals for 10 and up.
- Pet peeve: the filler word, "actually." To quote David McCollough: "Please, please do what you can to cure the verbal virus that seems increasingly rampant."

APPROXIMATE PAY: *nola baby & family* pays $25 for reprints; however, authors willing to localize their reprints with interviews with local parents and experts can expect more.

NORTH IDAHO FAMILY

Coeur D'Alene
nifamily.com
sales@nifamily.com

NORTH STATE PARENT

Mount Shasta, CA – monthly (18,000)
northstateparent.com
editorial@northstateparent.com

GUIDELINES: The email subject should include one of the following: Reprint Available, Query or Article. Also include the topic/title if applicable, e.g., *Reprint Available: Peggy Sue Rafts the Klamath.* If you are submitting an unsolicited query, please restrict each submission to one or two proposals that include a potential title, proposed premise/hook and your approach to the piece. Include potential interview sources you may use to localize and/or substantiate your premise (if needed). The number of submissions we receive hinders our response time to undeveloped queries. We plan magazine issues four to six months in advance; please keep this in mind when sending timed pieces. *North State Parent* reserves the right to edit copy and make final decisions on page layout. While we try to work with authors as much as is feasible, we are not able to provide the author with a final draft before printing.

General article submission tips:

- Before submitting, proof your work- use spell and grammar check, and if possible have at least one other person read your piece for clarity.
- Submit as a Word document in a 12-point font. Single spaced submissions are preferred.
- Double-space lines between paragraphs. (Don't indent paragraphs.)
- Include a word count for your piece; give sidebar word count separately. E.g., W/C 685, Sidebar W/C 89.
- Include a title (and subtitle if you like). We may change the title, but your piece is incomplete without one.
- Avoid excessive use of exclamations (!).
- Keep paragraphs relatively short.
- Avoid using he/she, her/his … pick a gender for your subject and stick to that; it's okay to change genders when introducing another subject.

We run both short (400-600 words "bits") and longer (700-1,000 words or more) articles. If you are writing an assigned article we will let you know the word count needed. Photographs may also be submitted via email as high-resolution (300 dpi) jpg images. Please include the photographer's name and a statement that the photographer gives permission to publish the photograph. Articles should be informative without being overly technical. Articles that carry a story line and/or present an interesting angle are preferred. Localizing the article is important; including interview comments from local residents is one way to do this. We serve four Upper California counties: Butte, Tehama, Shasta and Siskiyou, and we strive to represent editorial pertinent to all geographic areas we serve. We do not disclose full name and location information of minors, for privacy reasons. When including interview quotes from a minor, an example of how to do this is: "… said 7-year-old Benjamin of Redding, CA." or "…said, Trudy, age 7, of Chico." Check with adults you may be quoting to be clear about how much personal information they are comfortable having disclosed by way of their name and location. Articles with instructions, i.e., recipes or art projects, must have directions tested prior to submission. If articles mention historical or scientific facts, please be sure your information is accurate; document statistics where appropriate.

Article's Sidebar information:

- A sidebar may be included with your article, such as a resource list for the topic being presented. When presenting local resources, each county NSP served (Butte, Shasta, Siskiyou & Tehama) should be included when possible.
- Due to space constraints, sidebar information should be brief—include only the most relevant and quality resources that will inspire readers to research further—you may include both local and online resources.
- Sidebar information can also be a list of bulleted points key to the topic, or an inset box with "bit" info such a relevant quote not fitting within the article body; something cute, funny or interesting enough to be included.
- Sidebar information is often considered part of an article's overall word count; some exceptions are made on a case-by-case basis.

Author's bio:

- Please include a brief author's bio that relates in some way to the article you are submitting, i.e., let readers know (in a few words) why you wrote the article… how it relates to your life. If appropriate, humor is appreciated. E.g., *Author Tammy Trekker began hiking at age three and looks forward to introducing her two children to the experience as soon as they can walk without wobbling.*
- If you are local, feel free to indicate your location; if you are a parent, it's great to say so, since we are a family magazine. *Siskiyou County author Brenda Boeder is a mom and dedicated food revolutionary with the intention of inspiring peace one mouth at a time.*
- We do not publish author's website or contact info, unless by special agreement (e.g., a PR trade agreement with published book author or organization).
- Begin your bio with "Author Jane Smith…" to avoid the obvious "Jane Smith is a freelance writer who …"

Author's Picture: Please also submit via email a high-resolution (300 dpi) .jpg author's photo. A thumbnail picture of the author accompanies each author's bio in our publication.

Commissioned articles are by prior arrangement. Payments are as follows: Assignments under 600 words: $45; 600 up to 800 words: $75; 800+ words: $100. We generally do not publish articles over 1,200 words.

Reprint & unsolicited submissions rates: 1,000 words and over: $45; 500 up to 1,000 words: $35; "bits" pieces (under 500 words) $25.

Rights: We purchase one-time print rights with regional exclusivity for three months upon publication and electronic rights for use at www.northstateparent.com.

Author Invoicing

- Authors will receive an invoice request from us once the article has been published. Please do not submit your invoice prior to receiving an invoice request, as space limitations may happen in the final hour that require an article to be pulled last minute from a particular issue. We strive to avoid this, as it's like pulling a child off a school bus about to head onward to a fun field trip—it's disheartening.
- Once your author's invoice is received, we normally send out its payment by the end of the month the article runs in.
- If we do not have your social security number on file for 1099 tax form independent contractor requirements, please include it with your invoice.

APPROXIMATE PAY: $25-45.

NORTH TEXAS KIDS

Plano, TX – monthly
northtexaskids.com
mina@northtexaskids.com

GUIDELINES: *North Texas Kids* encourages and welcomes your submission of articles, children's artwork, photographs, and ideas. We reserve the right to edit all submitted material, and submissions will be printed at the sole discretion of the publisher. Recommended article length is 500-800 words.
APPROXIMATE PAY: $25 per reprint.

NORTHEAST OHIO PARENT

northeastohioparent.com
angela@northeastohioparent.com

NORTHEAST PENNSYLVANIA FAMILY

Kingston, PA – quarterly
nepafamily.com
pamela@nepafamily.com

GUIDELINES: All articles should be submitted in Word format. Articles should be no longer than 800-1,000 words. Please include a short two-sentence biography with submission. Include author's name, address, phone number and email with submission.
APPROXIMATE PAY: $35 reprints.

OFFSPRING

Australia
offspringmagazine.com.au
kate@offspringmagazine.com.au

OHIO FAMILY

ohiofamilymagazine.com
editorial@ohiofamilymagazine.com

OHIO VALLEY PARENT

Wheeling, WV – 10 times per year
ovparent.com
betsy@ovparent.com
APPROXIMATE PAY: $15 for reprints.

THE OLD SCHOOLHOUSE

Deborah Wuehler, Editor
thehomeschoolmagazine.com
senioreditor@thehomeschoolmagazine.com
GUIDELINES: The guidelines are HUGE, so please head to the links below, and a few of their guidelines are below the links:
http://thehomeschoolmagazine.com/writersguidelines.php
http://thehomeschoolmagazine.com/howtowritefortos.php
Please query us with a well-structured article proposal that includes a catchy lead, a summary of the article (including approximate length and sidebar ideas), and appropriate details. Users of HomeschoolBlogger.com should note their usernames on their query. Links to clips and portfolios are of assistance as well. All query and other submissions are subject to the Terms of Submission posted on our website. Query letters should be submitted electronically using the forms provided on our website. We strongly discourage multiple submissions of query letters (sending the same query to several publications at once). Queries to *TOS* should be written specifically for our publication. Check website for a list of annual themes. If you would like to contribute an article about any of these topics, or you would like to suggest additional topics that you would like to write about, please use the Query Submission button at the bottom of the page to share your ideas with the *TOS* editorial staff. We will acknowledge receipt of your query and attempt to make a decision to accept or decline the proposed article as quickly as possible. The review process normally takes between four and six weeks, but may be longer at times. Our editors will contact you if we decide to accept a queried article. Publication of accepted materials may take from three months to more than a year based on our needs and publication schedule. Terms of publication vary based on article length and content. At *TOS*, we slate authors' work for future issues as far in advance as possible, sometimes as much as two years before the issue will be published. Therefore, if you are interested in submitting a query, please do so immediately, so that your query may be carefully reviewed and considered prior to upcoming submission deadlines.
APPROXIMATE PAY: This publication does pay but would not give details.

OMAHA FAMILY
Omaha, NE – monthly (50,000)
omahafamily.com
editor@omahafamily.com
APPROXIMATE PAY: $30 for longer reprints.

ON THE COAST
Destin, FL – bimonthly (30,000)
onthecoastmag.com
otc@onthecoastmag.com
APPROXIMATE PAY: $25 per reprint.

ONLY CHILD
onlychild.com
onlychild@onlychild.com
GUIDELINES: We are always interested in articles specific to only children. As a policy, we do not open unsolicited documents (for obvious reasons), so please forward articles and queries in the text body of an email. *Only Child* is a publication devoted to one of the fastest growing segments of our society ... only children of all ages. There are an estimated 20 million only child households in the United States alone. Although we may not be advocates for having only children (possibly too much of a good thing!), we are advocates <u>for</u> only children. Our goal is to constructively address the concerns and interests of only children, their parents, grandparents, family and friends... from child care to eldercare. More and more people around the world are realizing the importance of one-child families. Over 10 years ago we started this website and newsletter to address the needs and concerns of only children from childhood through adulthood and into the senior years. Little did we realize that we had placed ourselves at the forefront of a new chapter in the history of the greatest shift in population demographics in the United States and the Western World. Like the tip of an iceberg, the mass of this movement lies hidden from view, largely as a result of ignorance about and prejudice toward only children. *Only Child*'s mission is to work with only children of all ages, their parents, relatives, friends, community organizations and educational institutions to provide support and information. Only children of all ages, parents, grandparents and friends of only children have written to let us know how helpful it is to finally have their own place to go for the information they need. The letters that have come to us from all over the world have touched us deeply and made us understand even more clearly the need that *Only Child* fills. Our goal is to provide a forum for the only child at all stages of life. We know that only children grow up and have a very unique journey through life. At

times they will have to manage many of life's joys and challenges alone. *Only Child* will be there to provide ideas about how to make that journey a smoother one.
APPROXIMATE PAY: Our pay structure is $100 (with one author edit) and must be accompanied be supporting Rights Granted illustration(s) and/or photos(s).

OREGON FAMILY

Eugene, OR
oregonfamily.com
info@oregonfamily.com

ORLANDO FAMILY

Orlando, FL – monthly (24,000)
orlandofamilymagazine.com
editorial@orlandofamilymagazine.com
GUIDELINES: Our editorial content is focused toward parents with children ages 0 to 15. We prefer articles which can be localized to the Central Florida area, but we will consider topics that relate to families in general. We look for pieces covering issues concerning today's parents, local family excursions, traditions, crafts, family fun, education and health & fitness. Featured articles require careful research, independent reporting and well developed story lines. Each monthly issue is focused around a particular theme, as well as a variety of regular departments: Family Fun, Traditions, Kids Korner, Making a Difference, Health and Wellness, Movie Review, Growing up Online, Book Buzz and Calendar of Events (see below, after Editorial Calendar). All items submitted shall become the property of *Orlando Family Magazine*, LLC and will not be returned. Articles that are sent via email must be sent in MS Word format. Manuscripts should include the author's name, address, daytime phone number, title or article, word count, and the rights you are granting to the magazine (First North American Serial Rights preferred), and a short bio (one to two sentences) on the first page. We expect writers to double-check their facts and be able to vouch for every phone number, Web address and name spelling in a story. We also request a list of sources with contact phone numbers, for fact-checking purposes. When granting First North American Rights, you are granting to *Orlando Family Magazine*, LLC the right to publish the article in the English Language in North America, both in print and digital versions of the magazine. You are also granting *Orlando Family Magazine*, LLC the right to archive the work in an online version of the magazine for an indefinite period of time. The editor reserves the right to edit for clarity, length and styles. We do not purchase articles from writers who are published by our competitors. For reprint offers, please inform us

of where the material has been published. No phone calls please. We assume no responsibility for unsolicited manuscripts. We do not pay for fillers, photographs and sidebars. Examples include short, humorous anecdotes about family or which fit into any of the regular departments, or practical sidebars with projects, tips or other suggestions for families to try. If the filler material that is being submitted has already been printed, indicate where and when the filler first appeared on the cover sheet of the submission. *Orlando Family Magazine* provides a copy of its printed issues online. All editorial submissions that are purchased will also be posted on our website www.OrlandoFamilyMagazine.com. *Orlando Family Magazine* does not allow for the online redistribution or republishing of the editorial submission. We will forward all reprint requests directly to the writer. All work must be submitted at least three months prior to the issue date. Prior to publication, we will ask you to sign a contract warranting that the work submitted is your original work, that you are granting to *Orlando Family Magazine*, LLC all of the rights set forth herein, and agreeing that you will not submit work to any other publication in the Central Florida area, and that you will not submit the work to any other family publication in North America for a period of 90 days following the expiration of the calendar month in which the article was published by *Orlando Family Magazine*, LLC.
In every issue:

- Family Fun: Every month we will provide fun filled ideas that the entire family can enjoy together from simple crafts, games and home activities to exciting, adventurous places to visit throughout Central Florida.
- Family Traditions: Readers share a favorite family tradition that brings meaning and enriches each family member's life. Holiday traditions will be featured in the same month they are celebrated.
- Kids' Korner: Local kids share their thoughts and favorite things from a variety of chosen topics.
- Making a Difference: A monthly column designed to offer charitable ideas that will inspire the entire family to work together to make a positive difference in the lives of others in our community.
- Health and Wellness: Editorial that focuses on a wide variety of valuable health and fitness topics that pertain to the entire family.
- Movie Review: Provides detailed information pertaining to the latest movie releases so that parents can make informed decisions.
- Book Buzz: Orange County Librarians recommend their top selections in the world of children's books.
- Growing up Online: Editorial that helps parents understand and guide the online activities of their children.

APPROXIMATE PAY: Fees vary depending on length and depth of the story. Original manuscripts for feature articles generally pay $50-$75 and reprints pay $25-$40. Payments are made (along with tear sheet) within the first month of publication for the article.

PTO TODAY

ptotoday.com
queries@ptotoday.com

GUIDELINES: *PTO Today* magazine is an essential resource for leaders of parent groups (often called parent-teacher organizations) at the 80,000 elementary and middle schools across the United States. Articles focus on helping the volunteer leaders of these groups run their organizations more efficiently and support their schools more effectively. The magazine is published six times a year, based on the school calendar; issues are dated January, March, April, August, September, and October. Parent groups go by many different names, including PTA, PTO, and PTC. PTAs are those groups formally affiliated with the National PTA. All other parent groups, more than 75 percent of the total, are independent organizations and are often referred to collectively as PTOs. We use "PTO" as a generic term—*PTO Today* writes about all parent groups, including PTAs. At the local level, all parent groups face similar challenges. For most of them, our magazine provides the only opportunity for volunteers to learn how similar groups (whether in the next town or across the country) run effective meetings and programs, solve problems, raise money, and otherwise enhance their children's school experiences. Our readers are the most active members of parent groups in K-8 schools. They are almost all women, and they are generally in their late 20s to mid-40s. Typically, they hold an office such as president, vice president, treasurer, or secretary. They chair one or more committees and are responsible for organizing specific events or programs. In most cases, they have little prior training or experience, yet a typical parent group raises tens of thousands of dollars each year for its school. We run how-to pieces, profiles of programs and people, and articles by experts. The tone is informational and informal rather than newsy. We never talk down to readers, we use PTO-specific examples to express concepts, and we prefer writers who can use the language of parent groups. We don't cover child-rearing issues, and we don't cover general education topics unless they have a very specific parent group angle. We focus exclusively on parent groups serving students in grades K-8; high school parent groups often take a form very different from that of elementary and middle school groups. Major topic areas we do cover include:

Parent involvement. The number one issue for most parent groups is how to get more parents to participate. More volunteers mean better events and programs and less work for those who do participate. We have published articles about reaching out to parents who are new to the school, making sure volunteers have a positive experience and want to come back, and communicating effectively with parents who aren't members.

Leadership. These articles focus on soft skills such as settling conflicts and developing good communication skills, as well as hard skills such as running meetings efficiently and managing volunteers effectively.

Fundraising. Fundraising is a major activity for parent groups, especially in these times of shrinking school budgets. Parent groups pay for everything from teaching positions to music programs to ice cream socials.

Group management and organization. Many groups have little understanding of the legal, financial, and tax aspects of running what is essentially a small nonprofit business. Topics include tax issues, applying for 501(c)3 (charitable nonprofit) status under the federal tax code, bookkeeping basics, and legal requirements for keeping meeting minutes and other documents.

Working with school staff. Successful parent groups have a strong working relationship with the school principal, teachers, and staff. Past articles have discussed topics ranging from teacher appreciation to tactics for strengthening ties with the principal.

Playgrounds. The largest and most complex project many parent groups undertake is building a new playground. A playground project typically costs $50,000 to $100,000 or more. Parent groups raise the money. They also participate in the playground design and, often, the construction. Safety standards, community involvement, and large-project logistics are all topics that relate to parent group playground projects.

Education. Our coverage of education topics extends only to the role of the parent group; PTOs often run field trips, bring in arts and enrichment performers, and sponsor other programs that complement or enhance the curriculum.

Queries

We recommend that you familiarize yourself with our previous content and our community before submitting a query. Archived articles are sorted into topic areas on our website, which you can find listed on the Topics A-Z page. Read the article "PTO vs. PTA: What's the Difference?" for an overview of the differences between these two types of organizations, and look through our active message boards to get a sense of the issues that are important to parent groups. Features run roughly 1,200-2,200 words, and the average assignment is 1,500 words. Department pieces run 600-1,200 words. Payment depends on the difficulty of the topic and the experience of the writer. We may ask writers to help us acquire appropriate art for articles, and we appreciate queries that offer art suggestions. We will review, but we do not encourage, unsolicited manuscripts. Send queries to Editor, School Family Media/PTO Today, 100 Stonewall Blvd., Suite 3, Wrentham, MA 02093, or email queries@ptotoday.com. Indicate the subject of your proposed article, the angle you plan to use, whom you plan to interview (if

applicable), and why you think the article is of interest to our readers. If you have been published before, please include several samples of your work with the query letter; if you have previous parent group leadership or volunteer experience, please let us know.
APPROXIMATE PAY: We pay by the assignment, not by the word; our pay scale ranges from $200-$700 for features and $150-$400 for departments. We occasionally pay more for high-impact stories and highly experienced writers. We buy all rights, and we pay on acceptance (within 30 days of invoice).

PALM BEACH PARENTING

Palm Beach, FL – monthly
pbparenting.com
info@pbparenting.com
GUIDELINES: Each month *PB Parenting* spotlights local family-friendly events and activities. We provide quick information and tips on parenting issues for families with children of all ages. Our editorial themes vary by month including special editions (Party Planning, Summer Camp, Beat the Heat, Back to School and Baby & Maternity).

PALMETTO PARENT

Columbia, SC
palmettoparent.com
palmettoeditorial@me.com
GUIDELINES: We don't accept unsolicited articles for print; we work with local freelancers only and offer stories to them to accept/reject; however, we do accept content for our website.
APPROXIMATE PAY: We don't pay much for those articles (free to $20 max) but we do byline them to credit the writer. We use them on our site as supplemental material.

PARENT EXPRESS

Keene, NH – monthly
parentexpress.net
editor@parentexpress.net
GUIDELINES: Please be sure to include your contact information, including phone number, mailing address, and email address. Articles should run between 400 and 800 words. We prefer articles that address a topic from a local perspective, focusing on the Cheshire County, NH and/or Windham County, VT regions. Articles that focus on a local issue, event, or organization work well, as do articles that explore a topic of general interest but include quotes and perspectives from local experts, organizations, and/or parents. We greatly appreciate photos to accompany articles. If you have photos, you may send them to our mailing address or send them in

digital versions via email (jpg, at least 300 dpi). In the event that we decide to use a submitted article, we will contact you directly. If we like the article but do not decide to run it immediately, we will keep it in our files for possible future use. If you have sent a hard copy or photos and would like them returned, please include a self-addressed stamped envelope. *Parent Express* expects all written, artistic and photographic submissions by staff members and freelancers to meet certain standards of accuracy, originality and independence, including the following:

- Sources of information will be identified by name.
- Quotations directly and indirectly attributed to sources will be actual quotations that have been spoken, written or otherwise expressed by that source in the time period of the focus of the article.
- Quotations that have been expressed as being "off the record" or "for background only" will not be published without approval of the editor.
- Events described in submitted articles will be actual events that occurred in the time period identified in the article—not fictional events that have been fabricated to illustrate a point. Any deviation from this policy must have the approval of the editor.
- *Parent Express* requires that the general rules of plagiarism will apply, meaning that words outside of quotations will be the words that were composed and actually written by the writer. Word-for-word duplication, or close paraphrasing of any other material (whether expressed orally or in writing, whether appearing privately or publicly or whether appearing in print or in other forms, such as the Internet) without clear attribution of the source is not permitted.
- Written works that have been published or written elsewhere may be republished in *Parent Express*, but only under terms approved by editor.

APPROXIMATE PAY: Payment will vary according to article relevance and length. Articles that address a topic from a local perspective thoroughly and serve as an important resource for area parents are more valuable. If an article is sold to us for publication, we ask that it not be sold to another local publication in Windham and Cheshire Counties. Likewise, please do not submit an article to us that has already been printed in a Windham or Cheshire County newspaper. We also like to share articles printed in our newspaper with local nonprofits, giving them rights to put relevant articles on their website.

PARENTLINE

Maryland
parentlineonline.com
parentline@comcast.net
APPROXIMATE PAY: Would not say how much, but they do pay.

PARENTMAP
Seattle, WA – monthly
parentmap.com
editor@parentmap.com
GUIDELINES: Take a close look at *ParentMap* and the type of content we use before drafting your query letter. This will give you a good idea of the different kinds of stories we publish, our voice and our audience. As a Puget Sound–based publication, we're interested in stories that will appeal to families throughout the Puget Sound region. You have the best chance of turning your query into an assignment if it fits within one of the departments that are a regular part of each issue of *ParentMap*. Here's an overview of departments that appear in all (or most) issues:

- **Ages & Stages.** This age-specific section forms the core of *ParentMap*. Over and over, parents tell us that an age section—which gives them content specific to the age of their child—is what they turn to first. Ages & Stages is divided into five age groups: 0-2, 3-5, 6-10, 11-14, 15-20. We're looking for short pieces (generally 700 words or less) that address a specific issue for an age group. Content runs the gamut from a first-person piece about a particular parenting experience, to concrete information on an enlightening study.
- **Out & About.** Reviews and ideas for places to go and things to do, locally and regionally.

Query letters can be emailed. When writing us, please detail the topic you'd like to address as well as your strategy for writing the story. Demonstrate that you are adept at doing research by mentioning the kinds of sources you intend to use. We generally work with writers who have some experience, so please make sure you list the publications in which your work has been published. Also include links to Web sites on which your work has appeared, and/or mail us photocopied examples of your published work. Do not send originals, as we can't guarantee their return. Payment for stories depends on length and placement of the article. *ParentMap* purchases first American rights, print and electronic, for articles and pays within 30 days following publication.

PARENT NEWS
Conway, SC
parentnewsmagazine.com
p-news@sccoast.com

PARENTING, PARENTING EARLY YEARS, PARENTING SCHOOL YEARS
New York, NY – 10 times per year (2,100,000)
parenting.com

Articles Editor
Time, Inc.
530 Fifth Avenue, 4th Floor
New York, NY 10036
Phone: 212-522-1212

PARENTING NEW HAMPSHIRE
Manchester, NH – monthly (65,000)
parentingnh.com
editor@parentingnh.com
GUIDELINES: *Parenting New Hampshire* welcomes submissions of non-fiction essays, poetry or vignettes for possible publication. Pieces should be no longer than 700 words, and the subject matter should be related to being a parent.
APPROXIMATE PAY: $35 reprints.

PARENTING OC
Anaheim, CA – monthly
parentingoc.com
editor@parentingoc.com
APPROXIMATE PAY: $35 reprints.

PARENTING PLUS
Wellington, FL – monthly
parentingplus.com
pplus000@aol.com
APPROXIMATE PAY: $20-30 per article.

PARENTS MAGAZINE
New York, NY
parentsmag.com
Articles Editor
375 Lexington Avenue
New York, NY 10017
Phone: 212-499-2000
GUIDELINES: Before you query us, please take a close look at our magazine at the library or newsstand. This will give you a good idea of the different kinds of stories we publish, as well as their tempo and tone. In addition, please take the time to look at the masthead to make sure you are directing your query to the correct department. When querying us, please send a one-page letter detailing the topic you'd like to address, as well as your strategy for writing the story. Demonstrate that you are adept at doing research by mentioning the kinds of sources you intend to use. Keep in

mind that all of our articles include expert advice and real-parent examples and also study data. It's unnecessary to send a completed manuscript; a query letter will do. We generally work only with writers who have some experience, so please make sure you list the publications you've written and include photocopied examples of your published work. Do not send originals, as we cannot guarantee their return. We receive many submissions for essays; typically, we only publish those that come from experienced writers and essayists. We're a national publication, so we're mainly interested in stories that will appeal to a wide variety of parents. For example, developmental service ideas for specific age groups are always welcome. In addition, we're always looking for compelling human-interest stories, so you may want to check your local newspaper for ideas. Keep in mind that we can't pursue stories that have appeared in competing national publications. We don't publish any unsolicited fiction or poetry; any children's books we excerpt are acquired strictly through book publishers. Because of the large volume of queries and manuscripts we receive, it generally takes about four to six weeks for us to reply, so please be patient. Always send a self-addressed, stamped envelope.

PARENTS' SOURCE

Berks/Lancaster Edition and Tri-County Edition
Douglassville, PA – bimonthly
parentssource.com
editor@parentssource.com
GUIDELINES: We publish parenting articles (serious and humorous) in the range of 750-950 words. Articles we publish in our book are also placed on our website ParentsSource.com. We do not have any restriction on where our writers live.
APPROXIMATE PAY: $25 reprints.

PEEKABOO

Bentonville, Arkansas – monthly
www.peekaboonwa.com
editor@peekaboonwa.com
APPROXIMATE PAY: Around $25 per article.

PHILADELPHIA FAMILY

(sister publication to *Main Line Parent*)
phillyfamily.com
melissa@familyfocusmedia.com
GUIDELINES: See *Main Line Parent*.

PIEDMONT PARENT

CAROLINA PARENT
CHARLOTTE PARENT

King, NC – monthly (36,000)
piedmontparent.com
editor@piedmontparent.com

GUIDELINES: *Piedmont Parent* and PiedmontParent.com welcome submissions from freelance writers. Each month we run several feature articles on topics related to our monthly theme and an article published exclusively on the website that goes along with this same theme. Features require thorough research (citing a minimum of three reliable sources), knowledge of our audience, and concise interviewing and writing skills. Articles on topics other than each issue's theme are also considered. We prefer articles and essays with local relevancy. Word counts for articles vary from 500-1,200 words. If you wish to query the editor, please include a story outline and previously published writing samples. Articles should be emailed, preferably as Microsoft Word documents. Include the author's name, address, Social Security number and daytime phone number on the first page of the story. Include the word count. We use the *Associated Press Stylebook* and *Webster's New World Dictionary*. If major revisions are needed, you will be contacted. Accompanying photographs (along with written permission) and electronic art are welcome (black and white or color). Deadlines are two or three months before the date of the issue.

APPROXIMATE PAY: Typically, we pay between $35 and $110 per story. We usually buy one-time print rights with exclusivity within our region and also post the story on our website. Reprints of articles from publications outside our region are considered.

PITTSBURGH PARENT

Bakerstown, PA – monthly
pittsburghparent.com
editor@pittsburghparent.com

GUIDELINES: Our editorial calendar is set up and assignments made each October for the following year. In addition, we accept articles (under 950 words) on spec for use when extra editorial space is generated through sales. We are always looking for teen, humor, camps, party, maternity and education stories. Feature stories must be under 950 words.

APPROXIMATE PAY: We pay $50 for 600-950 words and $25 for 375-600 word stories. Payment requires a W9 form and Social Security number and will be made from our Business Office 45 days after publication.

PORTLAND FAMILY (exclusive)

Beaverton, OR – monthly
portlandfamily.com

publisher@portlandfamily.com

GUIDELINES: *Portland Family Magazine* is a regional family magazine of arts, lifestyle, politics, environmental issues, holistic health and culture published monthly. Portland Family is an outlet for reportage and point of view that are not often found in the mainstream media. Our writers write the critiques, praises and personal anecdotes that provide the detail to the larger picture, the colors to the outline (often coloring outside the lines). We believe that Portland area families want to read something meaningful, something that enhances their relationship with each other and with their community. While we do, of course, want to entertain and enlighten our readers, above all we strive to convey substance with style and to make an emotional connection with our readers. We have an impassioned involved readership, and we embrace the opportunity to meet their high expectations. Our writers see the material with fresh eyes and real insight. We place a premium on surprise and good storytelling—the compelling anecdote, the colorful character, the lively quote, the telling detail. We are open to queries by email, (no phone queries, please) but you can endear us to your proposal if you pitch only developed ideas that fully describe the topic and your desired approach. Before you pitch a story to us, we recommend you read through a few of our back issues to get a feel for the type of articles we value and promote. At this point we do not envision adding regular/monthly columns. For all queries, indicate the availability of photos or artwork in your query letter or with your article. (Pertinent, high-quality photos can enhance an article's desirability.) If we are interested in your story idea, an editor will contact you within six weeks. We consider everything except a direct assignment to be submitted on a speculative basis. When an article has been assigned, we will contact you and then send a contract specifying terms and deadline. <u>Please do not submit work previously published or articles that have been submitted for publication elsewhere.</u> (☺ Kerrie says: I contacted the editor via email, and she said they <u>do</u> accept reprints, plus my Happy Hallogreen was published there … it wasn't technically a reprint then, but it was published other places at the same time.). We publish several features in each edition, from hard-hitting articles about weighty topics to pieces designed for entertainment. Activism, the arts, the community, education, the environment, family, fitness, health, nature, neighborhoods, outdoor activities, parenting, participatory sports, relationships, politics, profiles of interesting local people, recreation, renewable energy, sustainability, transportation, urban living, wellness, and many other topics—from the extraordinary to the off-the-wall—are good topics for features in *Portland Family Magazine.* We prefer to make writing assignments at least three months before they are due to give talented writers the time to do their best professional work. Barring unusual circumstances, articles are always published in the month scheduled, as indicated when assigned. By the same token, we do not over-assign features. We depend on writers to deliver assigned features in polished and professional form by the assigned deadlines. Writers will submit their article, tagline, 30-word biographical sketch, and their photo via email. Submitted articles must follow standard manuscript format. List your full name, address and telephone number in the upper left corner of the first page and an accurate word count in the upper right corner. The article should be emailed as an attached Microsoft Word file. The writer's color photograph should be attached as a .jpg or .tif, scanned at a resolution of 300 dpi, or a digital camera image of the same resolution. In addition, first-time writers must also furnish a mailing address, a Social Security number, and phone numbers where they can be reached. Our deadlines are assigned far enough in advance of press dates to provide sufficient time for thoughtful editing, ordering and obtaining necessary original art to illustrate the piece, proofreading, and doing the production work on a routine cycle that will result in an attractive, interesting and professional presentation.

Because *Portland Family Magazine* generally hires only experienced writers and will be reviewing writing samples before making an assignment, it is rarely necessary to kill a story. However, in the event a feature does not seem suitable even after editing or rewriting, a kill fee of 20% of the assignment fee (up to a maximum kill fee of $75) will be paid 30 days after the story was originally scheduled for publication. Generally, the writer bears all expenses associated with producing the assigned feature story. However, for unusual assignments, *Portland Family Magazine* may agree to cover certain expenses if negotiated at the time the assignment is being made, or subsequently approved by the editor while the story is being produced. *Portland Family Magazine* will not pay for expenses billed after the fact and not previously authorized by the editor. *Portland Family Magazine* purchases First North American publication rights for original material. The copyright reverts to the writer 90 days after publication.

APPROXIMATE PAY: Pays on a variable scale depending on length/complexity of the article based on a contract between the editor and the writer. Submit invoices for payment. We compile the necessary information for checks to be cut based on the assigned rates. We pay around 30 days after publication. $25 reprints.

PRACTICAL HOMESCHOOLING

Fenton, MO

practicalhomeschooling.com

GUIDELINES: We have no writer's guidelines per se. Rather, we ask you to briefly share your article idea with us and also your background — e.g., why you feel knowledgeable enough to write it. If we think it's appropriate and we have the space, we'll ask you to submit the article. If we then like the article, we send you our one-page Article Rights agreement for you to sign, which outlines your and our rights, the payment terms, etc. We are looking for practical articles (with resource lists and, ideally, photos) that explain how to meet some homeschool challenge or how to venture forth in to some new area. Ideally you are an acknowledged expert on the topic. We tend to run one to three freelance articles per issue.

WHAT WE DON'T WANT

- Theological articles
- Polemical articles about why everyone should homeschool (we write those ourselves!)
- "Why I Decided to Homeschool" articles
- Generic articles collecting ideas from other people's work (we prefer to hear directly from the original experts)
- Stories about local homeschoolers—we suggest the homeschoolers themselves submit these to our "Show & Tell" feature
- Articles on topics already covered by our columnists
- "Curriculum" articles—e.g., sample unit studies, artist biographies, historical pieces, etc.
- Self-promotional articles designed to tout a book, curriculum, or website. Articles must be of general interest and if resources are mentioned, they should not be yours.

Finally, we are only interested in unique and original work. So please let us know what topics and titles, if any, you have already submitted or had published on other homeschool magazines. If you're still interested, email us (using the online submission form only) your idea with the following information: Your name, address, phone number, email address, age, ages of your homeschooled children, how many years have you been homeschooling?, are you a homeschooled student or graduate?, your writing experience, your article idea and why you are qualified to write it, have you submitted this idea or article to any other homeschool publications (including print and online)?, what articles have you submitted or had published to date in other homeschool publications (print or online)?

APPROXIMATE PAY: $50 per article, and that includes any photographs to accompany the article.

PREGNANCY

10 issues plus four specials

editors@pregnancymagazine.com

GUIDELINES: *Pregnancy* is the leading monthly magazine for first-time moms. At a time when information about what to buy, what to wear, what's normal and what's healthy is voraciously consumed by first-time moms-to-be, *Pregnancy* is there to answer. With the most in-depth information available and frequent celebrity profiles, *Pregnancy* is fast becoming the most trusted and recognized publication serving the maternity market. Our audience of first-time moms is on a fierce mission of information gathering. They cannot learn enough about their new passion: becoming a mother. *Pregnancy* gives moms information about all aspects of life—health, relationships, parenting, fashion, green living, technology, shopping, and more—in one place. Our goal is to inform and comfort women about their new lives as moms and the first year of their baby's life. If you have an article idea you would like to pitch, please follow the guidelines below.

- Read the magazine: Before you send in a query, please read a few current issues of the magazine. Get familiar with our content—don't pitch a subject we just covered. Make your pitch as specific as possible, indicating in which department you feel it fits. Our voice mixes a friendly, familiar tone with humor, and we look for creative ways of packaging information. Word counts for articles: features 1,600-2,000; departments 350-800.
- Consider our readers: Please remember that the reader is already pregnant. *Pregnancy* does not cover issues of conception and fertility. Also, we do not cover child-care topics or products beyond the age of one year.
- Send a query letter: Please send a brief email explaining your topic and your approach for writing the story. Explain why your story would be important to our readers. Articles must include professional sources and real-life examples, so indicate your ability to conduct the appropriate research and, in general, who those sources would be. Do not send a complete manuscript; these will not be returned.
- Show us your work: If this is your first time pitching *Pregnancy*, please include published writing samples, links to clips posted on the Web, and your resume or bio. Writing samples cannot be returned.

We hire freelance writers for a small number of sections in the magazine. Please limit your pitches to these sections:

- Features
- Must Haves/Be Well (pregnancy wellness articles with related products, chosen by the writer or by us)
- Word of Mom/Dad is the new mom (articles for and from the dad's perspective)
- Word of Mom/Relationships

If we are interested in your idea, an editor will contact you. We keep pitches on file for up to six months.

PREGNANCY & NEWBORN

www.pnmag.com
editor@pnmag.com

GUIDELINES: We're glad you're interested in the prospect of working with *Pregnancy & Newborn* magazine—we're always looking to add to our pool of writers and are currently accepting freelance submissions! Please read and follow the guidelines below so you can query us effectively and we can respond efficiently. First, familiarize yourself with *Pregnancy & Newborn* both in print and online. Our targeted audience is comprised of women who are expecting or have a child under the age of 1. We strive to provide insightful, informative articles that discuss all things pregnancy- and baby-related in a casual, conversational, girlfriend-to-girlfriend manner. As a national magazine, we cover topics that are relevant to pregnant and new moms across the country. Each month, we print articles that fit into the following categories: prenatal health, prenatal nutrition, emotional well-being, labor & delivery, infant care and parenting. Examples of topics that might be of interest include, but are not limited to, baby's development month by month, alternative pain relief during labor, choosing a name for baby, healthy snacks for hungry moms-to-be, postpartum depression, maternity leave, finding childcare, vaccinations, raising a bilingual baby and more. We're always looking for new and creative story ideas—please send yours our way! We prefer to receive queries via email; you may direct them to editor@pnmag.com. Please send a detailed description of your proposed article, including topics you'll discuss, experts you'll interview, and sidebars you'll provide. Department articles are typically 750-1,000 words plus 2 sidebars; feature articles are usually 1,750-2,000 plus 4-5 sidebars. Keep in mind that we generally work under a 4 to 6 month lead-time. We appreciate when you include clips of your previously published articles. It's always nice to see the work you've done in the past. Please be patient as you wait for our response. Oftentimes we may not have a spot for your story immediately, but will file it away to have on hand when an opportunity arises—and rest assured that when one does, we'll be in touch!

PURCHASE AREA FAMILY

Paducah, KY – monthly (20,000)
purchasefamilymag.com
karen@purchasefamilymag.com

GUIDELINES: We publish on the first of each month; our submission deadline is the 15th of the month preceding publication. Our content is generally local in nature and features, events, activities and information for families and women. We do accept general parenting articles and publish them as and when we find space available. Generally, the articles should be between 650-1,000 words and provided as a Microsoft Word document in 12-point font, single spaced with a one-inch margin. We prefer that submissions do not contain many quotes from individuals outside of this area and if possible local sources. Too many quotes from other parts of the

United States only serve to point out to the reader that the author isn't local, and we are known for our local content. We prefer to receive the entire article, rather than a synopsis or outline. We suggest that articles are submitted three months ahead of the month they are intended for. We have an annual editorial calendar which is helpful for submissions. We also publish profiles of individuals who have noteworthy achievements or accomplishments. The Kids Bits section spotlights children who are engaged in creative or charitable endeavors or who have accomplished a significant achievement such as Eagle Scout. *Purchase Area Family* also includes paid advertorials in our usual content format and articles on, or authored by, local business professionals, health experts, etc. Prospective contributing writers should submit their work in a Microsoft Word document or the body of an email together with their name, address, phone number and email. If you have a website where your work can be viewed please include those details. You should send at least three samples of your writing for consideration, together with the details of prior publication if any. If you have graphics or photography to accompany your work please send those as a .jpg attachment. We typically include a picture of the author's face with each article to add a more personal touch. You will receive a .pdf of the article layout, via email, for final review and correction prior to publication.

APPROXIMATE PAY: Many of our authors send unsolicited submissions with the understanding that we will pay as we publish. Payment is made on the first of the month at publication and if your work is used, you will receive notification to send an invoice. We always mail a copy of the magazine with the check immediately. The going rate for one time reprint is usually $40 and I have writers willing to take less than that. Some will customize or localize the article for a few dollars more. Our rates mirror those of the national going rate for freelance writing. Please submit your rates with your sample work. We have a website, updated monthly, that includes a link to any writer with a website of their own.

RAISE

Visalia, CA

raisemag.com

karen@dmiagency.com

RAISING ARIZONA KIDS (only Arizona writers)

Scottsdale, AZ – monthly (30,000)

raisingarizonakids.com

editorial@raisingarizonakids.com

GUIDELINES: The theme behind *Raising Arizona Kids* magazine is that it be a place for sharing ideas about parenting. Its emphasis is on providing many viewpoints and ideas and encouraging parents to pick methods that work best for them. *Raising Arizona Kids* is targeted to caring, open-minded and intellectually curious Arizona parents within the 25-59 age range. Articles should be written to inform, enlighten, challenge, support, amuse or touch these parents as they grow within their new roles, seek ways to enhance their children's lives and face the pressure of combining careers and parenting. The magazine is geared to parents of children from birth through high school. Occasionally we run articles about the next stages in parenting: guiding children through the college years and adjusting to an empty nest. All submissions accepted for publication become the property of Raising Arizona Kids, Inc. and may not be used elsewhere without the written permission of the publisher. *Raising Arizona Kids* is a local publication, intended to foster networking and support among Arizona parents and professionals supportive of quality parenting. Articles should quote local expertise and, whenever possible, local parents. Articles should be well-researched and should conform to our standards and style. Writers are encouraged to submit queries and clips of previously published works before undertaking the work to produce an article. We recommend a thorough review of previously published work (available in our archives, found on our website) before submitting a query. Feature articles run from 1,000-3,000 words in length. Departmental submissions run 400-800 words in length. If your article is accepted for publication, you will be asked to provide it digitally, along with the following information:

- Your Social Security number.
- Your contact information (name, mailing address, phone, cell phone, email address).
- Your children's names and birth dates (for the bio that will appear at the end of your article), if applicable.
- The names and contact information (mailing address, phone number and email address) of any experts and/or parents you quote in your article. (because sometimes we will want to schedule a photo shoot with someone who is quoted; sometimes we will want to ask them to participate in our 12News version of the story. We also mail the magazine to each contact during the month the article in which they are quoted is published. We do not rent or sell our mailing lists to others.)

All assignments are made on speculation. Articles accepted for publication will be edited, when necessary, to enhance clarity and/or conform to style and space requirements. Submissions are welcome in any of the following departments—Ages & Stages, Community, Money, Sports & Fitness, Health Matters, Rant/Rave/Reflect and Journal.

APPROXIMATE PAY: Payment is negotiated per piece and depends on the complexity of subject, the desired length of the article and the writer's level of professional experience and/or track record writing for our publication.

Range: $150-500 for feature submissions that are accepted for publication. $25-150 for departmental submissions that are accepted for publication. Payment is made within 30 days of publication. Most of our photography needs are met by staff, but freelance digital photographs will be considered for publication with articles. Payment is $25-100 per photo published.

RED RIVER FAMILY
redriverfamily.com
RIO GRANDE FAMILY
riograndefamily.com
editor@redriverfamily.com
liz@redriverfamily.com
APPROXIMATE PAY: $20-35 (for both publications). Need 50-200 word fillers.

REDBOOK
New York, NY – monthly
www.redbook.com
GUIDELINES: *Redbook* is targeted to women between the ages of 25 and 45 who define themselves as smart, capable, and happy with their lives. Many, but not all, of our readers are going through one of two key life transitions: single to married and married to mom. Each issue is a provocative mix of features geared to entertain and inform them, including:

- News stories on contemporary issues that are relevant to the reader's life and experience, and explore the emotional ramifications of cultural and social change
- First-person essays about dramatic pivotal moments in a woman's life
- Marriage articles with an emphasis on strengthening the relationship
- Short parenting features on how to deal with universal health and behavioral issues
- Reporting on exciting trends in women's lives

Writers are advised to read at least the last six issues of the magazine (available in most libraries) to get a better understanding of appropriate subject matter and treatment. We prefer to see detailed queries rather than completed manuscripts, and suggest that you provide us with some ideas for sources/experts. Please enclose two or more samples of your writing, as well as a stamped, self-addressed envelope. Send queries to:
Articles Department
REDBOOK
300 West 57th Street, 22nd Floor
New York, NY 10019

RICHMOND FAMILY

richmondfamilymagazine.com

editor@rfmonline.com

GUIDELINES: *Richmond Family Magazine* is a full-size, full-color monthly magazine published for the Metro Richmond readership. Articles vary in length from 600 to approximately 2,400 words. Our articles are informative and topical with regional or local relevance and written for parents with kids of all ages – from babies to teens. Writing style is upbeat and informal. Our articles are never preachy and always unbiased. Content should answer everyday questions parents ask: family life, healthy living, education, working parents. Seasonal topics are welcome. No fiction or poetry, please.

Features

A full-length feature (1,800 words minimum) must explore a topic thoroughly and use quotes from real parents and/or anecdotal information from family life, and/or quotes from a Richmond-area expert. Credentials should be cited in context. Sources for statistics and research (books and websites) should also be cited within the article. When applicable, include resources for parents, i.e. local contact information, lists for parents, useful websites. Photos or artwork may be submitted with final for consideration. Sidebars may be submitted and should include information that does not appear in the article itself.

Profiles

We are looking for Richmond-area people with unique or inspirational stories to tell, such as parents with multiple multiples, families who have adopted internationally, parents who are serving in the military, etc. We are also interested in profiles on local celebrities who are parents: sports figures, business and political figures, and media personalities, for example.

Travel

Family travel pieces should inspire parents in a concise way to enjoy and explore destinations with the entire family. Content should be information based and should not use the words "I" and "me" excessively. We are looking for regional day trips, resort packages, and vacation destinations for families with kids of all ages. Sidebars should include information not related in the article itself: websites and email addresses, phone numbers, costs, hours of operation, dining opportunities.

No previously published material. We buy exclusive periodical rights and electronic rights. Payment is based on experience and quality of work and will be made at the time of acceptance.

Real Mom or Dad

This popular column is written every month for RFM by real parents who want to share valuable information with other parents. We offer a $50 Target gift card to say "thanks!" to our Real Parent contributors. Real Parent articles should be about 1,000 words. Here's some editorial help:

- Find your topic. 7 Things I've Learned about Toddlers; How To Connect With Your Teen; 8 Secrets to Smoother Bedtimes; How To Get Kids Hooked on Math; The 5 Best Films for Family Movie Night; 6 Ways Middle-Schoolers Can Have Fun in Richmond; 5 Things We Did Right—just button down your main topic. (The number of points used is up to the Real Parent writer.)
- Write your lead-in or introduction (usually about one paragraph). This will be the place to talk about your expertise in the area and/or personal experience with the topic. Why are you writing about this topic? Try to put a little of yourself and your family in here if you can.
- Start a list. Actually write down your item headers, which is really the first line of each point. For example: Read, read and read some more. Turn off the TV. Start a business. Cook dinner once a week. Short simple points that people can glance at and decide whether or not they want to read the whole thing. The beauty of this list format is that you don't have to transition from point to point. Just state your "reason, thing, or step," etc. and get on with it, explaining it in a few sentences (or more if necessary.) Then move on to your next point.
- At the end of the article, try to use a paragraph or a few sentences to wrap up your main point.
- Don't forget the endnote: "Real Mom or Real Dad" _________ teaches, works, whatever (if applicable) and lives in .... with son? daughter? ages?
- Generally, try to make your Real Parent piece personal. Tell the reader about you and your family and your experience. Be informative, but don't overwrite. Put anecdotal info in it. Try to put your kids and family in it. It will be helpful to go online and read past articles for direction.

RICHMOND PARENTS MONTHLY

Richmond, VA – monthly
richmondparents.com
rpmeditor@richmondpublishing.com

GUIDELINES: Considers article queries and submissions from local writers. Queries must be accompanied by three to five clips. Resumes are welcome but not required. Articles run 400-2,200 words, with payment appropriate to length. Writers new to the magazine are more likely to be accepted at the shorter end of the range. Submissions by local writers for the "Your Turn" essay feature should be 400-900 words and can be researched opinions or humorous or reflective thoughts on any aspect of parenting.

APPROXIMATE PAY: Payment appropriate to length. $35 reprints.

ROCHESTER & GENESEE VALLEY PARENT

ROCHESTER BABY GUIDE

New York – monthly
rocparent.com
editor@gvparent.com
APPROXIMATE PAY: $30.

ROCKY MOUNTAIN PARENT

rmparent.com
kristin.rmpublishing@gmail.com

SACRAMENTO PARENT

Auburn, CA – monthly (50,000)
sacramentoparent.com
shelly@sacramentoparent.com
GUIDELINES: We are currently accepting most submissions on spec; in other words, we generally need to see a finished (or nearly-finished) piece before agreeing to publication. Stories with the following qualities are particularly attractive to our publication:

Local

We look for stories with quotes from experts or parents in the Greater Sacramento region, or even a sidebar with local resources or related/upcoming event(s). Check website for the calendar.

Timely

Remember when… the vaccines-and-autism debate was all over the news? Hazardous toys were turning up in every store aisle? Research came out on the effects of BPA? The Sacramento Children's Museum announced it would open in 2010? (The list goes on.) Sac Parent offered coverage and local resources to our readers on all these topics and more, often weeks or months before many larger publications had answers. And we continue to strive toward serving up all kinds of stories to help parents—particularly moms—make sense of the latest issues, for themselves, their families and their communities.

Entertaining or compelling

Pretend you're a smart, hip mom with a great sense of humor, a sensitive side, and way too much to do most days. (96% of our readers are women, and over 80% of them are college-educated.) You're probably sleep-deprived and uber-busy. Ask yourself: would I have to read this? What would compel me? And what would I get out of it?

Lead time

Our editorial is planned around two to three months in advance. Issues are generally "put to bed" by the first of the month prior to publication (i.e., we finish up selections for the June issue in April, the October issue in August, etc.).

Length

- 300-500 words for short articles
- 600-900 words for medium-length articles
- 1,000+ words for long features (usually only allotted for narrative or in-depth stories)

Photos

Able to provide great photos along with your words? You rock! If we can use them (i.e., they're attractive, hi-res and BIG enough), we generally offer additional payment, and, of course, photo credit.

APPROXIMATE PAY: We have a limited monthly budget, and our rates vary (from $25 to $45 for reprints to around $50 to $200 for original articles) depending on the fit for our publication, and the amount of journalism, research, or travel, etc. required by a story. Not to mention how much additional work it needs before it's ready for layout. Whenever possible, we are happy to help new and emerging writers build their skills and portfolios, and we can offer pointers on picking up reprint fees in the parenting publications market. We require regional exclusivity (usually 6 months-1 year). If you submit a piece to multiple publications within the Greater Sacramento region, please ensure that it does not run in parallel publications within that time frame. We will notify you of intent to publish well in advance; if you agree, and you have submitted the piece to other local publications, please retract it from those other guys.

SAN DIEGO FAMILY

San Diego, CA – monthly (120,000)
sandiegofamily.com
editor@sandiegofamily.com

GUIDELINES: We are looking for articles between 400-1,000 words on topics relating to parenting and families: arts & crafts (performing & media arts); education; health & nutrition; holidays; home & garden; mommy/daddy diaries; parenting & child behaviour; parties & celebrations; pregnancy, babies; sports & fitness; technology; toddlers, preschoolers, school-age children, tweens & teens. Please review the guidelines from the pdf document on our website.

APPROXIMATE PAY: We pay upon publication per column inch (about 35 words). Cover story $3.50-4.00 per column inch; first rights $2.50-3.00 per column inch; reprint rights $1.25 per column inch.

SANTA BARBARA FAMILY LIFE

Santa Barbara, CA – monthly
www.sbfamilylife.com
production@sbfamilylife.com

APPROXIMATE PAY: Locals write for free. Others get $20 reprints.

SAVVY KIDS

Little Rock, Arkansas
savvykidsofarkansas.com
melanie@arktimes.com

SEATTLE'S CHILD

Lynnwood, WA – monthly
seattleschild.com
dzedonis@seattleschild.com
APPROXIMATE PAY: I have heard through the grapevine that they don't like reprints but they pay quite well for original pieces (in the $200+ range). I have also heard getting paid can be a challenge, so be careful. I'm leaving them in with reservations.

SI PARENT

Staten Island, NY – monthly
siparent.com
editorial@siparent.com
GUIDELINES: Articles should be between 600-800 words. Please be sure the story you submit is not advertorial in content, is your original work, and has not appeared in any other publication in our geographic area.
APPROXIMATE PAY: 3.5 cents per word for reprints.

SIMPLY FAMILY

Billings, MT – monthly
simplyfamilymagazine.com
jamie@simplyfamilymagazine.com
APPROXIMATE PAY: $40.

SOLO PARENT

soloparentmag.com
kate@soloparentmag.com
GUIDELINES: Thank you for submitting to *Solo Parent Magazine.* Your voice is a voice that we think would benefit parents raising their kids in non-traditional families around the world. Our mission is to create an online and real-time community for single, widowed, divorced, and non-traditional families so that they can share experiences, information, resources, and build community. We strive to empower a group of people who are struggling to raise their children in a culture where traditional, two-parent households are viewed as the norm. We envision a world where all families are whole, all families are "normal." We envision a world where parents can be proud of their choices, and can find the support to raise their children to

be proud of their upbringing and can thrive.

Solo Parent Magazine looks forward to members of the public submitting user published content or user content (e.g. articles and related links and images, etc.) to us in connection with our website ("User Submissions"). We are now accepting User Submissions in the following categories:

- Health (all areas—physical, mental, emotional, and spiritual)
- Wealth and money matters
- Separation, divorce, being widowed
- Choosing to raise kids outside of partnership
- Dating, relationships and sex
- Parenting, co-parenting and blending families
- Seasonal topics—relevant to holidays, events and time of year
- Legal matters pertaining to custody, personal rights, domestic violence and divorce.

User Submissions remain the intellectual property of the individual user. By posting content on our website, you expressly grant *Solo Parent Magazine* a non-exclusive, perpetual, irrevocable, royalty-free, fully paid-up worldwide, fully sub-licensable right to use, reproduce, modify, adapt, publish, translate, create derivative works from, distribute, transmit, perform and display the User Submission and your profile information, including your voice and/or likeness as contained in your User Submission, in whole or in part, and in any form throughout the world in any media or technology, whether now known or hereafter discovered, including all promotion, advertising, marketing, merchandising, publicity and any other ancillary uses thereof, and including the complete right to sublicense such rights, in perpetuity throughout the universe.

User Submissions are not confidential, and *Solo Parent Magazine* shall be under no obligation to maintain the confidentiality of any information, in whatever form, contained in any User Submission. We reserve the right to edit all submitted content without permission. We will respect the integrity of your submission, while matching it to the integrity of our magazine. By submitting to *Solo Parent Magazine* you acknowledge that you accept our terms and conditions which can be found on our website here, and any form of editing that might occur by the *Solo Parent Magazine* editorial team. Please note that Solo Parent LLC provides no guarantees that your post will be published and reserves the right in its sole discretion, which articles will be published and when they will be published.

General Writing Style and Suggestions

Every article we consider must answer the question, "why is this relevant to solo parents?" Our readers are people like you. We want to project an attitude of camaraderie. We want to be the friend next door who brings a bottle of wine and some good advice. Maybe we're a little snarky, maybe we're a little world-weary, but we're never cynical or mean. Please be concise in your articles, because our readers are solo parents, after all. They just don't have time to wade through every little he-said, she-said detail. Be informative. Be funny. Avoid using clichés, avoid rhetorical questions, avoid using filler words or words that aren't absolutely necessary. Try to find a conclusion that takes the reader to a higher place, or a deeper understanding of what they might be going through. We are creating a community, and we want people to keep coming back. For consistency and quality, we ask that writers adhere to the AP style.

Please send submission as an attachment (Word doc). Include your full name, email address, mailing address, and date of submission in the body of your email. Name the document and the subject line of the email clearly with the article title and your name. All submissions should be in Arial 12pt, single-spaced. Paragraphs should not be indented. Kindly include a suggested headline and one sentence sub-headline for your story. Please insert any hyperlinks in Microsoft Word. Articles should be 500-1,000 words, proofed and post-ready. Please include up to a 50-word bio with a photo. Image sizes should be the following:

- 150×150
- Jpeg format
- 72 dpi
- color (RGB) or black and white

Include any relevant photographs at the end of the story, along with captions and photo credit information, if applicable. Permissions or rights to any photos you submit with your stories are necessary. We will not accept material that is sexually explicit or contains hate language/slurs. This includes text, video, and/or photos that are part of submissions. When writing research-based posts, please make reference to any study that supports your site (e.g., "The 2013 Census Bureau report shows …"). All research must be available to the public. All original content must be original unless otherwise stated. You must own the content you submit, and it must be unique.

SONOMA FAMILY-LIFE
MENDO LAKE FAMILY LIFE

Philo, CA – monthly (28,000)
family-life.us
melissa@family-life.us
APPROXIMATE PAY: $40 for a reprint in both publications and online. Original assigned pieces pay 10 cents per word.

SOUTH FLORIDA PARENTING (exclusive to SE Florida)

Deerfield Beach, FL – monthly (110,000)
sfparenting.com

krlomer@sun-sentinel.com
GUIDELINES: In a typical issue, readers will find a variety of regular departments: Out & About, Baby Basics, Preteen Power, Family Money, Family Health and more. We also run feature articles of 800-2,000 words on topics of pertinence to South Florida parents. Features require careful research, independent reporting and well-developed interviews with South Florida sources. Our focus is on our three-county market, and we prefer features that use sources and settings in South Florida. Assignments, when given, go almost exclusively to writers who live in southeast Florida. However, we do consider insightful, captivating essays and features from outside our area, particularly those that deal with universal themes and issues. All stories must include clearly identified, real sources. Articles or essays that use only first names, composites or fictional examples will not be considered. We welcome your submission of material previously published outside South Florida, if offered to us on an exclusive basis in southeast Florida. No submissions or queries that are offered to other publications in southeast Florida will ever be considered. We do not buy work from writers who are published by our competitors. For reprint offers, send either typed manuscripts or clips and let us know where the material appeared. If you have an idea keyed to a particular issue, event or season, we suggest that you send it early. All articles accepted for publication must be submitted by email. Articles sent on spec may be typed and printed or sent by email attachment. An editor will contact you by phone or email if the article is accepted for publication. We cannot contact every writer in response to queries, but will inform you within a two-month time frame if we are considering your work for publication. We do not accept queries from writers who have not worked with us before. If your work is new to this publication, we will consider only completed articles submitted on speculation. Articles will be bought only when they meet our standards for clear, high-quality writing.
APPROXIMATE PAY: $150-300 for first publication rights to articles, based on placement within the magazine, length and quality of writing. We will ask you to sign a contract warranting that the work submitted is your original work and agreeing that you will not submit work to any other publications in South Florida. Writers are paid $30-50 for reprints of articles that are published elsewhere. Generally, these fees also include rights to use the article online at sfparenting.com.

SOUTH SOUND (locals)
Tacoma, WA
southsoundmag.com
lisa@premiermedia.net
GUIDELINES: We use local writers. Please send a resume and a couple of

clips.
APPROXIMATE PAY: Only pays for localized reprints on a case-by-case basis.

SOUTHERN FAMILY MAGAZINE
Madison, AL – bimonthly
southernfamilymag.com
sphillips103@aol.com
GUIDELINES: She has a local writer who does most of their pieces. Sometimes they might need a filler that has a maximum of 500 words. They sometimes have space to fill … send submissions, samples of work, author site, etc.

SOUTHWEST FLORIDA PARENT AND CHILD
Fort Myers, FL – monthly (25,000)
gulfcoastmoms.com
pamela@swflparentchild.com
GUIDELINES: *SWFL Parent & Child* magazine does use freelancers, mostly local writers. On the very rare occasion, we have used writers from outside our region. Word counts depend on the story. Most features are around 500 words, shorts are about 50-150, and cover stories can be around 1,200 words. Our pay structure depends on the story. We might pay $25 for a reprint or a short. Most feature stories are $75-150. And cover stories range from $150-250. We do get a lot of "personal account" submissions from people outside our area. We do not use those at all unless the writer lives in our region, which is Lee, Collier and Charlotte counties.
APPROXIMATE PAY: $25-200.

SOUTHWEST WASHINGTON FAMILY
Centralia, WA – monthly (9,000)
swwfamily.com
cwilson@swwfamily.com
GUIDELINES: We use local freelancers as much as we can.
APPROXIMATE PAY: Only pays for local content. If someone is from the area, has visited the area, or researches and gives the piece local ties they would consider it.

SPACE CITY PARENT
CY-FAIR PARENT
FORT BEND PARENT
KATY PARENT
PEARLAND PARENT
Houston, TX – monthly

spacecityparent.com
editor@spacecityparent.com
APPROXIMATE PAY: $35 for all publications.

STL PARENT
St. Louis, MO
stlparent.com
editor@stlparent.com

SUBURBAN PARENT
North Brunswick, NJ
njparentweb.com
editor@njparentweb.com
APPROXIMATE PAY: $10 per reprint.

TETON FAMILY (mostly locals)
tetonfamilymagazine.com
christina@tetonfamilymagazine.com

TEXARKANA PARENT
Nash, TX
texarkanaparent.com
publisher@texarkanaparent.com

THRIVING FAMILY (FOCUS ON THE FAMILY)
Colorado Springs, CO – bimonthly
thrivingfamily.com
thrivingfamilysubmissions@family.org
GUIDELINES: *Thriving Family* focuses on marriage and parenting from a biblical perspective. Most articles address marriage and the needs of families with four- to 12-year-olds in the home, but parenting preschoolers and teens are not ignored. The magazine is divided into the following departments:
FAMILY STAGES: Think immediate and practical applications for parents of preschoolers, school-aged children, tweens and teens. Submit a 50- to 200-word practical family idea or one way you proactively and successfully trained your child to do something. Each article must include the ages of the children mentioned and can be written in first or third person, but must be a true-life experience. Payment is $50 on acceptance for first non-exclusive rights. Send the complete manuscript, and use "Family Stages" as your subject line.
FOR FUN: Humor articles showcase the dynamics of marriage, parenting and routine family life with a hilarious, enjoy-the-journey tone (no

sarcasm).This true-life, funny narrative is written in first person and should be around 500 words. Payment is $175 on acceptance for first non-exclusive rights. Send the complete manuscript. Humor cannot be queried.
FAMILY FAITH & FAMILY ENTERTAINMENT: No freelance articles are accepted for "Family Faith" or "Family Entertainment" at this time.
FEATURES: Thriving Family includes 1,200-2,000-word articles that include well-known personalities in the Christian world. See our magazine for examples. Query first. Payment begins at 25 cents per word.
FAMILY LIFE: The following areas accept freelance queries, and payment begins at 25 cents per word. Please query your topic and ideas before submitting a manuscript:

- For Him — This 450-word article written by a man offers insight into one marriage or parenting issue from a male perspective.
- For Her — This 450-word article written by a woman offers insight into one marriage or parenting issue from a female perspective.
- Blended Family — This 800-word article covers one aspect of family life that is intrinsic to and exclusively about the issues and concerns of blended families.
- Extended Family — This 450-word article shows families how to stay involved and active in relationships with close and distant relatives.

All articles should:

- Be topical, timely and accurate.
- Not use fictitious or hypothetical anecdotes or composite characters.
- Avoid frequent scriptural quotations—biblical concepts should be implicit.
- Avoid Christian jargon and clichés.
- Include sources for statistics, facts or research.
- Include contact information and verifications for anyone who is quoted within an article.

ONLINE MARRIAGE AND PARENTING ARTICLES: *Thriving Family* will have an online presence that accepts 800-1,200-word articles. Review our themes list for more details.

All emailed submissions and queries must be inserted within the body of an email. No attachments are accepted.
APPROXIMATE PAY: See above.

TIDEWATER PARENT

Norfolk, VA – monthly (110,000)
mytidewatermoms.com
ss.acker@cox.net
APPROXIMATE PAY: I'm leaving this publication in because they are an award-winning magazine and I have to believe they pay, even though they didn't return my inquiry.

TODAY'S PARENT BABY AND TODDLER (favors Canadian writers)
Toronto, ON – twice a year
todaysparent.com
Send your query to (MAIL ONLY):
The Editor, *Today's Parent* Baby & Toddler,
One Mount Pleasant Road, 8th Floor,
Toronto, Ontario M4Y 2Y5
Phone: 416-764-2850
GUIDELINES: *Today's Parent Baby & Toddler* is a consumer magazine for parents with children up to the age of three. It is distributed as a "special edition" of *Today's Parent* through doctors' offices and to new subscribers to *Today's Parent* magazine who have babies. Currently there are two issues of *Today's Parent Baby & Toddler* a year. The tone of the magazine is positive and supportive, yet realistic. While for most articles it will be important to consult health or child-care professionals, we also want to include the experience and reflections of parents. We do not lecture or dictate to our readers; rather, we pass on to them the suggestions and shared experience we have gathered. We recognize that apart from basic matters of health and safety (e.g. using a car seat), there are a variety of positive ways to handle most parenting situations. *Baby & Toddler* does, however, have a parenting philosophy. We promote a gentle, nurturing parenting style that respects each child's unique personality, and also understands the normal developmental needs and limitations shared by all babies and toddlers as they grow. We encourage parents to interpret their babies' behavior in this context (my toddler is having a tantrum because she's frustrated and overwhelmed, not because she's "naughty"), and to stay on their child's side. We are advocates of breastfeeding as the best feeding choice for babies. At the same time, we respect the decision to bottle-feed, understanding that it may be the best choice for individual families. We also recognize that the first three years of parenting can be the most demanding, and the most hands-on, so we also address the needs of parents. Stories may range from the very practical (starting a playgroup) to the more introspective (coming to terms with your new identity as a parent). Please do not telephone, email or fax queries. Send a detailed query letter rather than completed manuscripts and, if it's your first contact with us, include samples of previously published work. When submitting a query, please indicate the word length you consider appropriate for the story. Responses will be mailed within six weeks, providing a stamped, self-addressed envelope is enclosed. *Today's Parent Baby & Toddler* accepts no responsibility for unsolicited material. Please note that we do not publish poetry or fiction. Because we promote ourselves as a Canadian magazine, we favor

Canadian writers.

- **BABY BULLETIN (every issue)**: provides news and tips on health, safety and development, plus crafts, activities and books. This department is written by a regular contributor.
- **HEALTH (every issue)**: deals with common health issues affecting children — everything from how to take a temperature to common baby ailments to ear infections. The tone should be helpful, not alarmist.
- **PLAYTIME (every issue)**: provides ideas for play, activities, crafts, outings and adventures that parents can share with their children.
- **BABY STEPS (every issue)**: deals with common developmental issues. Divided into four parts (0-6 months; 6-12 months; 12-24 months; 24-36 months). This department is written by a regular contributor.

Today's Parent Baby & Toddler runs features of varying lengths in each issue, with a balance between the practical and the philosophical, covering child care and development, breastfeeding, the parenting experience, consumer information, and resources for families. All articles should be grounded in the reality of Canadian family life. Without claiming to know all the answers, we try to leave the reader with a sense of positive direction. Feature topics range widely and can include such diverse stories as how fathers can support breastfeeding, night waking, making mealtimes happy for toddlers, choosing daycare, sex after childbirth, traveling with your baby, choosing a baby carrier and turning down parenting stress. Stay away from essay format and didactic prose. Use quotations. Unless you have been assigned to write a personal reflection article, restrict any first-person narratives to the occasional use of your own experience as an example or for a lead. The writing style should be lively and accessible. A light-hearted approach, where appropriate, is welcomed. Wherever possible, sources, statistics and anecdotal material should be Canadian. Since we are a national magazine it is important to avoid a local bias. When selecting parents to interview, please keep in mind that Canadian families have many configurations and many cultural backgrounds; we would like this diversity to be reflected in the pages of the magazine. Sidebars with supplementary information or practical tips are encouraged. We also like to include a list of resources for parents at the end of each article, and we encourage writers to recommend relevant books or organizations. We use the *Canadian Oxford Dictionary* for spelling. Numbers one to ten are spelled out and numerals are used for 11 and up. We would like the magazine to be read by mothers and fathers. Please don't assume an exclusively female audience. Also watch out for sexist language. Good non-sexist writing requires careful sentence construction (avoid using he/she or mixing singular and plural, as in "when a child cries, you should comfort them."). When discussing individual children, roughly balance girls and boys. If you are assigned an article, your handling editor will contact you by phone to discuss the direction of your assignment and will send you a contract letter specifying deadline and fee. We will reimburse telephone and some other expenses. Expenses other than long distance charges should be approved by the handling editor in advance. Writers must send an invoice with their manuscript; fees will be paid 30 days after acceptance. Include a list of your sources, with telephone numbers, with your manuscript. Be sure to include the full address of any source who has asked to receive a copy of your article and indicate that you wish copies sent. Please be diligent and double-check names and titles of sources.

APPROXIMATE PAY: Word length and fees vary depending on the complexity of the story—usually 1,000-2,500 words, $700-2,000.

TODAY'S PARENT PREGNANCY AND BIRTH

Toronto, ON – three times a year
todaysparent.com
Send your query to (mail only):
The Editor
One Mount Pleasant Road, 8th Floor
Toronto, Ontario M4Y 2Y5
Phone: 416-764-2850

GUIDELINES: *Today's Parent Pregnancy & Birth* is a consumer publication for expectant parents. It is published three times a year (April, August and December) and is distributed across Canada by members of the medical profession and childbirth educators. The editorial focus is on pregnancy, birth, postpartum care, and parenting the newborn. We believe in empowering our readers to make informed choices. It is our goal to provide readers with current research and to discuss new trends in a responsible and balanced way. We believe that childbirth is an important milestone in family life, and that the experience of birth has lasting effects on the lives of women, babies, fathers and families. We deal with both "baby care" and "parent care," recognizing that the transition to parenthood is a major life change. Because of the many benefits to both mother and baby, we are advocates for breastfeeding, while respecting the choice to bottle-feed. While the tone of the magazine is positive, we do also address the "dark side" of birth: postpartum depression, miscarriage, etc. We try to help parents understand these events and to provide them with practical resources to help them cope. *Today's Parent Pregnancy & Birth* publishes personal experience stories only in the Birth Story column, rarely publishes humor and never publishes fiction or poetry. Please do not telephone, email or fax queries. Send a detailed query letter rather than completed manuscripts and, if it's your first contact with us, enclose samples of previously published work. Responses will be mailed within six weeks, providing a stamped self-addressed envelope is enclosed. Today's Parent Group accepts no responsibility for unsolicited material. About 80% of the editorial is written by regular contributors. Editorial lineups are established one year in advance. About 40% of each magazine is permanent editorial, a three-part section called "Birthing Basics" which covers basic topics in pregnancy, birthing and the early postpartum. Each section is reprinted annually. Writers are asked to avoid duplicating topics in "Birthing Basics" when querying. "News and Views" offers short news items, pre- and postnatal care tips, book reviews, etc. This department is written by a regular contributor. Several features complete each magazine. They are designed to complement the core editorial with more specialized topics, in-depth treatments, current issues, etc. Each issue must have a mix of prenatal, birthing and postpartum topics, as well as a balance between difficult medical subjects and lighter articles. Articles usually run from 1,000-2,500 words. If you are commissioned to write an article, you will be given a word count. When querying the publication, indicate the length you consider appropriate for the subject. Stay away from essay format and didactic prose. Use quotations. First-person narratives are not encouraged (unless you have been assigned a personal reflection piece) but interpretive reporting is fine. We use *The Oxford Canadian Dictionary*. We use the British spelling for "paediatric," "labour," and "Caesarean." However, we are now using "fetus" instead of "foetus." "Breastfeeding" is one word. Numbers one to ten are written and numerals used for 11 and up. We use *The Canadian Style: A Guide to Writing and Editing* for reference. We would like *Pregnancy & Birth* to be read by mothers and fathers. An article on breastfeeding would usually be directed at the mother but, for example, sexuality during pregnancy should talk to both parents. Please watch out for sexist language. We don't want to see a manuscript full of he/she or she/he. Good non-sexist writing requires careful sentence construction. When discussing particular babies, try to roughly balance girls and boys. Sidebars and resource boxes are encouraged. A list of resources for parents should include access information: if you are recommending books give the title, author, publisher, and date of publication. Please check to make sure books are currently in print. If appropriate, give mail-order information including price and shipping/tax. For organizations give a contact name and address, telephone number and email address, if there is one. Please indicate if they are willing to take calls from the public. If not. We won't print the phone number. Sidebars can provide supplementary information or practical tips. Make the information useful. Please ensure that you research the subject thoroughly and, where applicable, give attribution. All information must be current and accurate. Research sources and statistics should be Canadian. When quoting, accuracy is essential. If the quotation is from an interview, double–check with the source before submitting your manuscript. *Pregnancy & Birth* is a national magazine so avoid giving a local bias. When selecting parents to interview, please keep in mind that "the Canadian family" has many configurations and many cultural backgrounds; we would like this fact to be reflected in the pages of *Pregnancy & Birth.* We do not employ a copy checker, so make sure names, addresses, etc. are correct. Include a list of your sources, with telephone numbers, with your manuscript. We can accept material on disk in most word processing formats. We work in Word for MacIntosh. We use a single space format, with one line between paragraphs, and paragraphs are not indented. If you are commissioned to write an article for *Pregnancy & Birth* you will be given an editorial deadline date. This is the date when the editors should receive the manuscript. *Today's Parent* Group reserves the right to cancel the assignment or reduce the fee if it arrives after the deadline. We will reimburse long distance telephone expenses associated with researching an article to a usual limit of $50. Other expenses should be approved in advance by your handling editor.

CONTRACT LETTER Your handling editor will contact you by phone to discuss your first assignment. Please make notes during this telephone conversation—you will be given guidance on the editorial direction and approach. A confirmation contract letter will be sent to you. If you have any concerns regarding the terms and conditions outlined in the contract, contact your editor immediately.

CORE EDITORIAL:

Your Changing Body

- Tips for a Healthy Pregnancy
- Pregnancy Discomforts
- Your Pregnant Body Image
- Labour Step by Step
- Caesarean Section
- Your Body Postpartum

Giving Birth Your Way

- Your Birth Plans
- Choosing Your Caregiver
- Pain Medication Options
- Medical Interventions
- Planning for Postpartum Support

Your Baby, Your Family

- Growing a Baby
- Becoming a Father
- Getting to Know You
- Why Breast is Best
- Your Changing Sexual Relationship

BIRTH STORY SUBMISSION
The Birth Story column is a place where parents and others who have witnessed the birth of a baby can share their story. The word length is no more than 500 words, and the fee will be paid on acceptance. Please note that we only publish three birth stories a year, and we cannot guarantee that your story will appear in the magazine. As is the case for all of our editorial content, we are looking for good magazine writing. We understand that the birth of your baby is probably one of the most moving experiences of your life. But what is it about the story you are telling that will be moving, compelling or entertaining for other readers of the magazine? Sometimes this is in an unusual or humourous turn of events, but not always. We are not necessarily looking for stories that are outlandish. The most "normal" of births can make compelling reading if it's told well. Also, please bear in mind that our readership is largely comprised of expectant parents who do not need to read birth stories that will frighten or horrify them.
APPROXIMATE PAY: The fee will be established when you are commissioned to write the article. Articles range from $700-$1,500 based on both length and the amount of research involved. Fees will be paid 30 days after the manuscript is accepted. We do not pay kill fees for editorially unacceptable material, nor do we pay extra fees for rewrites. Writers new to *Pregnancy & Birth* may be asked to write their first article "on spec," especially if they have limited experience writing for consumer magazines.

TODAY'S PARENT TORONTO (only Canadian writers)

Toronto, ON – monthly (190,000)
todaysparent.com
alison.wood@tpg.rogers.com
queries@tpg.rogers.com
GUIDELINES: Offers a mixture of straightforward service articles and more philosophical or issue-oriented stories. The tone is positive and supportive, yet realistic. There are rarely black and white answers to child-rearing issues and we believe in being informative without being dictatorial. We invite parents to adopt those suggestions that may work for their families. The magazine embraces a gentle, nurturing parenting style that respects each child's unique personality. We understand the normal developmental needs and limitations shared by all children as they grow. We respect parents' ability to understand their children and to make good parenting decisions. Mothers and fathers are "parenting experts" too, and we rely on their anecdotes and experiences as sources of wisdom in our articles. We recognize that good parenting depends, in part, on adequate social support. Thus the magazine is also a voice for change around social issues that affect the quality of family life.
DEPARTMENTS ASSIGNED TO FREELANCERS

- **YOUR TURN (every issue)**: a first-person forum for parents to share their experiences. Please note that we prefer to reserve this column for our readers rather than professional writers. (650 words; $200)
- **MOM TIME (every issue)**: recognizes that mothers are women, too and deals with topics not directly related to parenting, including health, fitness, wellness, relationships, beauty and fashion. (1,200 words; $1,200)
- **EDUCATION (every issue, except possibly July and August)**: tackles both straightforward subjects—helping with homework, field trips—and controversial or complex topics such as French immersion or phonics vs. whole language. The writer should avoid taking an academic or politicized approach. Education issues (e.g. standardized testing, public vs. private schools) are also occasionally covered in feature articles. (1,200 words; $1,200)
- **HEALTH (every issue)**: deals with common health issues affecting children—how to take a temperature, common baby ailments, ear infections—but also includes some investigative topics (e.g., are parents overusing the hospital ER?). The tone should be helpful, not alarmist. Health issues (including controversial ones) are also occasionally covered in feature articles. (1,200 words; $1,200)
- **BEHAVIOUR (semi–regular)**: focuses on child development and discipline. Again, experiences or problems common to many families are preferable to extreme cases. We're looking for a supportive, constructive tone that acknowledges a variety of parenting styles. (1,200 words; $1,200) Several departments are written by regular contributors and are not open to freelancers. These include Uncommon Sense, Nutrition, Cooking With Kids and Steps and Stages.
- **FEATURES**: *Today's Parent* runs features of varying lengths in each issue, with a balance between the practical and the reflective, the light–hearted and the investigative. All articles should be grounded in the reality of Canadian family life. Without claiming to know all the answers, we try to leave the reader with a sense of positive direction.

Feature topics can include such diverse stories as the evolving role of fathers, choosing the discipline technique that's right for your child, dealing with picky eaters, postpartum depression, returning to work, sex after childbirth, birthday party ideas, surrogate motherhood and child poverty. With some topics, the writer's personal experience as a parent adds a rich layer to the storytelling. Word length and fees vary depending on the length complexity of the story—usually 1,500-2,500 words, $1,500-$2,500. Send a detailed proposal by email, mail or fax rather than a completed manuscript (except for Your Turn). If it's your first contact with us, enclose samples of previously published work. Queries should have a specific hook, not just a subject area (e.g., the pros and cons of the family bed, not just "kids' sleep") and should have wide appeal for a national audience (camping in New Brunswick is too local; coping with cystic fibrosis too specialized). Please indicate the word length you consider appropriate for the story. Please note that if we are interested in your story idea, we will contact you within six weeks. Mailed queries should include a stamped, self–addressed envelope. *Today's Parent* accepts no responsibility for unsolicited material. Because we promote ourselves as a Canadian magazine, we favour Canadian writers. Writers new to *Today's Parent* may be asked to write their first article on spec, especially if they have limited experience writing for consumer magazines. If you are assigned an article, your handling editor will contact you by phone to discuss the direction of your assignment and will send you a contract specifying deadline and fee. *Today's Parent* reimburses telephone and some other expenses. Writers must send an invoice with their manuscript, including GST number. Fees will be paid 30 days after acceptance of the final article. *Today's Parent* routinely asks to secure the rights to publish articles online. The fee includes these rights, with details explained in the contract. Wherever possible, sources, statistics and anecdotal material in *Today's Parent* should be Canadian. Since we are a national magazine it is important to avoid a local bias. When selecting parents to interview, please try to include both mothers and fathers, and keep in mind that families have many configurations and many cultural backgrounds; we would like this diversity to be reflected in the pages of the magazine. Please be diligent and double-check names and titles, since not all stories are independently fact-checked. Include a list of your sources, with telephone numbers, with your manuscript and include the full address of any source who has asked to receive a copy of your article. Sidebars with supplementary information or practical tips are encouraged. We also like to include a list of resources for parents where appropriate, and we encourage writers to recommend relevant books, organizations and websites.

TREASURE COAST PARENTING
Port St. Lucie, FL
www.tcparenting.com
info@tcparenting.com
APPROXIMATE PAY: $35 reprints.

TULSA KIDS
Tulsa, OK – monthly (20,000)
tulsakids.com
editor@tulsakids.com
APPROXIMATE PAY: $25 reprints.

TWINS

Fort Collins, CO – bimonthly (55,000)
twinsmagazine.com
twinseditor@twinsmagazine.com
APPROXIMATE PAY: $25-250.

UTAH FAMILY
Salt Lake City, UT – monthly
utahdiscovery.com
editor@utahfamily.com
GUIDELINES: Please familiarize yourself with our editorial calendar. We are generally working at least a month or two in advance and would appreciate timely submissions that are thematically accurate. Duplicate submissions are not required, as we will keep a running file of articles that have been previously submitted. Our calendar can be found on our website.
APPROXIMATE PAY: Reprints $20-60. Make sure you check this publication monthly, as they have used my pieces twice without asking first then took quite a long time to pay.

VALLEY PARENT
Columbus, GA
valleyparent.com
callie@columbusandthevalley.com
APPROXIMATE PAY: $30.

VALLEY PARENT
Corvallis, OR – monthly (22,000)
valleyparentmagazine.com
valleyparent@comcast.net
APPROXIMATE PAY: We are in a relatively small market, so we pay $25 to $30 dependent on quality (people interviewed, research cited and so forth).
VANCOUVER FAMILY
Vancouver, WA – monthly
vancouverfamilymagazine.com
nikki@vancouverfamilymagazine.com
GUIDELINES: We look forward to reading article submissions, and ask that all submissions comply with the following guidelines in order to be considered for publication:

- Word length can vary, but is generally within 200-1,000 words.
- Microsoft Word file.
- 8-point Arial font, single spaced.
- Sources must be cited, with contact information for fact-checking.
- Include brief biography following article, in italics.

APPROXIMATE PAY: $35 reprints.

THE VILLAGE FAMILY

Fargo, ND – bimonthly (25,000)
thevillagefamily.org
magazine@thevillagefamily.org

GUIDELINES: If you have an idea for an article, submit a written outline of the idea to the editor. If we decide to use your submission, we will contact you. Article length for regular articles is approximately 1,500 words; feature article length is approximately 2,500 words. We often add quotes from local resources to articles written outside our distribution area. We reserve the right to edit articles; however, we show a final draft of the article to the writer. Please submit a short writer bio with your article. *The Village Family Magazine* is distributed to families in the Fargo, West Fargo, ND–Moorhead, MN area. We are the only local parenting magazine distributed in this area.

APPROXIMATE PAY: We pay freelance writers 7 cents per word. Our reprint fee is $30-50, depending on length of article.

WASHINGTON FAMILY MAGAZINE (exclusive)

Herndon, VA – monthly
washingtonfamily.com
editor@thefamilymagazine.com

GUIDELINES: We publish regional parenting publications with distribution throughout several metropolitan areas. For a current list of our publications, visit our website. Our readers are families with children, infants through age 18, and we strive to uncover issues that are important to their daily lives. Most of our writers are local professionals who share their expertise with our readers. We accept with enthusiasm work from freelance writers. Since we plan the editorial content for each magazine at least three to six months in advance, we request that all submissions arrive on disk or via email at least three months prior to publication. (Example: deadline for the May issue is Feb. 1). Our preferred feature-length story is 800-900 words, but if you have longer articles you feel would make an exceptional feature for our readers, we will be happy to review them. Please email our editor with a detailed query or brief outline concerning each topic before sending any articles. Electronic and disk submissions should be in Microsoft Word format with <u>no special formatting</u> (e.g., bold and italic fonts or underlining, additional spacing and words in all caps). *Washington Family Magazine* has an extremely loyal group of readers and advertisers. For this reason, we request exclusive rights inside our readership areas. We do not accept manuscripts that have been simultaneously submitted to other publications in our local regions. All purchases of one-time print rights include the right to place the article in the archive section of our website. If you do not want your article to appear on our website inside our archives, do not submit it to our magazine. We encourage email correspondence with our editorial department. This will ensure that articles and queries are received, reviewed, and responded to in a timely manner. Email correspondence also allows us to establish a friendly communications relationship with each contributing writer.

APPROXIMATE PAY: Our average payment for one-time reprint rights is $50 for average-length feature stories published in any or all *Family* magazines. Payment and one tear sheet will be sent following publication. Although the article may appear in more than one of our publications and will appear in the archives of our website, only one tear sheet will be sent.

WASHINGTON PARENT

Bethesda, MD – monthly (75,000)

washingtonparent.com

contactus@washingtonparent.net

GUIDELINES: *Washington Parent* serves as a local resource on topics of interest to parents of infants and children through age 18. Our chief purpose is to educate and support families living in the Washington, D.C., metropolitan area. Most of our writers are local professionals who share their expertise with our readers. We occasionally publish articles by syndicated columnists and freelance writers. We prefer solid articles of approximately 1,000 words, which may include sidebars and bulleted points. We rarely run slice-of-life stories. The deadline for all articles is the 15th of the month two months prior to publication (April 15 for the June issue). Please check all information in your article. If it contains a listing, be sure that it is complete and current and that all addresses, phone numbers, websites and other information are correct. This is especially important if the article previously appeared in another publication. Please proofread your work. "Spell check" is not sufficient. We just do not have the time to deal with sloppy grammar and punctuation. Please do not design your article. We will do that. Do not use fancy formatting, text boxes, hanging indents or back tabs. It is very time-consuming to remove these. It is fine to use bullets, and please supply us with subheads (which should be in bold). We use *The Associated Press Stylebook* and *Webster's New World College Dictionary*. We use one gender throughout each article. Do not write, "Let your child tie *their* own shoes." Choose "her" or "his. We will ask for your written permission to include your article on our site, in our e-magazine and in any future media.

APPROXIMATE PAY: $35 reprints.

WEST VIRGINIA FAMILY

WEST VIRGINIA BABY

Buckhannon, WV – quarterly (15,000)
wvfamilyonline.com
editor@wvfamilymagazine.com

GUIDELINES: In every issue of *West Virginia Family* you will find articles, columns and regular departments that touch on all areas of family interest, including the family calendar of local activities, family health news, parenting tips, education, child safety, children's book and product reviews, recreation, child care, home life, pregnancy, travel, fitness, finance, and more.

Deadlines for Editorials

Spring (March/April/May) December 31
Summer (June/July/August) March 18
Fall (Sep/Oct/Nov) July 1
Winter (Dec/Jan/Feb) October 1

Editorial Calendar

Spring (Mar/Apr/May)

Summer Camps; Programs Guide and Directory with Special Advertising Section for Camps, Birthday Party Directory, Environment, Gardening, Special Needs

Summer (Jun/Jul/Aug)

Camps Special Advertising continued, End of School Year activities, Summer Safety, Family Travel, Park; Museum Directory, Calendar of Family Events & Attractions

Fall (Sep/Oct/Nov)

Back to School Special Advertising Directory, After School Activities, Sports, Homework, Calendar of Fall Events and activities, Harvest, Halloween

Winter (Dec/Jan/Feb)

Holiday Gift Guide, Family Holidays, Family Traditions, Holiday Travel, Safe Winter Travel, Family Health, Family Pets, Resolutions, New Year Organization Tips

The editorial deadlines in the chart above are the absolute final deadline for us to receive editorial submissions. Please send complete manuscript. We are looking for articles and tips on the topics provided above. We are also looking for checklists related to the topics. Word count needs to be between 500-800 words.

APPROXIMATE PAY: We pay up to $25 per article, depending on word count. We also accept shorts on current events up to 100 words and must be material still current by the time the publication reaches the shelf. One-time rights. We accept reprints, but ask that we receive regional exclusivity.

WESTCHESTER FAMILY

Harrison, NY – monthly

westchester.parenthood.com
jean.sheff@westchesterfamily.com
APPROXIMATE PAY: $120 original pieces.

WESTCOAST FAMILIES (no reprints; locals only)
WESTCOAST BABY GUIDE
WESTCOAST MOM
Richmond, BC Canada – 8 times/year
westcoastfamilies.com
editor@westcoastfamilies.com
GUIDELINES: Please read through the following carefully before submitting queries or proposals. *WestCoast Families Magazine* is a free, full-colour, full-gloss family and parenting magazine, published eight times per year in British Columbia, Canada. Our publication promotes the unique, vibrant West Coast lifestyle popular among today's parents. Our readers are generally well-educated, affluent families with children ranging in age from birth to early teens. They are free thinkers, socially conscious, environmentally aware and eager for the best in everything, be it the latest non-plastic baby bottles and toys, organic products and foods, the latest in high quality children's wear or outdoor activities that take advantage of B.C.'s natural beauty. *Yummy Mummy* is a publication dedicated exclusively to parents and is published within every issue of WCF. Topics of interest include women's health, relationship and dating issues for married and single parents, fashion, interior design, profiles, and work/life balance. Our editorial line-up is planned out months in advance, so please be aware that time-sensitive content may not be appropriate. All queries should be related to families, parents or children and should be relevant to Canadian readers, particularly in the B.C. area. We accept freelance queries for regular columns (Health, Travel, Finance, etc.), as well as features and profiles. Please view our Editorial Calendar [site under construction as of the release of this ebook] to get a better feel for our content before submitting a query. *WCF* only accepts editorial submissions and queries via email. Please read through a few issues of our magazine (you can download current and past issues online), as well as our Editorial Calendar, before sending in your proposal. If we have not replied to your proposal within six to eight weeks, feel free to submit your ideas to another publication. We do not publish reprints. The deadline for articles (and photos) is set by the editor once the story is assigned to the writer. Story length can be anywhere from 600-1,200 words, and will be set by the editor. The editor reserves the right to terminate the work on any article in progress if the article is no longer relevant or needed. If a completed article approved for publication is not published within one year of submission, then the writer will receive a 50% kill fee. Stories may not be submitted to any publication defined by *WCF* as

sharing the same market area as *WCF* without prior written approval. *WCF* follows the *Canadian Press Stylebook* for spelling, grammar and writing style. Please make sure that your work follows the guidelines set out in the *Stylebook* and that you use Canadian spelling and grammar at all times. Please send a brief description of your proposal, your experience, and a writing sample via email to editor@westcoastfamilies.com. Please let us know if the proposal is time-sensitive. If you are writing a story on a particular issue or news topics, please include a list of research references and sources for quotes. The editor reserves the right to contact any and all references at any time to verify any information in the article. Microsoft Office Word file attachments are acceptable. If you choose to paste an article or proposal into the body of your email, please remove any extraneous formatting marks or characters before sending.

***WESTCOAST FAMILIES* REGULARS**: Health & Nutrition; Contests; Family Travel; WestCoast Finds; Great Reads/Art Projects; Community Events Calendar

***WESTCOAST MOM* REGULARS**: Health & Fitness; Local Profiles; Business/Career; Moms on the Street; WestCoast Mom Book Club; Events for Moms around Town

APPROXIMATE PAY: *WCF* generally pays freelance writers anywhere from $50-$100 per article, payable upon publication. Payment is negotiated once a proposal has been accepted, and is based on the length of the article, the amount of research involved and the experience of the writer.

WESTERN NEW YORK FAMILY

Buffalo, NY – monthly (25,000)
wnyfamilymagazine.com
michele@wnyfamilymagazine.com

GUIDELINES: Running 64-80 pages per issue, *WNY Family* is a 90% freelance-written, subscription and free courtesy copy publication. Articles submitted should address current parenting issues with a Western New York tie-in whenever possible. Each issue has an "Up Front" focus article with appropriate sidebars, as well as additional articles, regular columns (children's books, family travel, "The Newbie Dad," single parenting, tweens & teens, internet/technology, restaurant review) and a very popular centerfold calendar of events targeted to young, growing families. We are interested in well-researched, non-fiction articles on surviving the newborn, preschool, school-age and adolescent years. Our readers want practical information on places to go and things to do in the Buffalo area and nearby Canada. They enjoy humorous articles about the trials and tribulations of parenthood, as well as "how-to" articles (e.g., organizing a child's room, keeping your sanity while shopping with preschoolers, ideas for holidays and birthdays, etc.) Articles on making a working parent's life easier are of great interest as are articles written by fathers. We prefer a warm, conversational style of writing. Because this is a regional publication, local writers are given preference, but all authors are given equal consideration based on their writing skill, style and the appropriateness of subject matter. We publish an article anywhere from one month to 18 months after receipt. "Evergreen" articles are highly desirable. Seasonal pieces must be submitted at least three months in advance of the issue month. We prefer completed manuscripts over queries as our staff is small and our time is limited. We buy first rights or reprint rights. Simultaneous submissions to other parenting publications are accepted.

APPROXIMATE PAY: If your unsolicited article is used, you won't necessarily be notified in advance. You will promptly receive a check approximately 10 days after the print issue is published. Pays $35-200 depending on type and length of article. Pays $35 for up to 950 words or humorous pieces. Pays $40-60 for up to 1,500 words nonfiction, informational or creative pieces. Pays up to $100-200 for in-depth nonfiction main theme articles of approximately 2,500-3,000 words.

WHAT'S UP-CANADA'S FAMILY MAGAZINE

Ridgeville, ON – bimonthly (200,000)
whatsupfamilies.com
editor@whatsupfamily.ca
APPROXIMATE PAY: Not available, but pays 30 days after publication.

WICHITA FAMILY

Wichita, KS
wichitafamily.com
publisher@wichitafamily.com

WILMINGTON PARENT

Wrightsville Beach, NC – monthly (10,000)
wilmingtonparent.com
danielle.wilmingtonparent@gmail.com
APPROXIMATE PAY: $30 per reprint.

WOMAN'S DAY

womansday.com
womansday@hearst.com
GUIDELINES: Thank you so very much for your interest in writing for *Woman's Day*. Unfortunately, you are not alone. In fact, you have so much company, and we have such a small cadre of editors, that we have had to develop what you will no doubt find a rather tough policy on unsolicited

manuscripts. This is what you need to know: Our editors work almost exclusively with experienced writers who have clips from major national magazines. As a result, we accept unsolicited manuscripts only from writers with such credentials. There are no exceptions. If you do have significant national writing experience, and you have an idea or manuscript that you think might interest us, e-mail us at womansday@hfmus.com, and please include some of your most recent clips. For website inquiries/pitches, please email dailywd@hfmus.com. Please note that we cannot guarantee that your submission will be read or commented on; it is by far most likely that we will get in touch with you only if we are interested in pursuing the idea you propose. Please note as well that we said e-mail; hard-copy submissions will not be considered. If you do not yet have the national experience we outlined above, we look forward to hearing from you when you do.

APPROXIMATE PAY: From 2004 guidelines: Essays run about 650 words and they pay $2,000 on acceptance.

WORKING MOTHER

New York, NY
workingmother.com
editors@workingmother.com
See appropriate editor for email address, below

GUIDELINES: Our readers include full-time, part-time and sidelined moms who work at public and private companies of all types and sizes; who are entrepreneurs; and who are self-employed. The best way to pitch an idea that can work: Read *Working Mother* for content and tone.

Features

We do assign features to freelancers. Feature pitches should specifically relate to the working mom, whether geared to her work, family, personal well-being or a mixture of these. Features are also assigned to fit our initiative packages (100 Best Companies, Best Companies for Multicultural Women, Best Companies for Hourly Workers, etc.). We like tightly focused pieces that celebrate working moms while illuminating and sensibly solving a problem unique to our readers and/or their children and family. We assign features at about 1,000-2,000 words.

Columns

Most of our columns are staff written. We assign out LOL, Moms @ Work, My Money and other columns occasionally.

Please email queries. If possible, include links to or files of clips of your previously published work. Include all contact info so we can reach you if we need to. If pitching about a specific working mom, include recent photographs/jpegs (at least 300 dpi) if possible. Unsolicited manuscripts will not be returned. Please pitch queries/ideas to the correct editors:

- All Best Companies initiatives: krista.carothers@workingmother.com
- Non-initiatives features, working mom balance, parenting, travel, food, money and finance, LOL, IMHO, Moms @ Work: barbara.turvett@workingmother.com
- Celebrities, workplace issues, entrepreneur moms, child health, pregnancy, romance, family sleep, child care: lela.nargi@workingmother.com
- Beauty, mom and kid fashion, kid fitness and activities, mom and kid books, toys and games, apps: irene.chang@workingmother.com
- News, fashion, beauty, for online: maricar.santos@bonniercorp.com
- Other ideas: editors@workingmother.com

If we decide to pursue your idea(s), we will contact you directly to discuss. Due to the large volume of unsolicited queries we receive, we're unable to respond to every proposal. If you don't hear from us within 90 days, please assume that we're not interested. About blogs, please read about that on the website.

16. RESOURCES

This is just a tiny sampling of some great writing books and sites:

BOOKS AND EBOOKS

- *The Beginning Writer's Answer Book* edited by Jane Friedman
- *Cash in on Your Kids: Parenting Queries That Worked* by Kris Bordessa, Teri Cettina and Jeannette Moninger
- *The Everything Guide to Writing Nonfiction* by Richard D. Bank
- *The Renegade Writer* by Diana Burrell and Linda Formichelli
- *Starting Your Career as a Freelance Writer* by Moira Anderson Allen
- *The Well-Fed Writer* by Peter Bowerman
- *Writer's Digest Handbook of Magazine Article Writing* edited by Michelle Ruberg
- *Writer's Market* by Writer's Digest

WEBSITES

- Beyond Your Blog (beyondyourblog.com)
- The Dabbling Mum (thedabblingmum.com)
- Dollars to Deadlines (Kelly James-Enger) (dollarstodeadlines.blogspot.com)
- Get Published in Regional Parenting Magazines (GetPublishedParentingMags.com)
- Make a Living Writing (makealivingwriting.com)
- Mistakes Writers Make (mistakeswritersmake.blogspot.com)
- The Well-Fed Writer (wellfedwriter.com)
- The WM Freelance Connection (thewmfreelanceconnection.com)
- Writers Write (writerswrite.com)

17. CHANGES TO THE 2015/6TH EDITION FROM THE 2013/5TH EDITION

1. A Fine Parent paying market addition
2. Active Family market addition
3. ADDitude market addition
4. Alamo Area Kids and Family market addition
5. Alaska Parent paying market addition
6. Albemarle Family is now Charlottesville Family
7. Ann Arbor Family, Findlay Family, Toledo Area Parent email change
8. Augusta Family email change
9. Autism Notebook deletion
10. Baby Corner paying market addition
11. BabyFit paying market addition
12. Baby Times, Family Times and Grand Times defunct
13. Baltimore's Child email change
14. Bay Area Parent market addition
15. Black Hills Parent market addition
16. Boy's Life paying market addition
17. Brain, Child new submission guidelines and blogging opportunity
18. Central California market addition
19. Cincinnati Family, Northern Kentucky Family, Nashville Parent, Rutherford Parent, Sumner Parent, Williamson Parent email change
20. Colorado Parent email change
21. Columbus Parent email change
22. Dayton Parent market addition (with Hamilton County Parent in the Cincinnati Parent group)

23. Family & Parenting market addition
24. Family and Faith market addition
25. Family Australia market addition
26. Family Living market addition
27. Family Magazine of Michiana, Sassy, Boom email change and updated guidelines (no more MI Child)
28. Family Time IL email change
29. Family Times Syracuse market addition
30. First Coast Parent email change
31. Flagler Parent market addition
32. Fredericksburg Parent and Family email change
33. Genesee Valley Parent name and website change
34. Giggle market addition
35. Good Life Family market addition
36. Growing Up Chico market addition
37. Growing Up in the Valley market addition
38. Hamilton County Parent market addition (with Dayton Parent in the Cincinnati Parent group)
39. Hello, Darling (MOPS) market addition
40. Home Education Magazine email change and updated guidelines
41. Honolulu Family market addition
42. 'Hood market addition
43. IParent market addition
44. inBetween market addition
45. Inland Empire email change
46. Jersey Shore Family email change
47. Kids on the Coast market addition
48. Kids Vermont email change
49. Krazy Coupon Lady market addition
50. Lowcountry Parent market addition
51. Main Line Parent email change and added sister publication Philadelphia Family
52. MetroParent WI site and email change
53. Minnesota Parent market addition
54. NCW Kid Connect market addition
55. New York Family market addition
56. Northeast Ohio Parent market addition
57. North Idaho Family market addition
58. Offspring market addition
59. Ohio Family market addition
60. Omaha Family email change
61. Oregon Family market addition

62. Paducah Parenting changed to Purchase Area Family and new web and email address
63. ParentGuide Florida deletion
64. Parenting OC email change
65. PTO Today market addition
66. Parent News market addition
67. Parent Notebook deletion
68. Parent Paper changed to (201) family North Jersey
69. Parents' Source email change
70. Philadelphia Family market addition (sister to Main Line Parent)
71. Piedmont Family deletion
72. Playground deletion
73. Raise market addition
74. Richmond Family market addition
75. Richmond Parents Monthly email change
76. Saint Louis Kids deletion
77. San Diego Family email change
78. Savvy Kids of Arkansas market addition
79. Seattle's Child email change
80. Simply Family email change
81. Solo Parent market addition
82. Sonoma Family-Life/Mendo Lake Family Life email change
83. South Florida Parenting slight email change (hyphen)
84. St. John's Parent market addition (with Flagler Parent and Volusia Parent)
85. STL Parent (St. Louis) market addition
86. Tampa Bay Baby deletion
87. Teton Family market addition
88. Texarkana Parent market addition
89. Texas Parenting deletion
90. Tidewater Parent email change
91. Treasure Valley Family deletion
92. True North Parenting deletion
93. Upstate Parent deletion
94. Volusia Parent market addition
95. West Virginia Family website change
96. Wichita Family market addition
97. Working Mother guidelines update to include blogs plus some email changes

18. AT-A-GLANCE INFORMATION

Before you curse me for email bounce-back on the email addresses I provide, please keep in mind that editors come and go, as do magazines, so some emails may bounce back. Feel free to contact me and I can get you a replacement email address if the magazine is still in business.

More work-from-home ideas, as well as additions and updates to the markets in this ebook, can also be found at my blog Make Money From Home at GetPublishedParentingMags.com. Please sign up for a subscription there, as I find new markets all the time and will add those to the blog!

Kerrie

	PUBLICATION	**EMAIL**
1	(201)family North Jersey	editor@201magazine.com
2	A Fine Parent (new)	sumitha@afineparent.com
3	About Families	maric@aboutfamiliespa.com
4	Adoptive Families	submissions@adoptivefamilies.com
5	Active Family (new)	info@activekidsbayarea.com
6	ADDitude (new)	submissions@additudemag.com
7	Alamo Area Kids and Family (new)	graphics@hillcountrytravelguide.com
8	Alaska Parent (new)	editor@alaskaparent.com
9	American Baby	mail or see ebook recommendation
10	Ann Arbor Family	cjacobs@toledocitypaper.com

		nadine@adamsstreetpublishing.com
11	Appleseeds	Cricket Magazine Group
12	Arizona Parenting	todd.fischer@azparenting.com
13	Ask	Cricket Magazine Group
14	Athens Parent	editor@athensparent.com
15	Atlanta Baby	editor@atlantaparent.com
16 17 18 19	Atlanta Parent Big Book of Parties Big Book of Schools Camp Guide	editor@atlantaparent.com
20	Auburn-Opelika Parents	info@montgomeryparents.com
21	Augusta Family	kate.metts@augustamagazine.com
22	Austin Family	editor2003@austinfamily.com
23	Babble.com	See appropriate editor for email address
24	Baby Corner (new)	editor@thebabycorner.com
25	Baby New York	kbrown@cnglocal.com
26	Babybug	Cricket Magazine Group
27	BabyFit (new)	rachel@babyfit.com
28	BabyTalk	letters@babytalk.com
29	Baltimore's Child	editor@baltimoreschild.com
30	Baton Rouge Parents	amy@brparents.com
31	Bay Area Parent	jill.wolfson@parenthood.com
32	Bay State Parent	editor@baystateparent.com
33	BC Parent	info@bcparent.ca
34	Birmingham Parent	editor@birminghamparent.com
35	Black Hills Parent (new)	editorial@blackhillsparent.com
36	Boom (Michigan)	jessy@michianafamilymagazine.com
37	Boom!	jim@riverregionboom.com
38	Boston Parents Paper	deirdre.wilson@parenthood.com
39	Boys' Life	Mail query only
40	Boys' Quest	submissions@funforkidz.com
41	Brain, Child	editor@brainchildmag.com
42	Bronx Family	kbrown@cnglocal.com
43	Brooklyn Family	kbrown@cnglocal.com
44	Broward Family Life	info@browardfamilylife.com
45	Calgary's Child	calgaryschild@shaw.ca
46	Calliope	Cricket Magazine Group
47	Carolina Parent	editorial@carolinaparent.com
48	Central California Parent (new)	ccparent@ccparent.com

49	Central Penn Parent	editor@centralpennparent.com
50	Charlotte Parent	editor@charlotteparent.com
51	Charlottesville Family	editor@ivypublications.com
52	Chesapeake Family	editor@chesapeakefamily.com
53	Chicago Baby	chiparent@chicagoparent.com
54	Chicago Parent	chiparent@chicagoparent.com
55	Chicken Soup for the Soul	Submission form online
56	Child Guide	cis@childguidemagazine.com
57	Cicada	Cricket Magazine Group
58	Cincinnati Family	chad@daycommedia.com
59	Cincinnati Parent	editor@cincinnatiparent.com
60	Click	Cricket Magazine Group
61	Clubhouse	Mail only
62	Clubhouse, Jr.	Mail only
63	Cobblestone	Cricket Magazine Group
64	Coastal Family	publisher@savdailynews.com
65	Colorado Parent	edit@coloradoparent.com
66	Columbus Parent	jhawes@columbusparent.com
67	Connecticut Parent	editorial@ctparent.com
68	Coulee Parenting	cpclax@charter.net
69	Creative Child	editorial@creativechild.com
70	Cricket	Cricket Magazine Group
71	Curious Parents	editor@curiousparents.com
72	Cy-Fair Parent	editor@spacecityparent.com
73	Dabbling Mum	subs@thedabblingmum.com
74	Dallas Child	editorial@dallaschild.com
75	Dayton Parent (new)	susan@daytonparentmagazine.com
76	Dig	Cricket Magazine Group
77	Durham Parent	editorialinquiries@gmail.com
78	Eastern Shore Parents	info@montgomeryparents.com
79	Faces	Cricket Magazine Group
80	Fairfield County Parent	editorial@ctparent.com
81	Faith & Family	editor@faithandfamilymag.com
82	Family	editor@njfamily.com
83	Family & Parenting (new)	rensley@owatonna.com
84	Family and Faith (new)	familyandfaithmagazine@gmail.com
85	Family Australia (new)	editor@familyaustraliamagazine.com
86	Family Circle	Only have mailing address
87	Family Living (new)	beth@floridafamilyliving.com

88	FamilyFun	letters.familyfun@disney.com
89	Family Magazine of Michiana	jessy@michianafamilymagazine.com
90	Family Time (IL)	carrie@familytimemagazine.com
91	Family Times (Syracuse) (new)	editorial@familytimes.biz
92	Findlay Family	See Ann Arbor Family
93	First Coast Parent	editorial@firstcoastparent.com
94	Fit Pregnancy	mail
95	Flagler Parent	charlie@bradymediainc.com
96	Fort Bend Parent	editor@spacecityparent.com
97	Fort Worth Child	editorial@dallaschild.com
98	Fredericksburg Parent & Family	editor@fredericksburgparent.net
99	Fun for Kidz	submissions@funforkidz.com
100	Georgia Family	olyafessard@gmail.com
101	Giggle (new)	giggle@irvingpublications.com
102	Girls' Life	katiea@girlslife.com
103	Good Housekeeping	Only have mailing address
104	Good Life Family	sheryl@slpcompany.com
105	Good Living (new)	pam@goodlivingmag.com
106	The Green Parent	features@thegreenparent.co.uk
107	Growing Up Chico (new)	marne@growingupchico.com
108	Growing Up in the Valley (new)	josh@growingupinthevalley.com
109	Gulf Coast Parents & Kids	magazine@parents-kids.com
110	Hamilton County Family (new)	susan@hamiltoncountyfamily.com
111	Hawaii Parent	hpks@hawaii.rr.com
112	Hello, Darling (MOPS) (new)	content@mops.org
113	Highlights	only via mail
114	Home Education Magazine	editor@homeedmag.com
115	Homeschooling Today	management@homeschooltoday.com
116	Honolulu Family (new)	christiy@honolulufamily.com
117	'Hood (new)	hannah@thehoodmagazine.com
118	Hopscotch	submissions@funforkidz.com
119	Houston Baby Guide	editor@houstonfamilymagazine.com
120	Houston Family	editor@houstonfamilymagazine.com

121	Hudson Valley Parent	editor@excitingread.com
122	Hybrid Mom	allison@hybridmom.com
123	I Parent (new)	dbourgeois@iparentmagazine.com
124	Imperfect Parent	online submission form
125	inBetween (new)	rachel@inbetween.ca
126	Indy's Child	editor@indyschild.com
127	Inland Empire Family	iemail@iemag.bz
128	Irving Parent	editor@irvingparent.com
129	Island Parent	editor@islandparent.ca
130	Ithaca Baby Book	With Ithaca Child
131	Ithaca Child	jgraney@twcny.rr.com
132	Ithaca Parent & Teen	With Ithaca Child
133	Jersey Shore Family	pam@jerseyshorefamily.com
134	Just Kids	editor@atlantaparent.com
135	Kansas City Baby	editor@kcparent.com
136	Kansas City Parent	editor@kcparent.com
137	Katy Parent	editor@spacecityparent.com
138	Kern County Family	kerncountyfamily@earthlink.net
139	Kid Stuff	laurajean@uvkidstuff.com
140	Kids on the Coast (new)	editor@mothergoosemedia.com.au
141	Kids' Pages	ellen@kidspages.org
142	Kids Vermont	megan@kidsvt.com
143	Kiwi	sarahsmith@maymediagroup.com
144	Krazy Coupon Lady (new)	contributors@thekrazycouponlady.com
145 146	LA Parent City Edition Valley Edition	christina.elston@parenthood.com
147	Ladies' Home Journal	lhj@mdp.com
148	Ladybug	Cricket Magazine Group
149	Lowcountry Parent	cfossi@postandcourier.co
150	Mahoning Valley Parent	editor@mvparentmagazine.com
151	Main Line Parent (sister to Philadelphia Family)	melissa@familyfocusmedia.com
152	Melbourne's Child	editorial@melbourneschild.com.au
153	Memphis Parent	janes@contemporary-media.com
154	Mendo-Lake Family Life	melissa@family-life.us
155	Metro Baby	jelliott@metroparent.com
156	Metro Parent	jelliott@metroparent.com

157	Metro Parent	editor@metro-parent.com
158	Metrofamily	editor@metrofamilymagazine.com
159	Metrokids	editor@metrokids.com
160	MetroParent WI	epaulsen@jrn.com
161	Midwestern Family	jrudd@midwesternfamily.com
162	Minnesota Parent (new)	editor@mnparent.com
163	MommyThink	writers@mommythink.com
164	Montana Parent	leigh@mtparent.com
165	Montgomery Parents	info@montgomeryparents.com
166	Montreal Families	editorial@montrealfamilies.ca
167	Motherwords	jennifer.winn@motherwords.org
168	Muse	Cricket Magazine Group
169	My Child Magazine	editorial@poppetgroup.com.au
170	NCW Kid Connect (new)	nikki@ncwkidconnect.com
171	Nashville Parent	chad@daycommedia.com
172	Neapolitan Family	andrea@neafamily.com
173	New Jersey Family	njfamilyeditor@njfamily.com
174	New York Family (new)	emessinger@manhattanmedia.com
175	New York Special Child	kbrown@cnglocal.com
176	NOLA Baby & Family	editor@nolababy.com
177	North Idaho Family (new)	sales@nifamily.com
178	North Kentucky Family	chad@daycommedia.com
179	North State Parent	editorial@northstateparent.com
180	North Texas Child	editorial@dallaschild.com
181	North Texas Kids	mina@northtexaskids.com
182	Northeast Ohio Parent (new)	angela@northeastohioparent.com
183	Northeast Pennsylvania Family	pamela@nepafamily.com
184	Northshore Parents	nsparents@brparents.com
185	OC Family	schurm@churmmedia.com
186	Odyssey	Cricket Magazine Group
187	Offspring (new)	kate@offspringmagazine.com.au
188	Ohio Family	editorial@ohiofamilymagazine.com
189	Ohio Valley Parent	betsy@ovparent.com
190	The Old Schoolhouse	senioreditor@thehomeschoolmagazine.com

191	Omaha Family	editor@omahafamily.com or try lauren@hathawaypublishing.net
192	On the Coast	OTC@onthecoastmag.com
193	Only Child	onlychild@onlychild.com
194	Oregon Family (new)	info@oregonfamily.com
195	Orlando Family	editorial@orlandofamilymagazine.com
196	PTO Today (new)	queries@ptotoday.com
197	Palm Beach Parenting	info@pbparenting.com
198	Palmetto Parent	palmettoeditorial@me.com
199	Parent Express	editor@parentexpress.net
200	Parent Map	editor@parentmap.com
201	Parent News	parentnewsmagazine.com
202	Parenting New Hampshire	editor@parentingnh.com
203	Parenting OC	editor@parentingoc.com
204	Parenting Plus	pplus000@aol.com
205	Parenting	mail or see ebook recommendation
206	Parenting Early Years	mail or see ebook recommendation
207	Parenting School Years	mail or see ebook recommendation
208	ParentLine	parentline@comcast.net
209	Parents	mail or see ebook recommendation
210	Parents' Source	editor@parentssource.com
211	Pearland Parent	editor@spacecityparent.com
212	Peekaboo	editor@peekaboonwa.com
213	Philadelphia Family (sister to Main Line Parent) (new)	melissa@familyfocusmedia.com
214	Piedmont Parent	editor@piedmontparent.com
215	Pittsburgh Parent	editor@pittsburghparent.com
216	Portland Family	publisher@portlandfamily.com
217	Practical Homeschooling	online submission form
218	Pregnancy	editors@pregnancymagazine.com
219	Pregnancy & Newborn	editor@pnmag.com
220	Purchase Area Parenting	karen@purchasefamilymag.com
221	Queens Family	kbrown@cnglocal.com
222	Raise (new)	karen@dmiagency.com
223	Raising Arizona Kids	editorial@raisingarizonakids.com
224	Raising Teens	editor@njfamily.com
225	Red River Family	editor@redriverfamily.com
226	Redbook	Only have mailing address

227	Richmond Family Monthly (new)	editor@rfmonline.com
228	Richmond Parents Monthly	rpmeditor@richmondpublishing.com
229	Rio Grande Family	editor@redriverfamily.com
230	Rochester Baby Guide	editor@gvparent.com
231	Rochester & Genesee Valley Parent	editor@gvparent.com
232	Rocky Mountain Parent (new)	kristin.rmpublishing@gmail.com
233	Rutherford Parent	chad@daycommedia.com
234	Sacramento Parent	lisa@sacramentoparent.com
235	St. John Parent	charlie@bradymediainc.com
236	Saint Louis Parent (new)	editor@stlparent.com
237	San Diego Family	editor@sandiegofamily.com
238	Santa Barbara Family Life	production@sbfamilylife.com
239	Sassy	jessy@michianafamilymagazine.com
240	Savvy Kids (new)	melanie@arktimes.com
241	Seattle's Child	dzedonis@seattleschild.com
242	SI Parent (Staten Island)	editorial@siparent.com
243	Simply Family	jamie@simplyfamilymagazine.com
244	Solo Parent (new)	kate@solparentmag.com
245	Sonoma Family Life	melissa@family-life.us
246	South Florida Parenting	krlomer@sun-sentinel.com
247	Southwest Florida Parent & Child	pamela@swflparentchild.com
248	South Sound	lisa@premiermedia.net
249	Space City Parent	editor@spacecityparent.com
250	Spider	Cricket Magazine Group
251	Suburban Parent NJ	editor@njparentweb.com
252	Suburban Parent TX	editor@suburbanparent.com
253	Sumner Parent	chad@daycommedia.com
254	Sydney's Child	editorial@sydneyschild.com.au
255	Teton Family (new)	christina@tetonfamilymagazine.com
256	Texarkana Parent (new)	publisher@texarkanaparent.com
257	Thriving Family	thrivingfamilysubmissions@family.org
258	Tidewater Parent	ss.acker@cox.net
259	Tidewater Parent Baby	ss.acker@cox.net

	Guide	
260	Today's Parent Baby & Toddler	By mail only; favors Canadians
261	Today's Parent Pregnancy and Birth	By mail only
262	Today's Parent Toronto	queries@tpg.rogers.com
263	Toledo Area Parent	See Ann Arbor Family
264	Treasure Coast Parenting	info@tcparenting.com
265	Tulsa Kids	editor@tulsakids.com
266	Twins	twinseditor@twinsmagazine.com
267	Utah Family	editor@utahfamily.com
268	Valley Parent	callie@columbusandthevalley.com
269	Valley Parent	valleyparent@comcast.net
270	Vancouver Family	nikki@vancouverfamilymagazine.com
271	Village Family	magazine@thevillagefamily.org
272	Volusia Parent	charlie@bradymediainc.com
273	Washington Family	editor@thefamilymagazine.com
274	Washington Parent	contactus@washingtonparent.net
275	West Virginia Baby	editor@wvfamilymagazine.com
276	West Virginia Family	editor@wvfamilymagazine.com
277	Westchester Family	jean.sheff@westchesterfamily.com
278	WestCoast Families	editor@westcoastfamilies.com
279	Western New York Family	michele@wnyfamilymagazine.com
280	What's Up	editor@whatsupfamily.ca
281	Wichita Family (new)	publisher@wichitafamily.com
282	Williamson Parent	chad@daycommedia.com
283	Wilmington Parent	danielle.wilmingtonparent@gmail.com
284	Woman's Day	womansday@hearst.com
285	Working Mother	See guidelines for email addresses

ABOUT THE AUTHOR

Kerrie McLoughlin is a freelance writer and chaos-loving mom based in Kansas City. She is a homeschooler by day to her five kids and fits in an article-writing, ebook-writing and proofreading career by early morning and late night. Her writing credits include hundreds of published pieces in over 140 of the regional parenting magazines listed in this ebook.

She also sells Jamberry nail wraps and Younique cosmetics, and she also does social media projects for BlogHer.com.

When Kerrie isn't parenting, sleeping, playing, teaching, giving her husband grief or writing, she enjoys traveling, reading, walking, volunteering, avoiding chores, eating chocolate, drinking coffee, scrapbooking and learning new things.

The best place to find her is at her chaotic mommy blog called TheKerrieShow.com, and you can find all her offshoot projects from there.

Please also visit GetPublishedParentingMags.com for more writing fun and information about making money from home in general.

35445122R00127

Made in the USA
San Bernardino, CA
24 June 2016